Further praise for *Material Girls*

'Stock tackles several key axioms of trans activism, from the idea that everyone has an inner gender identity that might not match our biological sex to the pressure on people to acknowledge and legally protect gender identity instead of biological sex. Clear-sighted' *Evening Standard*

'*Material Girls* will help anybody bewildered by the complexity and anger of the debate to get their head around the objections gender-critical feminists have towards concepts such as gender self ID. It also provides a useful history of philosophical debates around sex and gender since Simone de Beauvoir' James Marriott, *Irish Times*

'Stock takes us on a whistlestop tour of ideas about sex and gender that shape the way we think today ... For me, what seems especially positive is Stock's plea to remember why feminism exists: to argue for women and girls, and to address the distinct challenges, oppressions and disadvantages they face in whichever culture or society they find themselves' Orlando Fretton, *The Lady*

'Unlike so many texts in the academic field of feminist studies, *Material Girls* is written in exceptionally clear and jargon free prose. It is aimed at a general audience trying to make sense of increasingly fraught public arguments about the social implications of gender identity ... [A] closely argued, courageous book and an indispensable read for all who want to make sense of this vitally important contemporary issue'
Sonya Andermahr, *Morning Star*

'A punchy, polemical read ... Stock is right to say there is a material reality to being a girl. And she is right to demand the space to say it' Ann Furedi, *Spiked*

'In her commitment to free speech, good-faith debate, clear and careful argument and upholding reason over dogma, Stock writes faithfully in the tradition of the Enlightenment'
Mary Harrington, *UnHerd*

MATERIAL GIRLS

WHY REALITY MATTERS FOR FEMINISM

KATHLEEN STOCK

FLEET

2022

To Laura

FLEET

First published in Great Britain in 2021 by Fleet
This paperback edition published in 2022 by Fleet

5 7 9 10 8 6 4

A CIP catalogue record for this book
is available from the British Library.

ISBN 978-0-349-72662-5

Typeset in Sabon by M Rules
Printed and bound in Great Britain by Clays Ltd, Elcograf S.p.A.

Papers used by Fleet are from well-managed forests
and other responsible sources.

Fleet
An imprint of
Little, Brown Book Group
Carmelite House
50 Victoria Embankment
London EC4Y 0DZ

An Hachette UK Company
www.hachette.co.uk

www.littlebrown.co.uk

Contents

Foreword

I wrote *Material Girls* as an opinionated guide for the public. The axioms of gender identity theory – the subject of this book – are often presented with a veneer of intellectual credibility and prestige. They are taken seriously by many academics, and consequently nodded through by politicians, medics, psychologists and lawyers. Though this book focuses on the UK, the reach of gender identity theory is international. Countries currently in the grip of it include Canada, Germany, Australia, Holland, the US, New Zealand and Spain. In these places, as in others, various authorities are making far-reaching decisions based on the assumption that gender identity theory is true.

And yet it is seriously questionable – or so I argue in this book. Its philosophical foundations are dubious, and it's a disaster when implemented in policy – for women, for children, for gay people and for trans people themselves. And even worse, proponents of gender identity theory often insist that it is not up for debate. To disagree is couched as unkind, exclusionary and transphobic. This silencing, along with a lack of fair representation in the progressive media, has frightened and infuriated would-be dissenters. The temperature of public discussion has been unnecessarily raised to boiling point, and mutual misunderstandings between polarised factions are rife. I wrote *Material Girls* as an attempt to calm things down: not by capitulating or soothing, but by standing my ground and explaining the reasons why.

I write this late in 2021. Exactly a year ago, I was editing *Material Girls* for hardback publication. I was used to controversy, having already written and spoken on the subject of gender identity theory, and I felt relatively sanguine about any ensuing fuss. I hoped that my book would help to open up dis-cussion, but I was also aware of the limitations of the written word in a culture increasingly dominated by the vanishingly ephemeral. What was needed, I thought, was a high-profile case persuasively demonstrating the degree of illiberalism within much current transactivism.

I did not expect that case to involve me. Four months after pub-lication, and after a sustained campaign of harassment on campus against me for my criticisms of gender identity theory, I left my post as Professor of Philosophy at the University of Sussex. Given the intensity and hostility of the campaign – involving threaten-ing communications, unannounced demos of masked men on campus, posters, graffiti and flares – I felt I had no choice but to resign. Headlines and TV reports followed, as did parliamentary questions, an investigation by the Office for Students, thousands of supportive emails to me from the public and a vastly increased public awareness of what was – and still is – at stake.

I would like to believe that the young protestors who harassed me out of my job have read this book. Unfortunately, I don't. They seem to think mere exposure to my writing is harmful. But prop-erly discussing these serious matters, in book form or otherwise, is the best hope we have of finding ways to accommodate the inter-ests of all. There is no viable alternative. Authoritarian, secretive attempts to railroad gender identity theory through parliaments, courts, health authorities, educational establishments, women's services and sports bodies have already produced huge resentment. If they continue, the backlash for trans people and perhaps even the LGBT world generally might be severe. The toxicity around gender politics needs to be reduced as a matter of urgency.

So: congratulations for reading *Material Girls*. Whether you agree or disagree with it, simply by reading with an open mind, you will have helped.

Kathleen Stock
December 2021

Introduction

This book is about sex, and about the mysterious thing known as 'gender'. It is about how, in the first quarter of the twenty-first century – quite unexpectedly – a philosophical theory about something called 'gender identity' gripped public consciousness, strongly influencing UK and international institutions, and causing protests and even violence.

In 2004, the UK government introduced a new law called the Gender Recognition Act. This allowed trans people to get a Gender Recognition Certificate, giving them what the official legal wording called an 'acquired gender' in line with their preferences. In 2004, it was estimated there were about 2,000–5,000 trans people in the UK.[1] Back then, the popular image of a trans person was mainly of a 'medically transitioned' adult trans woman, or 'male-to-female transsexual': an adult person of the male sex who had taken hormones over a long period of time to change many aspects of appearance, and who had also had 'sex reassignment' surgery to refashion natal genitalia. The Gender Recognition Act was brought in so that, among other things, transsexuals could get their birth certificates reissued to record their preferred sex instead of their natal one. In this way, they could protect themselves from accusations of fraud, and avoid being forced to disclose their sex in contexts where it might feel embarrassing or humiliating to do so. To get a Gender Recognition Certificate, applicants did not have to have undergone surgery or hormone treatment, but had to demonstrate they were serious about transition, having lived in their preferred gender for two years. They would also need official diagnosis of a profound and debilitating sense of unease about their sexed body, a psychological condition known as 'gender dysphoria'.

Six years later, in 2010, gender reassignment was officially made a protected characteristic under the Equality Act. This made it illegal to discriminate against someone because of gender reassignment. To count as eligible for protection, a Gender Recognition Certificate was not officially required. Instead, a person was protected under the terms of the Act if they were 'proposing to undergo ... [were] undergoing or [had] ... undergone a process (or part of a process) for the purpose of reassigning the person's sex by changing physiological or other attributes of sex'. In the Explanatory Notes, this rather opaque definition was further described as a situation 'where a person has proposed, started or completed a process to change his or her sex'.[2]

As I write this in 2020, sixteen years after the introduction of the Gender Recognition Act and ten years after the Equality Act, the situation on the ground has changed in several big respects. Most obviously, the number of trans people in the UK has rocketed. According to the LGBT charity Stonewall, their 'best estimate' is 'about 600,000'.[3] In 2018, the Government put the figure slightly lower and more cautiously, at '200,000–500,000', noting that only around 5,000 of these have received a Gender Recognition Certificate since 2004.[4]

Along with this increase, there has been a radical change to the public image of a trans person. For one thing – though we still don't know the actual proportions – the trans population now contains significant numbers of people of the female sex identifying as trans men or as non-binary (that is, as neither male nor female, or as both). For another, the trans population is no longer exclusively adult. Both of these changes are reflected in the fact the female sex has overtaken the male sex as the largest group of patients in gender clinics for children. In 2010, forty male and thirty-two female children were referred to the national NHS Gender Identity Development Service for children (GIDS); by 2019 that had risen to 624 males and 1,740 females. In 2018/19 the youngest patient seen by GIDS was three.[5]

In 2011, doctors at GIDS started to administer drugs called 'puberty blockers' to some patients at their clinic, in order to delay puberty and the physical changes it normally brings.[6] Though clinicians are licensed to prescribe these drugs for other conditions, they have not been licensed for use for children and adolescents with gender dysphoria. (According to the Health Research Authority, particularly in paediatric medicine it is 'common to use unlicensed medicine based on learning from clinical practice'.[7])

Evidence shows that many young patients who receive puberty blockers later proceed to cross-sex hormones when they reach the age of majority, and sometimes to surgery too. But these days not everyone in the trans community medically transitions – another way in which the 2004 stereotype of a trans person is now outdated. A 2019 study from the US notes that genital surgery has 'prevalence rates of about 25–50% for transgender men [i.e. females] and 5–10% for transgender women' [i.e. males].[8] Although we don't know the UK figures, it is clear that many trans people are not seeking surgery. Anecdotally it seems a significant proportion of trans people do not take hormones either. While medical practitioners often still think of being trans as a disorder, associating it with the condition of gender dysphoria and conceiving of it as something to be treated by drugs and surgery, many trans people now reject this idea, and with it the implication that any medical diagnosis or intervention is necessary for being trans.

As the size of the trans population has increased, its political voice has got stronger. Trans political interests are for the first time at the forefront of public consciousness. Prominent UK trans activist organisations such as Stonewall, Mermaids, the Scottish Trans Alliance, Gendered Intelligence, GIRES, Press For Change and All About Trans have made coordinated and effective pushes for a number of new measures, and have met with some success. Since 2015, as a direct result of lobbying, the main English and Scottish political parties have all supported proposed changes to the 2004 Gender Recognition Act that would make getting a Gender Recognition Certificate a matter of 'self-identification' or 'self-ID', withdrawing the requirements of a medical diagnosis of gender dysphoria and of evidence of having lived in the acquired gender for two years beforehand. On the proposed new terms, getting a GRC, and so also changing one's birth certificate, would be a purely administrative and relatively instantaneous matter. The Conservatives, initially enthusiastic, have now rowed back on the proposal, but apparently the Labour, Liberal Democrat and Scottish National Parties all still officially support it, and it was included in each of their 2019 general election manifestos. Were Labour to get back into power, it is reasonable to assume they would seek to implement this change. As I write, the Women and Equalities Select Committee is again examining the question of gender recognition reform from an apparently sympathetic perspective.

The focused lobbying for gender recognition reform has

sprung from the newly perceived importance of something called 'gender identity' in trans activist thinking. According to this theory, it is not the process of gender reassignment that makes you trans but, as Stonewall puts it: 'A person's innate sense of their own gender, whether male, female or something else ... which may or may not correspond to the sex assigned at birth.'[9] That is, it's an inner feeling. It is your gender identity rather than your sex that is considered to be what makes you man, woman or non-binary. It also determines your preferred pronouns: that is, whether you wish to be referred to as 'she', 'he' or (in the case of non-binary people) 'they'. Some supportive academics add that binary sex does not materially exist for humans in nature anyway. Educators in schools and universities are now advised by trans activist organisations to teach pupils and students about innate gender identity, and that sex is 'assigned at birth'.

For at least five years, alongside proposed changes to the issuing of Gender Recognition Certificates, trans activist groups have been lobbying the Government to change the protected characteristic of 'gender reassignment' in the Equality Act to 'gender identity'. They have also pressed to have exemptions removed from the Equality Act that allow discrimination on the basis of sex in certain circumstances – exemptions that might exclude trans people from single-sex spaces belonging to the opposite sex.[10] At the same time, some of these activist groups – most notably Stonewall – have been advising institutions and organisations that existing Equality Act exemptions do not go far enough, and that if they want to be inclusive they should not apply the exemptions in most ordinary cases of public facility and resource provision. Many of those in charge of facilities and resources across the country have listened. So right now, within multiple national organisations, the policies that govern women-only facilities – for instance, changing rooms, hostel dormitories, public toilets, sleeper carriages, school facilities, student accommodation, rape crisis centres and domestic violence refuges – have been explicitly changed to include anyone, male or female, who self-identifies as a woman. Similar policies, citing self-identification as a man, now apply to many men-only facilities. There has also been a big rise in 'gender neutral' facilities (in older terminology, unisex).

One striking consequence of this change is that since 2016, trans women – some without GRCs – have been housed in the female prison estate on the basis of identity. Also strikingly, in some amateur and professional sporting competitions, trans women now compete alongside females. Meanwhile, resources originally set up to try to establish equal opportunities for women in the workplace and public life – for instance, all-women training and mentoring events, shortlists or prizes – are now often explicitly open to anyone who identifies as a woman. Even in data collection, gender identity is replacing sex. For instance, despite protests from some academics and some hesitation over a similar plan in England, at the time of writing Census authorities in Scotland and Northern Ireland still plan to instruct respondents to their 2021 Census survey that they may answer the question about their sex as a question about their gender identity[11]. By common consent of many powerful national bodies, it is gender identity that now determines what public spaces you may enter, what resources should be available to you, and how you should be categorised for the purposes of data collection.

Simultaneously there has been a widespread reduction of public references to biological sex. It has become commonplace to hear from politicians, officials and other public figures that 'trans women are women, and trans men are men', and that there should be 'no debate' about it. It has become unexceptional for non-trans and trans people alike to announce their pronouns, indicative of gender identity, in email signatures or social media bios. In some workplaces, asking about or commenting upon the sex of a fellow trans employee risks your being classed as 'transphobic' by official HR policies. The trend in favour of gender identity and away from sex has reached public health communication, with some national health bodies starting to talk about 'menstruators' and 'cervix-havers' rather than women and girls.

These changes in social organisation and public language have been rapid and have caused enormous disquiet among some sections of the public. A generational divide has opened up. Many younger people cheer on the changes in the name of progress and see dissent as a measure of societal hatred of trans people. Many older women feel concerned or even outright panicked by what seems rapidly to be disappearing, without their having had any real say in the process. While mainstream feminist groups have either kept out of it or straightforwardly supported trans activist demands, grassroots women's organisations have sprung up to discuss how best to fight the proposed changes. Young activists have protested at these meetings with megaphones, smoke bombs, graffiti and, at one point, a bomb threat.[12] Women attendees have been screamed at from close quarters, had water thrown at them, been shoved and blocked from entering. I know, because I am one of them.

As I write this in 2020, the public row has just gone global. After J. K. Rowling wrote a blog post in defence of attending to women and girls' interests during any discussion of trans activist demands, the backlash was intense.[13] Accusations of 'transphobia' flooded in from around the world, often accompanied by threats and insults. Stars such as Daniel Radcliffe and Emma Watson, whose reputations were made in the films of Rowling's books, scrambled to distance themselves from her and to repeat the mantra that 'trans women are women'.[14] Employees of Rowling's own publishing house asserted that they would not work on her latest book.[15] Public attention is on the conflict as never before.

The thinking behind the rise of gender identity originally came from academia. I'm an academic too, employed in a philosophy department in a UK university. For most of my professional life, I have focused on exploring questions to do with fiction and imagination, and I have occasionally published in feminist philosophy too. Both of these areas of expertise – fiction and feminism – are highly relevant to the discussion of trans activist claims. Still, it's worth noting that, despite my recent professional turn towards sex and gender, I'm still mostly considered an outsider to the area. Although I have been writing and speaking on the topic in public for a couple of years now, and have authored academic papers about it, I don't work in a Gender Studies department, or in the field of queer theory, or in Trans Studies. I'm not trans myself. I'm not even a proper feminist philosopher; at least, I didn't used to think I was.

This means that academics already working in these fields often consider me unqualified. When I write opinion pieces for magazines or speak on TV, I can almost feel the eye rolls. I am characterised as a clumsy, intellectually unsophisticated rube, making old mistakes in my thinking that they have long since put behind them. 'Hasn't she read *the literature*?' they ask. 'How can she be so naïve?' Another common response is to say that I must be arguing with strawmen: academics don't *really* think what I think they think. 'Nobody thinks there isn't a distinction between sex and gender, Kathleen,' I am told, often by the very same academics who are telling me that referring to trans women generally as biologically male, for the purposes of discussing the impacts of sex, is transphobic. Or, even more basically, it's complained that – whether I mean to be or not – I am a transphobe who shouldn't be listened to.

Yet my outsider status in this area has many benefits. As far as I can see, standard academic norms for the production of knowledge are not often observed in fields that deal with matters of sex and gender. The whole area has become unacceptably politicised. Particular articles and books are treated like sacred texts rather than the opinionated, potentially fallible or myopic arguments they actually are. As one trans author, Andrea Long Chu, puts it, the result is 'warmed-over pieties' and 'something like church'.[16] There are small things you may question or criticise, and then there are the fundamental orthodoxies it is considered transphobic to deny. Evidence or facts are considered relevant only when they help what is perceived to be the political cause of trans people. Any philosophical critiques that do sometimes (rarely) emerge – especially by non-trans academics – are regularly treated as equivalent to *actual attacks on trans people* rather than as critiques of *views about* trans people, or of *trans activist commitments*. It's assumed these critiques are not worthy of rational engagement but should be met only with strong moral disapproval and suppression. This sort of judgement floats down from on high, via academic managers, journal editors and referees, to make sure that, on the ground, no dissenting voice gets into 'the literature' without a huge struggle. Even worse, it helps ensure that hardly any seriously dissenting voices get into the discipline areas in the first place.

In this suffocating context, I definitely count as a heretic. And that suits me fine. I didn't become a professional philosopher to go to church. In the article I just quoted from, Andrea Long Chu also describes a lot of academics in Trans Studies as secretly 'itching for a fight'. I'm more than happy to provide an intellectual one here. I do so partly in the name of academic rigour, and partly on behalf of the women and girls whose lives – as I will document – are adversely affected by policies based on gender identity. I also do so on behalf of the many trans people whose objections to political demands made in the name of gender identity, and also in their name, are routinely ignored. Trans people deserve lives free from fear. They deserve laws and policies that properly protect them from discrimination and violence. But as I will argue, laws and policies based around gender identity are not the right route.

A note on pronouns: In this book I've made the decision to use preferred pronouns for trans people in a way that tracks their gender identity and not their sex. I will discuss my route to this choice, and its implications, in Chapter 6. I'll also defend the right of others to choose differently.

A Brief History of
Gender Identity

Here are four axioms of modern trans activism, which I'll be examining from different angles in this book.

1. You and I, and everyone else, have an important inner state called a gender identity.

2. For some people, inner gender identity fails to match the biological sex – male or female – originally assigned to them at birth by medics. These are trans people.

3. Gender identity, not biological sex, is what makes you a man or a woman (or neither).

4. The existence of trans people generates a moral obligation upon all of us to recognise and legally to protect gender identity and *not* biological sex.

Though it might seem surprising, these count as philosophical claims. Philosophy is popularly imagined as involving a lot of dry reading, incomprehensible words and chin-stroking. In its academic guise, this isn't far wrong. But most of us have philosophical thoughts every day. When you wonder what makes you the same person you were ten years ago, or whether your cat has a mind and what that is like, or whether you're technically responsible for what you did last night after eight beers, or how you *really know* you're not in *The Matrix* right now, you're doing philosophy. You're also doing philosophy when you try to work out what sort of organisational structure is best for society, and what rights and protections should be granted to people in it.

As an easy way of identifying them, I am calling these four axioms 'gender identity theory'. I am critical of gender identity theory – but not of trans people, for whom I have friendly sympathy and respect. When criticising a philosophical position, it's a good idea to start with a fairly neutral presentation of it. You should try to describe the position as its supporters would, without aspersions. That way, you aren't lazily setting yourself up for cheap wins later. So here are eight key moments in the rapid intellectual onset of gender identity theory, which give a brief but instructive history of the popular and influential cultural phenomenon we encounter today.

Moment 1: Simone de Beauvoir says, 'One is not born, but rather becomes a woman'

Early in her 1949 book *The Second Sex*, the French existentialist and feminist Simone de Beauvoir wrote this resonant phrase. As de Beauvoir scholar Céline Leboeuf puts it: 'to intone this sentence at the beginning of a work of feminist theory is tantamount to genuflecting at the family pew'.[1] From the last quarter of the twentieth century onwards, de Beauvoir's famous phrase has been taken up enthusiastically to convey the idea that being a woman is not the same as being born biologically female.

De Beauvoir devoted a lot of *The Second Sex* to pointing out the different ways in which women and men are treated by society, describing how, as the female infant turns into the girl turns into the woman, she's increasingly exposed to images and stereotypes concerning how she *should* behave, think and feel. In other words, girls and women are exposed to something called 'femininity'. De Beauvoir argued that cultural representations of femininity are mostly formed by, and largely in the interests of, men. A woman is expected to be whatever a man wants, needs, subconsciously fears, craves or hates. Woman is 'the Other' in relation to the central figure in the human universe, Man. In building her case, de Beauvoir described perennial images and myths of womanhood throughout history, constructed through the consciousnesses of men: the fertile Earth Mother, the chaste Madonna, the lustful Whore, the beguiling Nymph and the terrifying Crone. She wrote: 'There is ... no feminine figure – virgin, mother, wife, sister, servant, lover, fierce virtue, smiling odalisque – capable of encapsulating the inconstant yearnings of men.'[2] In other words, the expectations around femininity are inconsistent. Women are expected to be kind, domesticated, submissive, modest, selfless and responsible, but also exciting, sexually available, 'frivolous, infantile, irresponsible', and other contradictory things too.[3]

In the 1960s, 70s, and 80s, partly taking a lead from de Beauvoir, so-called 'Second Wave' feminists – some of them in newly formed Women's Studies departments in universities – became particularly interested in femininity and masculinity, understood as the different bundles of expectations, stereotypes and norms faced by men and women respectively. They gave femininity and masculinity, understood in this way, a special name: 'gender'. For many feminists, it was important to think of gender (in this sense) as purely social, without foundation in biological generalisations about women and men. The conceptual distinction between 'sex and gender' was born. Here is British feminist sociologist Ann Oakley writing in 1972: '"Sex" is a word that refers to the biological differences between male and female: the visible difference in genitalia, the related difference in procreative function. "Gender" however is a matter of culture: it refers to the social classification into "masculine" and "feminine."'[4]

In the decades that followed, some feminist commentators moved beyond this distinction to a much more radical position. They started approvingly to interpret de Beauvoir as having meant that womanhood itself is essentially social not biological: not a matter of being female but rather a matter of having projected on to you, and perhaps also internalising, the restrictive social expectations, stereotypes and norms of femininity. They took women and girls to be, by definition, the set of people who have a feminine 'social role' projected upon them. And perhaps tellingly, though it isn't really mentioned much, it followed that men and boys must be the set of people who have a masculine 'social role', understood as the distinctive expectations of masculinity – being tough, brainy, decisive, competitive, unemotional, boisterous or whatever – projected by society upon *them*.

It looks like a consequence of this view that – at least potentially – being a woman doesn't require being female, nor being a man, being male. A male can be a woman, as long as he has systematically projected upon him – or rather, perhaps, upon her – a feminine social role. So this apparently opens up the possibility of a trans woman counting as a woman – quite literally – as long as she occupies a feminine social role just as other women do.

Whether or not de Beauvoir actually intended the conceptual separation of being female from womanhood is moot. I don't think she did. Nonetheless, the idea of womanhood as occupation of a feminine social role was received like manna from heaven by many feminists. This was not because their direct goal was to produce a theory that accommodated trans women as women. Rather more self-interestedly, it was to get away from the spectre of what is known as 'biological determinism'. Feminists wanted to escape the historically persistent idea that a woman's personality, behaviour and life options are determined by her female biology, making her naturally suited for home life rather than professional work or intellectual life. The idea of biological determinism was and is used by some traditionalists to justify a relatively limited role for females: domestic, maternal, submissive, and so on. An apparently neat way to defeat the constricting idea of biological determinism seemed to be to argue that women, as such, weren't necessarily female after all – so how could their biology determine anything significant about them *as women*? As French feminist theorist Monique Wittig put it in 1981: 'by admitting that there is a "natural" division between women and men, we … naturalize the social phenomena which express our oppression, making change impossible'.[5] Best then get rid of the natural division altogether, it was thought. As philosopher and later Gender Studies guru Judith Butler wrote in 1986: 'The distinction between sex and gender has been crucial to the long-standing feminist effort to debunk the claim that anatomy is destiny … With the distinction intact, it is no longer possible to attribute the values or social functions of women to biological necessity.'[6]

As argumentative gambits go, this is a bold one, a bit like arguing that an asteroid isn't about to hit Earth by redefining the word 'Earth' as 'thing incapable of being hit by an asteroid'. Whether or not arguing this way persuaded traditionalists to stop justifying the exclusion of women from workplaces, universities and private members' clubs, what it certainly did do was start to open up conceptual space for the idea that some trans women could literally count as women too.

Moment 2: John Money and Robert Stoller introduce the concept of 'gender identity'

While feminists in the 1960s were starting to insist sex was separate from 'gender', medical clinicians were bringing about changes in the way people thought about the relation between biological sex and identity. The New Zealand psychologist and paediatrician John Money is perhaps most well known for his involvement in an ethically dubious clinical case: the involuntary medical 'sex reassignment' of male child David Reimer after a severely botched circumcision, whose tragic story ended in his suicide as an adult. What is less well known about Money is how influential his clinical work has been in shaping later discourse about trans people. In the course of this work, Money emphasised two important interlinked theoretical concepts: *gender role* and *gender identity*.

A 'gender role', Money wrote, 'is ... all those things that a person says or does to disclose himself or herself as having the status of boy or man, girl or woman, respectively'. They include 'general mannerisms, deportment and demeanor'.[7] So a gender role is behavioural. It isn't quite the same thing as having a set of 'feminine' or 'masculine' expectations projected upon you by society, as described by de Beauvoir. It's more like the feminised or masculinised set of behaviours a developing child and adult comes to adopt, perhaps at least partly in response to such projections. Your gender role is supposed to be whatever it is you do to act in the world 'like a man' or 'like a woman'.

Though, according to Money, we all adopt gender roles, he first developed this concept to apply to so-called intersex people with whom he worked – known today as people with Disorders (or Differences) of Sexual Development (DSDs). In some individuals, chromosomes don't line up neatly with expected bodily characteristics. Money worked with children like this. As he saw it, the outward 'gender roles' of some people with DSDs – whether they behaved 'as girls' or 'as boys' – are sometimes misaligned with relatively hidden facts about their biological status.

A second concept, *gender identity*, then emerged from that of gender role. As Money tells it: 'Gender identity is the private experience of gender role, and gender role is the public manifestation of gender identity.'[8] A gender identity was thought of as a psychologically internalised gender role. It was assumed that during early development, we each come to psychologically relate to ourselves in a wholesale 'gendered' way, which may or may not match facts about our sex. Money thought that gender identities could be male, female or neither, in which case they were 'androgynous'.[9] Another influential American clinician working in this area, Robert Stoller, talked of 'hermaphroditic' gender identities – 'not male nor female, but both (or neither)'.[10]

For both Money and Stoller, the idea of gender identity first emerged from working with people with DSDs. They assumed that people with DSDs often have 'inner' gender identities that don't match the relatively complicated 'outer' facts about their sex. However, this idea of an inner gender identity misaligned with outward sex also seemed to them to apply to chromosomally and morphologically standard people, whose gender identities strongly clashed with facts about their sexed bodies: that is, in modern terminology, to trans people. And they explicitly made room for an 'androgynous' or 'hermaphroditic' gender identity: neither male nor female or perhaps both. Money and Stoller recognised that, untethered to biology, the number of available gender identities needn't be confined to two. In this, their ideas prefigured the emergence of an explicitly 'non-binary' gender identity decades later.

Moment 3: Anne Fausto-Sterling argues biological sex is a 'continuum'

For centuries the assumption was that there are only two possible states for human beings, male and female, and all humans are born cleanly and clearly belonging to either one or the other. By common consent these days, that isn't right. Since the late 1980s, Anne Fausto-Sterling, a Professor of Biology and Gender Studies at Brown University in the US, has been influential in convincing the public that biological sex is not a natural binary division.

Largely thanks to Fausto-Sterling, general public understanding of people with DSDs has increased vastly over the last fifty years, challenging conventional wisdom about relations between chromosomes and bodies. In most human bodies, chromosomal configuration is either XX or XY, and each of these lines up with one of two sets of primary and secondary sex characteristics. For instance, possession of XY chromosomes normally lines up with possession of penis and testicles; and possession of XX chromosomes normally lines up with possession of labia, vagina, ovaries and post-pubescent breasts. Yet a DSD baby with XY chromosomes might also have Complete Androgen Insensitivity Syndrome (CAIS), so that external genitalia consist of labia, clitoris and vagina rather than penis and descended testicles. A child with XX chromosomes might have Congenital Adrenal Hyperplasia

(CAH), resulting in genitalia with a highly 'virilised' appearance resembling a penis and testicles. Those born with ovotesticular disorders might have both ova and testicular material in their bodies. There are many varieties of DSD, and the numbers of babies born with DSDs are much higher than you would think, Fausto-Sterling tells us: even as high as 1.7 per cent of the population.[11]

On the basis of DSDs, Fausto-Sterling proposes an intellectual position on biological sex. She suggests there are at least five sexes rather than only two. Alongside standard-issue males and females, there are also 'hermaphrodites' (e.g. those with ovotesticular disorder), 'male pseudohermaphrodites' (those who possess XY chromosomes and 'feminised' bodies), and 'female pseudohermaphrodites' (those who possess XX chromosomes and 'virilised' bodies).[12] She also seems to suggest that every way that humans try to carve sexed variety up into groups – including her own – is relatively arbitrary. In an op-ed for the *New York Times* she endorses an earlier distinction of John Money's between different stages or 'layers' of sexed development, consecutively occurring at different points from conception onward: 'chromosomal', 'fetal gonadal', 'fetal hormonal', 'internal reproductive', 'external genital', 'pubertal hormonal' and 'pubertal morphological'. Her suggestion seems to be that we should abandon talking about sex as a homogenous, overall state, and instead talk about how someone is sexed in terms of these various layers. The same person may be sexed 'M' according to one layer and 'F' according to another.[13] Sex, she tells us, is 'a vast, infinitely malleable continuum'.[14]

If Fausto-Sterling is right, we should be much more cautious about talking about sex being 'recorded' at birth. A practical point is that midwives and doctors might get it wrong. A more thoroughgoing conceptual point is that simply writing down 'male' or 'female' for a baby might not reflect any genuinely pre-existing single homogenous state. In that case, we had better say binary birth sex is a fiction, 'assigned' by a doctor rather than recorded, or at the very least, massively oversimplified.

Moment 4: Judith Butler tells us gender is a performance

In 1990, the American academic Judith Butler published her book *Gender Trouble: Feminism and the Subversion of Identity*. The book had a huge impact both on the emerging academic fields of queer theory, Gender Studies and Trans Studies and on the liberal intelligentsia generally. Broadly speaking, Butler took tenets from French post-structuralist and deconstructionist philosophy and applied them to the notions of 'female', 'woman', 'male' and 'man'.

Butler makes the general assumption that anything at all humans can meaningfully think about is socially constructed, 'all the way down' as it were. This means she thinks there are no material facts before language – that is, prior to culturally specific linguistic and social constructions of them. Linguistic categories, including scientific and biological ones, aren't a means of *reflecting* existing divisions in the world, but a means of *creating* things that otherwise wouldn't have existed. According to Butler, scientific language in particular creates 'hierarchies' of dominance and subordination, entrenching power relations between social groups. And this also applies to the categories of male and female: they are arbitrary, artificial and do not reflect any prior material division. What they *do* reflect is 'exclusionary' power relations, dictating who gets to count as a 'real' woman or man, and who does not (for instance, gay or feminine-looking males don't, nor do lesbian or masculine-looking females).

What is left of notions like 'female', 'woman', 'male' and 'man' once the radical weapon of post-structuralism has been applied to them? For Butler, the answer is 'gender as performance': being a woman or female, for instance, is not a materially stable state, but rather, a kind of repeatable social performance. A drag queen, a trans woman and a traditional housewife are all performing the 'gender' of woman in their own ways. No single kind of performance is more authentic or appropriate than any other.

This radical and transgressive line of thought sent thrilled shockwaves through humanities departments in universities at the time of publication, and the aftershocks have been felt ever since. In the 1990s, the academic discipline of queer theory was forged: a branch of critical theory applied to sex, gender and sexuality, with *Gender Trouble* a foundational text. One by one, Women's Studies departments founded in the 1970s and '80s started to rename themselves as Gender Studies departments, interested in *all* gender performances and not just the narrow, heterosexual, white and Eurocentric performances of womanhood with which many feminists had mostly concerned themselves to date. In many quarters, feminism became thought of as a political project aimed at critiquing 'exclusionary' gender practices generally, rather than at the liberation of the female sex in particular – or even at all. After all, if the female sex is merely a social construct propping up hierarchical power relations, then to make it a focus of political activity is to give that social construct apparent validity and so further to entrench it. Better then to try, positively, to 'queer' sex subversively, via transgressive, unexpected performances of masculinity and femininity such as drag and trans; or, if you can't do *that*, then ignore it altogether.

Moment 5: Julia Serano says gender identity is what makes you a woman or man

The 2000s was a crucial decade for the modern trans movement, in which apparently separate theoretical concepts from previous decades were synthesised into more cohesive bodies of ideas and disseminated into popular culture. This is when gender identity theory really got going. It is worth remembering that, at least according to some, the word 'transgender' received its contemporary meaning only in 1992, while 'trans' person reportedly first came into formal usage only in 1998.[15] Prior to both, the term 'transsexual' was much more familiar. The first decade of the 2000s is where modern trans activism – political activism in favour of trans people – got off the ground in a significant, organised way. A newly rejuvenated concept of gender identity was now a crucial component of the trans activist narrative.

Gender identity, we know from earlier discussion, is – roughly – an internalised psychological representation of oneself, consciously conceptualised as female or male or as something else altogether. From the 2000s on, it started to be a relatively commonly held belief in progressive circles that it is not your biological sex nor even your 'social role' that makes you a woman or man – it is having a *female or male gender identity* that does it.

It is hard to pinpoint exactly when this idea took hold in popular imagination, but one influential text was the 2007 book *Whipping Girl* by American biologist and trans woman Julia Serano. A notable contribution of *Whipping Girl* to popular culture is the idea that trans women are a kind of woman like any other. The term 'trans', Serano argues, should be treated as an adjective like 'Catholic' or 'Asian', rather than 'trans woman' being thought of as a compound noun.[16] Relatedly, *Whipping Girl* did much to popularise an adjective for people who are not trans: 'cisgender', later shortened to 'cis', and standing for those people whose gender identity and sex are 'aligned'.[17]

For Serano, the general category of women is composed of trans women and cis women. Both are kinds of women. The category of men is composed of trans men and cis men. Both are kinds of men. Serano makes clear she thinks trans women are defined, as such, in virtue of their possession of a female gender identity, and not by any medical or legal process, or physical features or behaviour. When you put all this together – that trans women, as such, are those with female gender identities; that cis women also have female gender identities; and that cis and trans women are both different kinds of women, on equal taxonomical footing – you get the clear implication that possession of a female gender identity is what makes you a woman, whether cis or trans.

This idea is deeply radical. When some twentieth-century feminists talked in de Beauvoir-esque vein about 'becoming a woman', they meant having a set of social norms or expectations about femininity imposed upon you, not having an 'inner' identity of a certain kind. And when John Money and Robert Stoller talked about gender identity, they didn't think having a gender identity was what *made you* a woman or a man. Twenty-first-century trans activists like Serano effectively took from Money and Stoller the idea of gender identity, and from feminism the thought that something other than (just) being 'born female' made you a woman, put these together and decided that the thing that made you a woman was an inner female gender identity; and that correspondingly, the thing that made you a man was an inner male gender identity. Fausto-Sterling and Butler helped, insofar as it was assumed they had jointly debunked the idea that anyone was 'really' biologically female or male anyway.

Another influential feature of Serano's *Whipping Girl* relates to a significant change in cultural understanding of what sexual orientation is: what counts as being gay or lesbian, bisexual or straight. Your sexual orientation used to be categorised fairly straightforwardly as whatever relation existed between your own biological sex and the biological sex(es) of the people to whom you're attracted. This gave us either: same-sex (homosexual, gay, lesbian) orientations, opposite-sex (heterosexual, straight) orientations and bisexual orientations. Yet in *Whipping Girl*, trans woman Serano – by traditional accounts a male, attracted to females – self-describes as a 'lesbian'. This implication follows from the logic of gender identity. If having a female gender identity is what makes you a woman, and you, with a female gender identity, are habitually sexually attracted to other people with female gender identities, then – since lesbians by definition are women attracted to women – you must be a lesbian. A gay man, meanwhile, is now understood as someone with a male gender identity attracted to others with a male gender identity, irrespective of the assigned sex of either. A straight man is someone with a male gender identity attracted to those with a female gender identity, and so on. As trans man Max Wolf Valerio wrote in his autobiography *The Testosterone Files*, published the year before Serano's book: 'As a woman, my sexual orientation was ostensibly lesbian. As a man, it is heterosexual.'[18]

This departure from a traditional understanding of sexual orientation has – perhaps surprisingly – since been enthusiastically taken up by organisations whose original mission was to lobby for the rights of gay people. For self-styled progressive organisations, thinking of sexual orientations in terms of attraction between members of given biological sexes – same-sex or opposite-sex or both – is now considered old fashioned. For instance, the US organisation GLAAD writes on its website, 'a person who transitions from male to female and is attracted solely to men would typically identify as a straight woman. A person who transitions from female to male and is attracted solely to men would typically identify as a gay man.'[19] In the UK, campaigning group Stonewall's website now asks (my italics), 'So, could a *lesbian* have a trans woman as a *lesbian* partner, or a gay man be with a trans man?' The reply then comes: 'Of course.'[20] Stonewall's current definition of sexual orientation is: 'A person's sexual attraction to other people, or lack thereof. Along with romantic orientation, this forms a person's orientation identity.'[21] Sexual orientations are 'identities' now. They follow from, and depend upon, a prior and more fundamental one: gender identity.

Moment 6: The Yogyakarta Principles recommend recognition of gender identity as a human right

It is now a dictum of modern trans activism that we each have a gender identity. Gender identity is treated as a basic and even supremely important determinant of who we are; a fundamental aspect of the individual, generating distinctive human rights. Nowhere is this conception of gender identity more obvious than in the 2007 Yogyakarta Principles, published in the same year as Serano's *Whipping Girl*.

In 2006, an international group of experts in law, health and human rights met in Yogyakarta, Indonesia, and produced what have become known as the 'Yogyakarta Principles': an influential set of recommendations about human rights in relation to sexual orientation and gender identity, heavily cited in international legislation since.[22] As philosopher and sociologist Heather Brunskell-Evans has put it: 'Though not legally binding, the Yogyakarta Principles have been understood as an authoritative interpretation of international law and provide a definitional point for academic papers, bills, resolutions and other documents. They are not incorporated into any UN convention or declaration, yet they are regularly cited and used as a reference point in the UN.'[23] For instance, when the UK Parliament's Women and Equalities Select Committee delivered their Report on Transgender Equality to the Government in 2015, they recommended that 'the Government must also make a clear commitment to abide by the Yogyakarta Principles ... This would provide trans equality policy with a clear set of overall guiding principles which are in keeping with current international best practice.'[24]

People whom Serano defines as 'cisgender' can talk about and otherwise express their gender identities casually to others without stigma or fear. Trans activists argue that this privilege isn't available to trans people, who, if they decide to come out to others about their non-standard gender identities, may face shaming, hostility and abuse. Equally, governments officially recognise standard binary gender identities in laws and administrative policies – for instance, in issuing passports, or in asking questions about sex in data collection – because it's assumed, wrongly according to trans activists, that outward biologically-influenced appearances are a good guide to inner gender identity. This is considered discriminatory to those with misaligned gender identities, who effectively aren't officially recognised for who they are.

Early on in the Yogyakarta Principles, this stirring sentence sets the scene: 'Sexual orientation and gender identity are integral to every person's dignity and humanity.' The document goes on to propose twenty-eight human rights for those with non-standard sexual orientations or gender identities. Many of these, completely unproblematically, are versions of familiar general human rights, tailored to specify gay and trans people and their particular needs in an often hostile world: rights to life, equality and non-discrimination; freedom from torture; rights to education, social security and housing, and so on. One right in particular stands out as a bit different, though. This is Principle 3: 'The right to recognition before the law'.

Principle 3 starts by reiterating the fundamental nature of gender identity, describing both gender identity and sexual orientation as 'integral to . . . personality' and 'one of the most basic aspects of self-determination, dignity and freedom'. It recommends that 'no one shall be forced to undergo medical procedures, including sex reassignment surgery, sterilisation or hormonal therapy, as a requirement for legal recognition of their gender identity' – an echo of Serano's assumption that it is gender identity and not any outward bodily modification that makes you trans or cis. The Principles continue: 'No one shall be subjected to pressure to conceal, suppress or deny their . . . gender identity'. Moreover: 'all State-issued identity papers which indicate a person's gender/sex – including birth certificates, passports, electoral records and other documents – [should] reflect the person's profound self-defined gender identity.' Each of these recommendations apparently aims to create a world in which those with misaligned gender identities feel they can express this fundamental part of the self and be officially recognised for it rather than ignored.

Since publication of the Principles, this vision of gender identity as a fundamental part of the self, not under any cir- cumstances to be suppressed, has filtered down into legislation and policymaking in numerous countries and states. In the UK, it has influenced the campaign to have the Gender Recognition Act altered in favour of 'self-ID', removing medical gatekeeping or any other substantive prerequisite for the acquisition of a Gender Recognition Certificate. In the background here is the assumption that it is inner gender identity and nothing else that determines being trans. This vision is also behind attempts in various countries including the UK to have equality law altered to protect gender identity. And it is behind concerted attempts of trans activist organisations to remove what is colloquially known as the 'spousal veto' from the GRA: the clause in the legislation that specifies that the spouse of a transitioning person must formally declare their consent to the marriage or civil partnership continuing, in order for a GRC to be issued to the partner. In practice, this clause mainly applies to the wives of late-transitioning trans women. Activists want it removed because it is viewed as potentially stopping a trans person from fully realising their gender identity. Speaking at the Liberal Democrat conference in 2019, MP Layla Moran proposed, on behalf of both her own party and trans activist organisations, that the condition be abolished, saying, 'You should not be defined by anyone else other than you, and that's what makes the spousal veto such an injustice ... the fact is your identity has nothing to do with anyone else. This is deeply personal and no one, no government, no spouse, should be able to veto who you are.'[25] In Scotland, activists have succeeded in getting the condition removed.[26]

The thinking behind Principle 3 has also had an apparent influence on clinical medical and psychological settings, and, specifically, the prohibition of 'conversion therapy' of those with non-standard gender identities, including children and teens. In 2017 several professional therapeutic bodies, including the British Psychological Society and the Royal

College of General Practitioners, signed off a Memorandum of Understanding prohibiting conversion therapy, understood as 'any model or individual viewpoint that demonstrates an assumption that any sexual orientation or gender identity is inherently preferable to any other, and which attempts to bring about a change of sexual orientation or gender identity, or seeks to suppress an individual's expression of sexual orientation or gender identity on that basis'.[27] The memorandum describes such therapy, whether for sexual orientation or gender identity, as 'unethical and potentially harmful'. The thinking seems to be that if gender identity is a fundamental part of identity, it would be destructive for a medical practitioner to try to undermine it. Instead, the gold-standard clinical approach is now considered to be 'gender-affirmative' or 'trans-affirmative' care, defined by the American Psychological Association as 'the provision of care that is respectful, aware, and supportive of the identities and life experiences of [trans and gender nonconforming] people'.[28] In affirmative care, you simply 'affirm' and so nurture what was always within. You allow the 'real' and fundamental identity to come to the surface, unimpeded.

Moment 7: The concept of a TERF was invented

Since the late 2000s, it has become increasingly common to see intellectual criticism of gender identity theory dismissed on the grounds that it inevitably comes from a bigoted place. In *Whipping Girl*, Julia Serano variously dismisses possible objections to her ideas as products of 'transphobia', 'homophobia', 'trans-misogyny', 'oppositional sexism' and 'gender anxiety'. In a 2009 interview, Judith Butler talked of 'the feminist police force who rejects the lived embodiment of transwomen', calling their claims 'transphobic discourse' and a form of 'mutilation'.[29] UK charity Stonewall's online glossary currently defines transphobia as (my italics): 'The fear or dislike of someone based on the fact they are trans, *including denying their gender identity or refusing to accept it.*' To spell this out: Stonewall's definition explicitly places 'denying' someone's gender identity, or 'refusing to accept it', as inevitably issuing from fear or dislike, *no matter what the grounds*. Even if you have reflected on the intellectual background for gender identity theory, find it lacking, and for that reason 'refuse to accept' gender identity, the *real* reason must be a deeper fear or dislike.

In 2008, denigrating the motives of critics of gender identity theory was given a big boost with the invention of a 'TERF'. TERF stands for 'Trans Exclusionary Radical Feminist'. It was reportedly coined by American Viv Smythe.[30] In 2008 Smythe was running a feminist blog. In a post, she promoted the Michigan Womyn's Musical Festival, also known as Michfest. When founded in 1976, Michfest had been conceived by its radical feminist organisers as for females only – or, as organisers named them, 'Womyn-born-womyn'. There was a heavy lesbian presence, in the traditional same-sex sense, amongst attendees. Latterly, the festival had become controversial for its explicit exclusion of trans women from the event. (Indeed, eventually Michfest closed in 2015, partly due to this controversy.) Smythe was quickly taken to task by blog readers for her promotion of Michfest, and in the course of her subsequent public apology, coined the acronym TERF. She wrote, of her promise not to promote any 'trans-exclusionary feminist event' in future: 'I am aware that this decision is likely to affront some trans-exclusionary radical feminists (TERFs).'[31] The term TERF rapidly took off, as memorable acronyms often do – perhaps helped by its ugly phonetics and capacity to be easily barked out as an insult or threat. Though in Smythe's original construction, TERFs were, by definition, feminists, later popular usage of the term widened to refer to any person at all who had, for whatever reason, an even mildly critical perspective on the bundle of ideas that constitutes gender identity theory. Indeed, trans women and trans men *themselves* came to be called TERFs, whenever they worried that gender identity alone was not what made you a woman or man.

What explains the generally aggressive approach to criticism on the part of defenders of gender identity theory? At least part of the answer seems to lie in the intellectual priors of gender identity theory, and specifically with the philosophical world-view of Butler. Butler thinks the categories of *man* and *male*, *woman* and *female*, are inevitably 'exclusionary'; i.e. they prioritise certain restrictive ideals or stereotypes about what is natural and 'right' for men and women. So effectively on this view, *whenever* you try to assert that there's such a thing as females or women, as a natural and pre-given category – *for whatever reason* – you are effectively 'excluding' socially marginalised people who don't meet the implicit ideal and you should be criticised accordingly.

A further influence in the background here is what is known in philosophy as 'standpoint epistemology'. This is the idea that some forms of knowledge are socially situated, so that only if you are in a particular social situation are you able to easily acquire that kind of knowledge. The term originally comes from Marxism and the idea that oppressed people can have insight into two perspectives or 'standpoints' at once – their own and their oppressors' – whereas oppressors can have only one perspective (their own). Since the workers are subject to bourgeois rules and a bourgeois worldview, they get insight into the bourgeoisie's standpoint. Additionally, though, workers have intimate knowledge of their own socially situated standpoint, which the bourgeoisie lacks.

This idea has been adopted by several social justice movements, including feminism, critical race theory and trans activism. As developed by trans activists, standpoint epistemology says there are special forms of standpoint-related knowledge about trans experience available only to trans people, not cis people. For instance, only trans people can properly understand the pernicious effects of 'cis privilege', and how it intersects with other forms of oppression to produce certain kinds of lived experience. As with some versions of feminism and critical race theory, when transmuted through popular culture this has quickly become the idea that only trans people can legitimately say anything about their own nature and interests including on philosophical matters of gender identity. Cis people, including feminists and lesbians, have nothing useful to contribute here. Their assumption that they *do* have something useful to contribute is a further manifestation of their unmerited privilege. In the words of trans philosopher Veronica Ivy, 'cis folks' – including TERFs – just need to 'sit down and shut up'.[32]

Moment 8: An explosion of identities

Two decades into the twenty-first century, an outdated stereotype of a trans person still lingers in the popular Western imagination. This represents her as a glamorous post-operative trans woman, otherwise known as a transsexual male-to-female (MTF): someone who – the stereotype goes – started life as a man, but later had operations to remove natal genitalia and create a synthetic vagina. She 'passes' – that is, she is visually indiscernible from a woman. She's committed to the lifelong taking of oestrogen to suppress male-associated physical traits and enhance female-associated ones such as breasts. She dresses in women's clothes and wears make-up. Alongside this physical stereotype, there's a psychosexual one: she's very likely sexually oriented towards males. Had she not transitioned, she would have been considered a gay man. Prior to transition, in light of her obvious misalignment with masculine bodily norms and heterosexual ideals, she suffered from gender dysphoria, a condition that caused her unbearable psychological distress.

Yet once inner gender identity, misaligned with 'outer' assigned sex, is taken to be the determining factor in being trans rather than any medical or legal or behavioural fact, this stereotype is revealed to be wholly inadequate as a complete picture of contemporary trans life. Not only does the stereotype fail to accommodate trans men, it also ignores how being trans comes in a rich variety of cultural, behavioural, physical and psychosexual manifestations, and under many different further sub-headings. As trans academic Stephen Whittle summed it up in 2006, the same year he was involved in the writing of the Yogyakarta Principles: 'A trans person might be a butch or a camp, a transgender or a transsexual, an MTF or FTM or a cross-dresser; they might, in some parts of the world, consider themselves a lady boy, katoey, or even the reclaimed Maori identities whakawahine or whakatane.'[33] What used to look like historically and culturally disparate phenomena are now bundled up together under the heading 'trans', and understood as unified in relation to the central idea of having a misaligned gender identity. 'Passing' is no longer seen as a necessarily desirable state for a trans person either. Instead, broadly in line with Judith Butler's ideas about gender as performance, failure to pass is now represented as productively disrupting and subverting – in the words of influential trans scholar Sandy Stone – 'the old binary discourses of gender'.[34]

In 2020, the number of gender identities has exploded. A particularly popular one is being non-binary: having a gender identity that is neither exclusively male nor exclusively female, neither masculine nor feminine, but either switches fluidly between these or rejects both. Since gender identity determines womanhood and manhood, it follows that if you are non-binary, you are neither a woman nor a man, or perhaps you are a bit of both. There is more to gender identity than male, female or non-binary, however. Stonewall's online glossary describes 'trans' as an 'umbrella' term, 'including (but not limited to) transgender, transsexual, gender-queer (GQ), gender-fluid, non-binary, gender-variant, crossdresser, genderless, agender, nongender, third gender, bi-gender, trans man, trans woman, trans masculine, trans feminine and neutrois'.[35] Facebook offers the user a choice of seventy-one 'gender options'.[36] For a grasp on what the really cutting-edge gender identities currently are, it's always worth looking at official university trans policies. For instance, University of Kent policy currently officially recognises and protects the gender identity 'demifluid' – that is, the policy states, people 'whose gender identity is partially fluid whilst the other part(s) are static'. Kent also recognises the 'demiflux' – that is, people 'whose gender identity is partially fluid, with the other part(s) being static'. Though the unwary might confuse demiflux with demifluid, these are not the same, we are told, for 'flux indicates that one of the genders is non-binary'.[37] University of Essex policy, meanwhile, recognises the 'pangender', understood as people who identify 'with a multitude, and perhaps infinite (going beyond the current knowledge of genders) number of genders either simultaneously, to varying degrees, or over the course of time'.[38] Perhaps not surprisingly in light of all this, the University of Roehampton notes in its trans policy that 'Terminology is continually evolving and by the time this policy is published, some definitions may be out of date'.[39]

A further source of non-standard gender identities is thought to be non-Western cultures. In the quote I used just now, Stephen Whittle mentioned the Thai katoey and the Maori whakawahine or whakatane. In recently published educational material for schools, Stonewall highlights 'the Hijra community in India; the Calabi, Calalai and Bissu genders in Indonesia; the Mashoga of Kenya; and two-spirit people from Native American cultures'.[40] Increasingly we are told by academics that the idea of a natural binary division between females and males is a pernicious product of Eurocentrism, colonialism or even white supremacy.[41] It has also become possible to speculate that famous cross-dressing or otherwise ambiguous figures from the past were actually trans, with inner gender identities misaligned with assigned sex. Dr James Barry, Anne Lister, Joan of Arc and Queen Hatshepsut are just a few of those names offered.[42]

Children, too, are considered as potentially having non-standard gender identities that require external recognition and affirmation from society, and which should not be repressed. Between 2009 and 2019 the number of male children treated at the NHS Tavistock Gender Identity Development Service (GIDS) rose by 1,460 per cent from 40 to 624, and the number of female children by 5,337 per cent from 32 to 1740.[43] From 2011 to 2020, forty-four UK children between the ages of ten and fifteen diagnosed as having misaligned gender identities were prescribed 'puberty blockers' – gonadotropin-releasing hormone agonists, licensed for prostate cancer, endometriosis, uterine fibroids and central precocious puberty, but not for children with gender dysphoria. Following a Judicial Review in 2020, a report revealed that for forty-three of these patients, cross-sex hormone treatments followed.[44] In the US, female children as young as thirteen are having radical double mastectomies, known as 'top' surgery.[45] In many countries, including the US and UK, trans teenagers reaching the age of majority have major reconstructive surgery on genitalia.[46] In line with gender identity theory, these events are celebrated by some as allowing the children and teens concerned to be who they 'really' are.[47] At the same time, it's assumed that adults with currently misaligned gender identities must have always had them, even in childhood and even if undetected; so that where for example a trans woman used to be, ostensibly, a boy child, all the while she was 'really' a girl.

The ever-expanding list of kinds of trans people can seem incomprehensible to outsiders, but it needn't be, as long as we understand that they all have something in common: namely, gender identities misaligned with assigned sex. Gender identity is expressed through many possible ways of dressing, acting and modifying one's body, from having surgery to doing nothing at all. As Stephen Whittle writes, being trans can involve 'occasional or more frequent cross-dressing, permanent cross-dressing and cross-gender living, through to accessing major health interventions such as hormonal therapy and surgical reassignment procedures. It can take up as little of your life as five minutes a week or as much as a life-long commitment to reconfiguring the body to match the inner self.'[48] Equally, being trans may not involve any outward behavioural change at all. Just as you can be gay before you ever come out and start to tell people, you are also trans even if you haven't started to change your outward presentation in any way whatsoever. And in fact, you might never start. Some trans people reject alteration of their bodies or appearances as reinforcing stereotypical expectations about femininity and masculinity in a pernicious way.[49] Nonetheless, they are still trans. Their gender identities make them so.

So concludes my whistle-stop tour of big moments in the history of gender identity theory. I turn now to some house-keeping matters for what is to come.

The many meanings of 'gender'

Readers may have spotted that, even at this early stage in the book, the word 'gender' has already appeared in several different guises. In Moment 1 alone, it popped up twice with two different meanings. It is a standing feature of almost any argument between feminists and trans activists that the word 'gender' will appear there in several different senses, often unnoticed and in a way that increases confusion and toxicity exponentially. Cultural historian Bernice Hausman captures the confusion well when she writes how, at a certain point, she began to realise that: 'although most people adhered to a distinction between "sex" and "gender" that relegates the first term to nature and the second to culture, some were beginning to use "gender" to refer to both realms. Instead of "sex discrimination" people used the term "gender discrimination"; on some affirmative action forms, applicants were asked to enter their gender – male or female. Thus, although "gender" originally was used by researchers to refer to social attributes of sexed identity, it was beginning to dominate popular discourses to such an extent that its older usage – as a direct substitute for the word "sex" – was being revived.'[50]

I will disambiguate four senses of 'gender' now. Readers should return to this section if they later come across a use that confuses them. Just as the English word 'bank' can refer to the land beside the river, or the institution that looks after your money, the following are four different meanings of the English word 'gender' – etymologically related, no doubt, and overlapping in terms of people they apply to, but standing for different things. Here they are.

GENDER1: A polite-sounding word for the division between men and women, understood as a traditional alternative word for biological sex/the division between biological males and females. This word is thought to have the benefit of an absence of embarrassing connotations of sexiness in the copulatory sense. When a passport application, say, asks for 'gender', it's intended in this sense. In Elizabeth Gaskell's *Cranford*, a character refers to the 'masculine gender', meaning males/men.

GENDER2: A word for social stereotypes, expectations and norms of 'masculinity' and 'femininity', originally directed towards biological males and females respectively. These can and do differ from culture to culture, though there are many overlaps too.

GENDER3: A word for the division between men and women, understood, by definition, as a division between two sets of people: those who have the social role of masculinity projected on to them, and those who have the social role of femininity projected on to them. This is the view of womanhood and manhood, as such, discussed in Moment 1 above. As mentioned, in the late twentieth century it was enthusiastically endorsed by some feminists as a putative shield against accusations of 'biological determinism': the idea that female anatomy is domestic destiny. It will be examined critically in Chapter 5.

GENDER4: A shortened version of the term 'gender identity'. What exactly a gender identity is will be investigated in Chapter 4, but a common idea is that it is the 'private experience of gender role' – roughly, whether you relate to yourself psychologically as a boy or man, girl or woman, or neither, in a way that has nothing directly to do with your sex.

Keeping these different senses in mind is crucial when trying to decipher various claims made by feminists and trans activists. Even though Yogyakarta Principle 3, discussed just now, is mostly concerned with the primacy of *gender identity*, when it refers to 'all State-issued identity papers that indicate a person's gender/sex', confusingly it means GENDER1 not GENDER4. Presumably when therapists talk about 'gender dysphoria', strictly speaking they mean GENDER1: feeling distressingly dysphoric about your sex, i.e. being male or female. When feminists say there's a difference between 'sex and gender', they can't possibly mean GENDER1, and they definitely at least mean GENDER2. They quite possibly also mean GENDER3, though you can coherently talk about GENDER2 without implying GENDER3. When parents say they are raising their children 'gender-free', they seem to mean GENDER2. When the term 'transgender' was originally introduced, meaning 'across' or 'on the other side of' gender, users presumably meant GENDER2 or GENDER3 and not GENDER1, or, at least, should have done (for, as I'll argue in the next chapter, you can't actually change or 'trans' sex, literally speaking). Similarly, as I'll discuss in Chapter 6, when the law talks about 'gender recognition' or 'gender reassignment', it presumably doesn't, or at least shouldn't, mean GENDER1. When Butler talks about 'gender performance' it's harder to classify her, but she probably means something close to GENDER3. When therapists talk about 'gender-affirmative care' they mean GENDER4, as does Stonewall when it says on its website that 'If you aren't recognised as being the gender you know you are, it's extremely damaging' and 'you can use the bathroom that fits your gender'. Equally, when people talk about being 'gender-fluid', or the University of Essex talks about 'a multitude, and perhaps infinite ... number of genders' they mean GENDER4.

Because of all this confusion, it will be policy in this book to avoid the word 'gender' wherever possible, and in each case substitute more concrete, clearer terms that do whatever job I want them to at the time. So, for instance, I'll always say 'sex' for GENDER1. Rather than say GENDER2, I'll talk about 'sex-based' or 'sex-associated' stereotypes, making clear when I mean purely social ones, and when I don't. I'll also talk about 'sex conforming' or 'sex nonconforming', rather than 'gender conforming' or 'gender nonconforming' behaviour. I won't use GENDER3 at all, except to explicitly criticise the ideas behind it. And for GENDER4, I'll always use 'gender identity'.

A final, related caveat. Quite apart from the trans-activist-versus-feminist wars, there's another culture war raging simultaneously that sometimes gets in the way. Its forerunner was the battle between feminists and biological determinists described in Moment 1. These days, skirmishes tend to be between 'blank slate' feminists, who think all sex-associated stereotypes of femininity and masculinity must be social, so that in effect there are no natural or innate behavioural or psychological differences between males and females at all, and those 'innatist' evolutionary psychologists who think at least some behavioural and psychological stereotypes accurately represent pre-existing average biological differences between the sexes.[51] In this book, I want to steer clear of this second front in the gender wars where possible. Usually, when I say 'sex-associated stereotypes' I want to leave room for the idea that at least some of those are grounded in biological reality. Equally, though, it seems obvious that some are not. Part of my argument will depend on that.

In defence of debate

In this book, I take on gender identity theory. I argue that much of it is intellectually confused and concretely harmful.

First, though, I tackle the charge that any criticism whatsoever of gender identity theory or trans activism must be 'transphobic'. Obviously I need to get this out of the way.

A first thing to note, in case it's unclear, is that I am not arguing against legal protections for trans people against violence, discrimination or coercive surgeries. I enthusiastically support these protections.

A second thing to note is that, in their own ways, not just professional philosophers de Beauvoir and Butler, but also Money, Stoller, Fausto-Sterling, Serano and Whittle are each endorsing sometimes complicated and abstract philosophical theories, despite sometimes presenting them with a gloss of straightforward scientific observation. Take Fausto-Sterling: she speculates both that there are at least five sexes and that sex is a 'continuum'. Now, she certainly didn't read these conclusions straightforwardly from data in a lab. Other people can and do look at the very same data and come up with different rational conclusions. Equally, when John Money hypothesised about the existence of 'gender identity', he was hypothesising a new, contestable theoretical concept to try to better explain what he and others observed. Ditto for Serano's proposal of the concept of 'cis'. As such, then, all of these theoretical postulates should be available for robust critical examination, just as theoretical postulates in general should be.

It's standard practice in philosophy and academia more generally to subject theories and their postulates to trenchant critique. Does a given theory explain the evidence well? Are there rival theories that might explain the evidence better? Does the theory help us explain and predict what people care about? Does it have other explanatory virtues such as simplicity, and is it a good fit with other existing productive theories? To rule these questions out as automatically 'transphobic' is potentially to give a free pass to bad theorising. As an academic I can't responsibly do that, and others shouldn't either. It is standard for academics to subject their work to rigorous critique by peers: papers get torn to shreds in seminars and referee reports, and experiments pored over to look for potentially confounding variables. And for good reason: history is littered with bad theories and empty theoretical concepts, from inner demons to bodily humours to phlogiston. There's no reason to think there isn't room for similar error here – in fact, there is extra reason to think there is, inasmuch as some (though not all) trans people so clearly desperately want gender identity theory to work, which might be affecting their neutrality. Many trans people assume – wrongly, as I will eventually argue – that the existence and recognition of their political and legal rights depends upon gender identity theory's correctness.

To critics who would say that, as a cis person, I am unacceptably encroaching on trans people's accounts of their own lived experience by arguing about gender identity, I would first say: do they not assume that I, as a cis person, have a gender identity too? More importantly, I would add that I don't believe the insights of standpoint epistemology, rehearsed earlier, take us anything like that far. It's plausible to say, as standpoint epistemology does, that the workers can understand the concrete impact of bourgeois rules upon them better than the bourgeoisie do; and that by extrapolation, only trans people can really understand what it's like to live as a trans person in a mostly cis world. But it's a wild leap from there to saying that only trans people can legitimately comment on the philosophical nature and practical consequences – for everybody – of gender identity. As a lesbian and as a sex-nonconforming woman I too have skin in this game – not to mention as an academic who cares about ideas, and as a feminist who cares about other women. In any case, trans people reasonably disagree among themselves about gender identity.

Trans people aren't an intellectual monolith, and misaligned gender identity, understood as a general concept, is not something lived experience delivers straight to trans brains in a transparent and uninterpreted way.

A final objection to all this might be: in the end, what does it really matter? Can't we just give trans people a free pass on gender identity theory if it makes them happy? Am I not just playing abstract philosophical games with real people's lives? Shouldn't I try to be more kind? It will be the argument of much of this book that, unfortunately, the relatively uncontested prominence of gender identity theory in many circles matters very much, for trans and non-trans people alike. Its consequences are far from 'abstract'. They do material harm to many, including to some trans people themselves. Trans people, and future trans activism, are better off without it.

Gender identity theory doesn't just say that gender identity exists, is fundamental to human beings, and should be legally and politically protected. It also says that biological sex is irrelevant and needs no such legal protection. In a straight fight between gender identity and sex, as it were, gender identity should win. So, I need to talk about sex.

What is Sex?

In the past five years, UK campaigning charities such as Stonewall, the Scottish Trans Alliance and Gendered Intelligence have lobbied politicians both to change the law to recognise gender identity and to remove political protections for the female sex from the Equality Act.[1] Why do trans activists think we must choose between gender identity and sex? Partly, it's assumed to be psychologically important to trans people that others don't refer to sex at all. This thought, pushed hard by lobbying groups, has led to the development of a cultural taboo around mentioning it. But another important contributory factor has been academics arguing that there are not in fact two distinct biological sexes after all. If this were true, it would indeed be a good reason to think legal protections should focus only on gender identity. So there's an immediate need to scrutinise such claims.

The topic of this chapter is, directly, *being female or male*, and not (directly) *being a woman or man*. As we have seen, for some theorists, being a woman is not the same as being female: according to them, some males can be women, and some females, men. I will discuss these views later, but for the moment I don't want us to get distracted, so: whatever you now think about whether you have to be female to count as a woman, or be male to count as a man, bracket those thoughts. We are talking only about being female or male, which is to say, about sex – and, to be clear, not the fun kind. For now, concentrate only on the claim that humans are divided into females and males, and that this binary division is a natural state of affairs rooted in stable biological fact.

For many readers, it might seem surreal that I'm bothering to spend a whole chapter on establishing that binary sex exists. They will take this to be blatantly obvious. For others, my arguments will seem outrageous and heretical. Such is the strange intellectual climate we now live in. Even for those falling into the former camp, it is worth finding out how the other half lives, and what background intellectual commitments are fuelling current disputes.

Before we get to claims that binary sex doesn't exist, we need to find the best available positive account of what sex is. There are three candidates on the table. Each of them holds that males and females are naturally found in the world and always have been, for as long as there have been humans. I find all three equally plausible; each has some drawbacks, but no drawback seems devastating, and I won't choose between them. In any case, the common objections made to the idea of two sexes do not threaten any of them.

What are the sexes?

The gamete account

A first account of the sexes, recently spelled out by philosopher Alex Byrne, aims to account for females and males in every species where they occur: human, animal or plant.[2] Let's call this the 'gamete account'. An organism's reproductive cells are called its gametes. The gamete account says males, by definition, are those organisms on a developmental pathway to produce small gametes for the purposes of sexual reproduction. Females, meanwhile, are those organisms on a developmental pathway to produce larger gametes for the purposes of sexual reproduction. 'Larger' here is relative to the small gametes produced by males in the same species. Females produce relatively few, static, large gametes. Males produce relatively many, mobile, small gametes. In some organisms, male parts and female parts are present simultaneously: for instance, in flowers that produce both pollen and ova. In most species, though, males and females are separate organisms. Equally, in species such as clownfish – sometimes cited as a species of relevance to whether humans can change sex – organisms can change from male to female, given exposure to the right external circumstances interacting with internal mechanisms. But here, too, what makes a clownfish at a given point in its development male or female is whether it is on a developmental pathway (immediately, next) to produce smaller or larger gametes.

Why insist on the wording 'on a developmental pathway' (etc.) rather than simply make actual possession of small or larger gametes the criterion of being female or male? The answer, as Byrne recognises, is that developmental pathways can go awry. Gametes are not always produced. Disease and variation can interfere, as can environmental influences and old age. Yet we do not normally say organisms subject to such interference are no longer female or male. When we talk about females and males, we are talking about a capacity that a given organism either *actually has* or at least *would have had under certain given circumstances* (e.g. had *that* particular variation not occurred; had *that* particular environmental factor not interfered, etc.). We can reasonably say: had it not been for this interfering factor, large gamete production would have occurred for this organism given the rest of its internal workings. So it is still a female, even if it doesn't actually produce large gametes now.

This account of sex has nothing to say about chromosomes. It doesn't mention XY or XX at all. Nor does it specify primary or secondary sex characteristics or other morphological features (roughly: physical characteristics). Its aim is to cover any biological species whatsoever that has a division between males and females for the purposes of sexual reproduction. Such species vary in chromosomes and morphologies. But what they all share, in this view, is two separate developmental pathways, each producing a certain relative size of gamete at the end of it, if all goes according to plan.

The chromosome account

A different account of the sexes takes as its focus *human* males and females. This view seeks to classify human males and females, as such, in terms of whatever physical factor(s), specifically, send them down one gamete-producing pathway or other. This factor, it turns out, is possession or lack of a Y chromosome in cells. It's the SRY gene on the Y chromosome that, in a seven-week-old human embryo, normally triggers development of a small-gamete-producing body rather than a large-gamete-producing one. A human male is a human with a Y chromosome. A human female is a human without a Y chromosome. I'll call this account of the two sexes the 'chromosome account'. The chromosome account doesn't say females necessarily have XX sex chromosomes and males XY. That is the standard distribution, but rare Disorders of Sexual Development (DSDs) mean some females are X, XXX, XXXX or XXXXX, and some males are XXY, XXXY or XXXXY. It is rather the presence or absence of a Y chromosome in cells that is counted as defining the two groups.

On both gamete and chromosome accounts, there are occasional cases of DSDs not easily characterised as either male or female. One such case is individuals produced by the early merging of non-identical twin embryos in the womb. They have some cells that express XX and others that express XY. This condition is called 46,XX/46,XY. Some, though not all, of these people have ovotesticular disorder – that is, both ovarian and testicular tissue in their bodies. The gamete account would struggle to classify such people as definitively male or female since it is unclear precisely which gamete-producing developmental pathway they are on. And the chromosome account would struggle too, as there seems no particular reason to favour possession of a Y chromosome in some cells but not others as definitive for classification.

Both gamete and chromosome accounts characterise human males and females from a narrow range of explanatory interests – mainly, the interest in locating them in biological and medical explanations. Both are also 'essentialist' accounts – that is, each prioritises one particular feature (respectively: developmental pathway; Y chromosome or lack of one) as essential to, and also sufficient for, membership of a given sex. The lines of these accounts are not completely clean, but still, for the majority of humans, there will be a clear answer as to whether someone is male or female.

Yet that answer may seem counterintuitive, relative to what an ordinary non-scientific person might say. Take the case of people with XY chromosomes who also have a DSD called Androgen Insensitivity Syndrome (AIS). They have testicles, sometimes partly or fully undescended, and are 'male' according to both the gamete and the chromosome accounts. Yet they are also partly or wholly unable to respond to testosterone, and so can develop either an 'undervirilised' or even a thoroughly 'feminised' external morphology (in plain terms: breasts, vulva and clitoris, as well as post-pubescent muscle and fat distribution and facial structure within female-associated ranges). Some people with the extreme form, Complete AIS, grow up thinking of themselves as female, as do those around them – yet wrongly so, according to the gamete and chromosome accounts. Alternatively, there are people with XX chromosomes and ovaries, identified as female on both the gamete and chromosome accounts, yet who have a condition, Congenital Adrenal Hyperplasia, resulting in some cases in a highly 'virilised' external morphology, including a phallic-like clitoris, and the appearance of an empty scrotum.

Another case that apparently produces counterintuitive identification concerns individuals with a condition called 45,X/46,XY mosaicism. Embryos with this condition start with an XY chromosome, and so technically are on a small-gamete-producing pathway, at least at the beginning. Hence they count as male on the gamete account, and – though it is less clear – perhaps also on the chromosome account too, depending upon what stage of Y chromosome possession is judged most relevant to classification. However, early on in the cell division process, a Y chromosome is lost from a cell leaving only an X. This cell is then copied and recopied, reproducing exponentially. The result is a foetus with both X and XY cells. Here, as with 46,XX/46,XY there's a possibility of having both ovarian and testicular tissue in the body. Yet the gamete and perhaps also the chromosome account would classify people in this group as male.

The cluster account

This third model of the sexes contains resources for a different answer to some of these cases. I will call this the 'cluster account'. The cluster account takes its inspiration from a particular account of what a species is.

It used to be an article of faith that all members of a given species must share a common trait or 'essence', guaranteeing membership of that species. It was assumed that what makes, say, tigers all members of one species is that they, and only they, share some particular features in common. Though the features differ in each case, the same was assumed to go for common earthworms, oyster mushrooms, Scots pine trees and so on, for all species. In practice, however, scientists were often unable to find any features that might count as the 'essential' ones shared by all and only members of a given species. Natural selection tends to generate species with genetic diversity, through processes such as recombination, mutation and random drift. Morphological characteristics – physical characteristics of an organism like a tiger's stripes or dense, short fur – can vary profoundly within a species, given both genetic variation and differences in how particular genes are expressed in particular environments. Some tigers are born without stripes, for instance. Making things more complicated, different species can share genetic material and/or morphological characteristics.

In response to such facts, the philosopher Richard Boyd proposed a 'Homeostatic Property Cluster' account of biological species (HPC).[3] According to HPC, species are defined in terms of relatively stable *clusters* of morphological characteristics plus underlying mechanisms producing those characteristics.[4] Morphological characteristics tend to cluster together in a species either because of certain underpinning mechanisms – genetic or environmental or developmental – or because some of the characteristics are made more likely by the presence of other characteristics in the cluster; or both. But crucially, according to HPC, *no particular characteristic in the cluster, nor underpinning mechanism, is counted as essential for an individual's membership of the species.*[5] That is, particular members of species can lack particular characteristics and/or particular mechanisms (remember the example of some tigers having no stripes). Nonetheless, as long as the individual possesses *enough* of the important properties in the cluster, and those properties are caused by *enough* of the relevant mechanisms, it still counts as a member of the species in question. Hence there is room for genetic and morphological variation within a species, unproblematically.

What counts as having 'enough' of the 'important' properties in a cluster is in some sense a practical decision, relative to wider collective theoretical goals. Although Boyd doesn't to my knowledge say this, presumably our collective goals in categorising entities in the natural world might sometimes be other than strictly scientific or medical. If so, perhaps we can adapt the HPC account to explain the basis of two naturally occurring categories, male and female, in which humans have interests from a number of perspectives that aren't just medical and scientific ones.

The 'cluster account' of sex first identifies a cluster of morphological characteristics relevant to identifying people as male or female in ordinary life. From birth to old age, females and males respectively tend to have certain distinctive general physical features, relative to each other and within certain ranges. They have distinctive reproductive organs and genitalia at birth (primary sex characteristics), and also, after puberty, a certain distinctive kind of facial structure, skeletal structure, muscle and fat distribution, breasts or lack of them, body hair or lack of it, vocal tone, and so on. These are called secondary sex characteristics.

So effectively, there's one cluster of morphological characteristics relevant to counting as male, and another cluster relevant to counting as female. It's important to note the 'relative to each other and within certain ranges' in my formulation just now. I am not, of course, saying all or even most females, say, have exactly the same face and body. The claim is about features *within a range*, where features within this range are more statistically likely for one kind of people than the other kind. Each cluster of features is characteristically associated with a set of underlying causal mechanisms: distinctive kinds of gene expression, levels of hormone production, and other developmental mechanisms. Unlike on the gamete or chromosome account, though, on the cluster account, *no individual characteristic is treated as essential for being female or male*. Equally, there's no requirement that an individual exhibit *all* of the features in a given cluster. So the possibility of variation is anticipated and dealt with. Rather, what's required for being female is that one exhibits *enough* of the important features in the female-associated cluster, underpinned by enough of the right sort of mechanisms. The same goes for being male, in relation to the male-associated cluster. Most people will exhibit all of the characteristics in a particular cluster, but not everyone will. Still, this won't make them any less male or female, because on the cluster account, there was never any requirement that they have the full set, as it were.

What counts as 'enough' of the 'important' features in a cluster, as with the HPC account, is in a sense a practical decision, to be made in relation to wider theoretical goals. And as mooted in relation to HPC, perhaps these goals need not be exclusively medical/biological, and so might conceivably place heavier emphasis on the 'outer' observable features of a person in the everyday than on chromosomes or inner reproductive organs. This might seem reasonable, given that 'outer' features are the ones people are directly acquainted with most often, used in everyday identification of sex, including self-identification. If this is right, it might leave the door open for a person with CAIS – a person with XY chromosome but who was born with a vulva and clitoris and who in puberty develops breasts and other female-associated physical features – to count as female, in at least one coherent sense: if, say, we collectively decided to weight external bodily characteristics as more important than internal ones. After all, the external morphology associated with Complete Androgen Insensitivity Syndrome is at least partly due to an underlying causal mechanism shared with females generally.[6]

Perhaps, for similar reasons, there's also room on the cluster account for a person with XX chromosomes but with Congenital Adrenal Hyperplasia and a resulting extremely virilised external morphology to count as male, given at least one underlying mechanism shared with males: exposure to high levels of androgens. And in the case of 45,X/46,XY mosaicism, what classification we eventually make might be tailored to best fit particular aspects of the individual morphology. These classifications would not necessarily be suitable for medical or biological contexts, but there are other important human contexts too.

I don't pretend establishing what to say in such cases is easy. Some DSDs and resulting morphologies push us to the limits of our concepts. But in any case, we now have our three contenders for defining what being female or male is. So are there, as the critics would have it, any good reasons to think that, in fact, the belief that there are (only) two naturally given sexes is a mistake or a fiction? Let's look at the reasons given most often and see if any of them are a threat. I will start with an easy one.

We normally don't know what people's chromosomes are or what their genitals look like

This objection proceeds from the fact we don't know what someone's chromosomes/gametes/genitals are to the claim that these can't be counted as conditions relevant to their membership of one sex or other. Biologist Julia Serano, encountered in Chapter 1, makes this argument in *Whipping Girl*. She seems to argue that there is no such thing as a 'genetic' male or female because 'we are unable to readily see other people's sex chromosomes'.[7] She is similarly scathing about the idea that being a 'biological' male or female could have anything to do with genital possession because we don't typically see strangers' genitals and yet we usually still know what sex they are. She apparently concludes that, because we usually identify the sex of strangers only on the basis of *observable* secondary sex characteristics like breasts and facial hair, or their absence, they must be what make you one sex or other.[8]

This argument confuses *how you usually infer* something is in a particular category with *what makes it* belong to that category. Compare: I see you're wearing a wedding ring and infer you are married – correctly as it happens, because you *are* married. However, wearing a wedding ring is not what makes you married. You could wear one and be single. As this demonstrates, there can be a distinction between the evidence used, usually reliably but not infallibly, to assess membership of a particular category, and actual conditions of membership. When people go through a marriage ceremony, they often though not always get a wedding ring. So it's not crazy to use a wedding ring as reasonable evidence of someone being married. Similarly: females usually gain breasts but not facial hair in puberty. So usually we can use the appearance of breasts and the non-appearance of facial hair to help assess someone's sex. Still, though, it's not having an appearance of breasts or a lack of visible facial hair that makes you female, just as it's not the wedding ring that makes you married. You could have acquired each of these things by other means. There's no real threat here to any of the three models of sex I have offered.

Some people exhibit Differences of Sexual Development

As described in Chapter 1, Anne Fausto-Sterling has been influential in promoting the view that sex isn't a binary but, in her words, 'a vast, infinitely malleable continuum' .[9] Her books are best-sellers, and her opinion pieces make the *New York Times*. Her reasoning to this conclusion mostly derives from discussions of people with DSDs. This is a slightly harder challenge.

Following others before her, Fausto-Sterling tends to call people with DSDs 'intersex'. She is fond of saying that 1.7 per cent of the population is intersex.[10] If she is right, that would be a huge number – nearly one in every fifty people. But in fact, this figure of 1.7 per cent includes the 1.5 per cent of the population who have a condition called late-onset (non-classical) Congenital Adrenal Hyperplasia. This is different from the classical CAH discussed just now, and involves an enzyme deficiency that potentially affects both sexes and is accompanied by no ambiguity in genitalia or in reproductive organs. It's even compatible in females with carrying a baby to term.[11] This condition easily can be accommodated on any of the three models of the sexes we've looked at.

Other DSDs easily accommodated on those models include:

Klinefelter's, where individuals with a Y chromosome, on the small-gamete pathway, and with a virilised morphology (i.e. males) have two or more X chromosomes rather than one; Turner syndrome, where individuals without a Y chromosome, on the large-gamete pathway, and with a feminised morphology (i.e. females) only have one X chromosome in some or all cells, rather than two; and MRKH, which produces an underdeveloped or absent vagina in people without a Y chromosome, on the large-gamete pathway, and with a feminised morphology (i.e. females). Once these conditions are subtracted from Fausto-Sterling's 1.7 per cent, we're left with the rather less eye-catching figure of 0.018 per cent – that is, 1.8 people in 10,000.[12] And this is important to note, because the inflated figure of 1.7 per cent has done a lot of rhetorical work on its own to persuade people that sex isn't binary but a continuum or 'spectrum'.

On further investigation, it turns out that what Fausto-Sterling means by 'intersex' is 'an individual who deviates from the Platonic ideal of physical dimorphism at the chromosomal, genital, gonadal, or hormonal levels'.[13] This implies that what it is to count as male or female must be to meet a chromosomal *and* genital *and* gonadal/gametal *and* hormonal Platonic ideal, and that if one fails in any of these essential respects, one is therefore intersex. This places preposterously over-demanding conditions on sex category membership. (I lost an ovary in my early twenties, so it would make me intersex, for a start.) The gamete account focuses only on gonadal/gametal developmental *pathways* – not even *actual* gamete or gonad possession – and makes no other requirements for sex classification. The chromosome account focuses on the presence or absence of the Y chromosome and makes no other requirements. The cluster account focuses on primary and secondary sex characteristics but crucially, makes no particular configuration of these essential to being female or male, for it isn't an essentialist account.

Despite statements that 1.7 per cent of people are intersex, in fact Fausto-Sterling's explicit arguments that sex is an 'infinitely malleable continuum' focus mostly on what are, by her own admission, a very rare subset of DSDs. Although she later described it as written with tongue in cheek, in her 1993 article 'The Five Sexes: Why Male and Female Are Not Enough' Fausto-Sterling suggests that alongside males and females, there are three more human sex categories.[14] I described these in Chapter 1 but it's worth revisiting them. First, there are 'true hermaphrodites': those with both ovarian and testicular material in their bodies as described earlier. Second, there are 'male pseudohermaphrodites': those with a Y chromosome on a small-gamete-producing path, but also with a feminised external morphology, as with CAIS. Third and finally, there are 'female pseudohermaphrodites': those without a Y chromosome on a large-gamete-producing path, but also with a virilised external morphology, as with classical CAH.

Positing five discrete categories hardly establishes an 'infinitely malleable continuum'. A 'continuum' suggests adjacent entities that are only subtly distinguishable from one another, which is not the case here. But more to the point, there is no need to call Fausto-Sterling's last three categories 'sexes' at all because they are all accounted for on all three models of the sexes canvassed above.

On both the chromosome and gamete accounts, 'male pseudohermaphrodites' are still male because they have a Y chromosome and are on a small-gamete-producing pathway, albeit disrupted and with a non-standard sexed body shape, relative to the norm. Equally, 'female pseudohermaphrodites' are female because they lack a Y chromosome and are on a large-gamete-producing pathway, again with the caveat above.

It's true these results are at odds with what some people with CAIS and CAH would say about themselves, but that is not necessarily a reason to reject the conclusions. On the cluster account, meanwhile, 'male pseudohermaphrodites' and 'female pseudohermaphrodites' can potentially count as male or female, depending on how we collectively decide to weight the importance of external morphology over other characteristics in the female and male clusters.

This leaves us only with 'true hermaphrodites', comprising an exceptionally rare 1.2 people in 100,000.[15] For instance, people with 46,XX/46,XY are difficult to classify on both the gamete and chromosome accounts, and perhaps for the cluster account as well. But it is unclear why such difficulties should lead us to think of sex as non-binary, let alone a 'continuum'. Fausto-Sterling, crucially, seems to ignore the fact that *difficulty about borderline cases is absolutely standard for biological categories*. At the metaphorical edge of *every* biological category there are so-called hard cases. For instance: where is the precise boundary between one existing biological species and another new species, evolving out of the former? There will obviously be cases that don't clearly belong to either, or seem to belong to both. Similar ambiguity occurs in species that split along geographical lines. Hybridisation between species poses another challenge. Are tigons and ligers members of the species tiger or lion, or both, or neither? Our existing biological categories struggle to provide a definitive answer.

Arguably, though, this issue isn't even limited to biological kinds. According to some philosophers, many or even all of our concepts are 'underdetermined' when it comes to outlying hard cases and what we should say about them. Take 'planet', as discussed by the philosopher Peter Ludlow.[16] 'Planet or non-planet?' looks like a binary question. But is Pluto a planet or not? Some say yes (on grounds that it's massive enough to form a ball and orbit the sun), some say no (on grounds that it's made of ice and not on the same plane as other planets). Or, more mundanely, take Jaffa Cakes: are they a cake (after all, they are sponge-like) or a biscuit (after all, they are small and biscuit-shaped)? The UK courts once found that Jaffa Cakes were cake, but it is easy to imagine the judgment being later reversed. Our ordinary concepts of *cake* and *biscuit* just aren't set up to cover that sort of case.

So, hard cases are not a special fact about the categories *male* and *female*. Many categories are bound, eventually, to run into hard cases that can't be automatically settled one way or the other on present understandings of the category. We mostly form our categories as conceptual tools to help us negotiate the everyday world and the sort of cases we encounter most. So it's not surprising that, when an unusual case turns up, we don't always know how to classify it.

So do what Fausto-Sterling calls 'true hermaphrodites' show that sex isn't a binary? Only if 'binary' means that every entity in the world must clearly fall into one state or the other. Properly understood, the 'sex binary' requires only that the vast majority of people fall into one category or the other. And on the three understandings of sex offered above, they do.

In a recent opinion piece for the *New York Times*, 'Why Sex Is Not Binary', Fausto-Sterling has one more go. This time, following John Money, she distinguishes between different stages or 'layers' of sexed development, consecutively developing at different points of life, from conception on: 'chromosomal', 'fetal gonadal', 'fetal hormonal', 'internal reproductive', 'external genital', 'pubertal hormonal' and 'pubertal morphological'.[17] She implies one layer can be 'female', and a different layer 'male', in the very same person. One immediate question is what exactly 'male' and 'female' mean here, if we're no longer talking about whole sexed individuals. But leaving that aside: given the three models of the sexes we've looked at, there's no good reason to think that talk about 'sexed' layers must replace any overall judgements about whether a given individual is male or female. Once again, Fausto-Sterling seems to have as her imagined antagonist someone who thinks of a female or a male as embodying a comprehensive 'Platonic Ideal', essentially involving perfect configurations of chromosomes *and* gonads, gametes *and* hormones *and* reproductive organs *and* genitals *and* pubescent features too. But to repeat: none of the above accounts are anything like this demanding.

The sexes are socially constructed (part 1)

Another intellectual behemoth in the world of sex denial is the American philosopher and Professor of Comparative Literature at Berkeley, Judith Butler. Mostly via her 1990s books *Gender Trouble* and *Bodies that Matter*, Butler has had a huge influence on the fields of queer theory, Gender Studies and Trans Studies. She is endlessly cited by modern trans activists as having 'shown' that biological sex is a 'social construct'.

Straight away we need to distinguish this statement from a less radical one with which it might easily be confused. Hers isn't just the familiar observation that the categories of males and females respectively each have a whole load of cultural and social meanings, expectations and norms contingently attached to them. In some Western cultures, for instance, males are culturally expected to be more powerful, active, loud, aggressive, otherwise emotionally repressed explorers of the world (and so on); females are culturally expected to be more caring, submissive, reconciliatory, emotionally open, domestic (and so on). We can argue about whether some of the meanings taken to be socially produced are in fact biologically determined, but surely we can agree that not all of them are, as shown by their significant cross-cultural and historical variation. She's saying something much more radical and subversive: that the categories of male and female are nothing but social meaning, as it were. There is no natural division in the world underneath, corresponding to the sexes. There are just two sets of social meanings that humans have contingently and arbitrarily assigned to two groups of people. If cultures and societies had ascribed social meanings differently, we could have a different configuration of sexes, or even no sexes. Sex is wholly socially constructed.

How does Butler arrive at this startling conclusion? As indicated in Chapter 1, an important assumption of hers is that any binary theory of the sexes must inevitably be 'normative' and therefore 'exclusionary' in a way that props up power imbalances between groups. It must appeal to two 'heteronormative' paradigms of ideal male and female bodies, minds and sexualities. As such, she thinks such a theory must perniciously 'exclude' people – for instance, gay people – who don't fit neatly with either respective set of norms.

In fact, no such norms are built into any of the three models of the sexes described above. It is not an exclusionary norm to insist that males, as such, possess a Y chromosome or be on a small-gamete-producing pathway. Rather, it is a way of conceptually differentiating between two kinds of entity, assumed to be naturally found in the world. Simply noting that some people fulfil such facts and others don't is not a value judgement about superiority or inferiority, or any other positive or negative connotations. Meanwhile, the cluster account is explicit that not all characteristics associated with maleness and femaleness need be possessed by an individual to count as one or other, and is clear that male and female characteristics are expressed across a range. Again, this is hardly obviously 'normative' in any sense that presupposes or entrenches pernicious power relations. Nor are there implications from any of the models we have looked at for the value of heterosexuality or otherwise. True, the gamete view is tied to thinking of females and males in terms of their evolutionarily-bestowed reproductive function, but this is not a claim about individual psychologies or sexual orientations, and so is compatible with perfect relaxation about various individual sexualities including homosexuality.

Butler's conclusion is embedded in a much wider philosophical worldview from which it cannot really be unmoored.[18] Intellectual commitments include the idea outlined in Chapter 1 that there is nothing intelligible in the world before it is referred to in language. Linguistic categorisation doesn't refer to prior reality, but is rather 'productive' or 'constitutive' of it. Because languages differ in their concepts, so too do 'constructions' of reality vary socioculturally and historically. Language doesn't reflect what was already there.[19] There are no pre-existing human kinds or types whose natures are to be discovered via philosophical or scientific analysis. Biology is itself just a 'medico-legal alliance emerging in 19th century Europe [that] has spawned categorial fictions' – i.e., the two sexes – 'that could not be anticipated in advance'.[20] Concepts such as the self or human nature or the 'natural' human body are also fictions, shifting in their details from society to society. There's nothing 'underneath' or 'before' language that would secure linguistic reference to something 'outside' of it.

To academic philosophers like me, keen to connect philosophy with working science in fruitful ways and to make appropriately nuanced distinctions between what is discovered by humans in the world as opposed to what is put there by them, Butler's worldview looks adolescently, simplistically monotonic. In short: she thinks it's all put there. Yet long experience tells me that, to some students and lecturers – mostly, it has to be said, in fields other than academic philosophy itself – Butler's worldview is hugely seductive. For those of a certain mindset, Butler is the Harry Potter of philosophy, transforming boring old truisms about the material world into something alchemical, shifting and sexily impermanent. This effect is heightened by the famous opacity of Butler's prose style, which can make people think they must be accessing *really deep* truths, and by the fact Butler rarely spells out the consequences of her view, coyly offering with one sentence what she then seems to take away with another. On a single page, she can imply both that there are no human bodies prior to various contingent sociocultural constructions of them, and that, somehow, there *is* such a thing as 'materiality' after all.[21]

To debunk the general social-constructionist worldview presented by Butler would take me very far from the central concern of this book – and besides, others have already done so.[22] What I can do is spell out in stark terms the consequences of Butler's worldview in a way she never does, and no doubt would at least half-heartedly disclaim.

So: it follows from the logic of Butler's worldview not only that there are not two naturally pre-given, stable biological sexes, but also that there are no pre-given facts about natural selection. There is no sexual reproduction. There are no pre-given chemical elements or biological species. There is no climate change, at least not as commonly understood. There are no molecules, atoms or quarks. There are no viruses and no bacteria; no successful drugs nor placebos. Talking about oxygen as a cause of combustion is ultimately no more rationally justified than talking about the eighteenth-century concept of phlogiston (which was thought to reside in every flammable substance and be released as it burned). Talking about neurons as causes of behaviour is neither more nor less accurate, ultimately, than talking about bodily 'humours'. Creationism is neither worse nor better a theory than Darwinism. There is no ahistorical, non-relative truth, in fact, nor 'accurate' scientific theory or representation.

I might be told, in response to the above précis, that I've got it wrong: in fact, there is still some coherent way in which, within the Butlerian picture, all of these things can be said 'really' to exist, *whilst also* understood as 'socially' and 'linguistically' constructed. In which case: phew, what a relief; in that case can we have the sexes back too, please?

The most plausible versions of social constructionism about science are not sceptical about the existence, full stop, of the things they conclude are socially constructed. As philosopher Ian Hacking says of those who claim airplanes are 'socially constructed': they still 'expect airplanes to get you there, and know that science, technology, and enterprise are essential for air travel'.[23] But even arch social constructionists about science, Bruno Latour and Steve Woolgar, say they do 'not wish to say that facts do not exist nor that there is no such thing as reality'.[24] Butler's social constructionism about sex is not like this. She apparently supposes she has debunked the concepts of binary sex, specifically. And yet she does so on general grounds that would logically extend this scepticism, completely implausibly, to any scientific grouping whatsoever.

The sexes are socially constructed (part 2)

Butler published *Gender Trouble* in 1990. Also in 1990, cultural historian Thomas Laqueur published his influential book *Making Sex: Body and Gender from the Greeks to Freud*, in which he argues that nearly all claims about the differences between the two sexes are culturally and historically relative, including our own. If true, this would clearly be good reason to deny the ahistorical reality of two sexes, or the accuracy of any of the three models of the sexes I have described above. So it's worth taking a look, not least because, apparently on the basis of reading Laqueur, UK Gender Studies professor Sally Hines tweeted in 2019 that 'Before the Enlightenment the female skeleton didn't exist'.[25]

In his book, Laqueur argues that, prior to the eighteenth century, most people had a 'one sex' rather than a 'two sex' model of the sexes. Females were conceptualised as imperfect, only slightly different versions of males, rather than as fundamentally different kinds of human. The 'boundaries between male and female' were taken to be of 'degree and not kind'.[26] After the eighteenth century, a rival 'two sex' model emerged, according to which the sexes display prominent differences.[27] But *either way*, Laqueur argues, 'there is no "correct" representation of women in relation to men and ... the whole science of difference is thus misconceived'.[28] Whether the female body is conceived as very like the male body or very unlike it, both conceptions have equal validity in their context, and neither possesses ahistorical truth.[29] Indeed, Laqueur would see the gamete, chromosome and cluster models of the sexes as, at most, only relatively true to a post-Enlightenment way of thinking, and ultimately no more ahistorically accurate than the 'one sex' model of pre-Enlightenment times.[30] In the eighteenth century, 'two sexes were invented' largely to service narratives about social differences.[31] He thinks the idea of two pre-given sexes fitted dominant cultural narratives at the time which favoured the 'natural' for political and strategic reasons: mainly, to prop up unequal power relations between two groups of people (the powerful ones called 'male' and the less powerful ones called 'female').

Like Butler, Laqueur does a delicate dance from such radical conclusions back to safer, more commonsensical ground, sometimes on the very same page. For instance, he says he has 'no interest in denying the reality of sex or of sexual dimorphism as an evolutionary process'.[32] At the same time, though: 'Science does not simply investigate, but itself constitutes, the difference ... of woman from man.'[33] And he talks of 'the fundamental incoherence of stable, fixed categories of sexual dimorphism, of male and/or female'.[34]

For our purposes, his most interesting claims are that post-Enlightenment two-sex models – such as the gamete and chromosome and cluster accounts – are ultimately no more or less accurate than pre-Enlightenment models, and that eighteenth-century thinkers *created* two sexes rather than found them. To my mind, Laqueur doesn't establish that increasing scientific attention in the eighteenth century to two functionally and morphologically different sexes must have been an 'invention' out of nothing, rather than, at most, the strategically useful emphasis of *newly discovered, newly interesting, but already existent facts*. It is certainly true that, at a given point in history, prevalent cultural and political preoccupations make the discovery of certain facts newly possible, while the discovery of other facts will be effectively impossible or at least very hard. For instance – apparently easily using the language of 'discovery' in at least some contexts – Laqueur relates how the clitoris was only discovered as such by anatomists in the Renaissance. It also seems true that dominant cultural and political preoccupations in a given period can make certain facts seem more interesting, more germane to certain preferred narratives, and hence riper for uptake. Perhaps then, it is true, as Laqueur says, that in the eighteenth century there were politically strategic reasons for emphasising the distinctness of the male and female forms. But all this is compatible with the existence of predictable, observable and ultimately scientifically explicable differences in human bodies – long before humans started to notice them, show interest in them, or to represent them in various ways.

What about the female skeleton? Does Laqueur show that before the Enlightenment, it 'did not exist'? No. What he shows, at most, is that when the female skeleton was represented for the first time as such in eighteenth-century textbooks, models and imagery – that is, when it was (allegedly) first depicted as an obviously different form to the male skeleton – artists and model-makers were influenced by aesthetic ideals of canonical femininity and beauty in the concrete forms they chose.[35] But this is a claim about human imagery that has no implications for prior facts about skeletons themselves.

At various points, Laqueur reveals his own philosophical background, partly explaining the radical conclusions he draws. For instance, at one point he says we can't assess the accuracy of modern theories of the sexes, or otherwise compare them with earlier theories, because, in fact, there are no shared, stable terms to refer to what both theories have in common, and so nothing in practice to compare. He says that without 'modern terms' like 'vagina, uterus, vulva, labia, Fallopian tubes, clitoris' there was, in pre-Renaissance times, 'in an important sense no female reproductive anatomy', and such terms 'cannot quite find their Renaissance equivalents'.[36]

What Laqueur apparently assumes here is that the identity and meaning of a word or phrase is *holistic* not *atomistic*: it depends fundamentally on its connection to the wider background theory in which it is embedded.[37] So because pre- and post-Renaissance thinkers had very different theories of the nature and function of the vagina, they could not in principle share a term for that organ with a single meaning. As Laqueur says of pre-Renaissance thinkers supposedly tied to the one-sex model, '[T]he fact that [they] saw only one sex made even words for female parts ultimately refer to male organs.'[38] Laqueur's apparent belief in the holism of meaning also entails we can't easily translate a sentence containing a single pre-Renaissance term (e.g. 'cunt') into a sentence employing a post-Enlightenment word like 'vagina' – he apparently thinks extraction from the original background theoretical context, in each case, is impossible. This means we can't say either that the post-Enlightenment sentence is non-contextually, ahistorically true. At most, we can say each sentence, post- or pre-Enlightenment, is true or false only relative to its own respective set of commitments.

This all takes us into deep waters philosophically, but we can at least say three things in response. The first is that other, more plausible accounts of word meaning are available.[39] These allow terms with stable meanings to be shared or translated between different background theories, opening up the possibility of comparative judgements about the truth or falsity of different sentences from different theoretical paradigms. Secondly, even if meaning *did* turn out to be holistically tied to a given background theory, ways of judging whether a new theory was better than an old one would still be available. For instance, a new theory can count as better than an old one if it is better at solving problems and puzzles people care about, or at explaining and predicting phenomena we're interested in. Clearly this is true of modern theories of the sexes, as compared to their primitive pre-Enlightenment counterparts.

Finally, if Laqueur is right, like Butler, he would seem to be making a point that generalises *way* beyond theories of the two sexes. Do big differences between ancient and modern conceptions of cancer mean present-day cancer was invented by scientists rather than discovered by them? Did Copernicus 'invent' the modern Earth and Sun when he first theorised the former went round the latter, and not vice versa? Were there no black holes before Einstein's theory of general relativity predicted them? If you baulk at these conclusions, as I do, you might also baulk at the related conclusion about the sexes and so seek alternative theories of meaning and truth to the ones relied upon by Laqueur.

The sexes are socially constructed (part 3)

I turn now to a third influential attempt to convince the world that the sexes are not natural but social. For some Second Wave and radical feminists in the 80s, the two sexes were an entirely artificial social division created by 'oppression' or 'dominance'. French feminist Monique Wittig writes: '[T]here is no sex. There is but sex that is oppressed and sex that oppresses. It is oppression that creates sex and not the contrary.'[40] And US legal theorist Catharine MacKinnon writes: 'Male and female are created through the erotization of dominance and submission.'[41]

Like Butler and Laqueur, these thinkers apparently conceived of males and females as socially constructed, all the way down, with nothing pre-given corresponding to the division. Had we a different sort of social structure, we would have no males and females. But they add a twist. The division was instigated and then artificially maintained purely in the services of propping up the power of the people called 'males'. As Wittig puts it: 'Every system of domination establishes divisions at the material and economic level ... The masters explain and justify the established divisions as a result of natural differences.'[42] According to this so-called 'dominance' model of the sexes, it is as if, long ago, there was only a blooming, buzzing confusion of flesh, and perhaps also of sexual parts of different shapes. Then one day, a group of people came along and artificially moulded this proliferation into two categories for their own nefarious purposes, calling it 'natural': the dominant males and the dominated females.

One immediate problem with this model is one of origins: how exactly was the oppressive pattern supposed to start? Or perhaps more to the point, who, exactly, was supposed to have started it? Did a random group of people start oppressing random others? Or was it rather that there was one group better able, on average, to dominate the second group, due to genetics and associated tendencies to relatively superior physical strength? And if that, then how could the oppression or dominance itself have 'created' such characteristics? Not much of this makes sense.

One motive for embracing the dominance model is connected to the feminist desire to rescue females from the spectre of 'biological determinism' – the idea that behavioural and psychological traits such as submissiveness, modesty and domesticity are determined by female biology or otherwise natural to females. This view was and still sometimes is used to justify the promotion of certain restricted social roles for females, usually associated with home and family. Assuming they rejected this, some 70s feminists then seemed to reason in a couple of defective ways about biological determinism and sex. On the one hand, some assumed all binary theories of sex must imply determinism: that is, that these theories *must* be saying something about the fundamental individual 'natures' of males and females in terms of dominance for males, and passivity and submission for females. Working backwards, they therefore concluded that, since biological determinism isn't true, binary sex must be a myth. Meanwhile, an alternative feminist response from some seemed to go roughly: 'If there were no natural differences at all between males and females, biological determinism would obviously be false. We all want biological determinism to be false. Hence there are no natural differences between males and females.' Compare: Jed really wants it to be false that he's got cancer. If there were no such thing as cancer, it would be false that he's got it. Hence, Jed concludes, there's no such thing as cancer.

In fact, a binary model of two natural sexes could be accurate, and biological determinism still utterly false. These feminists overlooked the fact that definitions of the sexes can be relatively minimal and refer only to a *few* structural and/ or physical aspects of the body as defining conditions, as all of the models I've looked at do. They don't have to build in any particular behavioural or psychological traits – active or passive, dominant or oppressed, or otherwise – as essentially connected to maleness and femaleness. Whether some given behavioural or psychological traits *are* actually biologically rooted in sex continues to be a bitter dispute, and one I'm mostly trying to steer clear of. But we don't need to take any stance on that issue, either way, to be able to assert simply that there are two naturally pre-given sexes.

There's no such thing as 'natural' vs 'artificial'

This attack on the binary existence of biological sex says that any distinction between 'natural' sex and 'artificial' sex is arbitrary, and that there's no real distinction between them.

As most people do, philosophers often distinguish between natural kinds of thing and artificial kinds of thing, known as 'artefacts'. Artefacts, unlike natural objects, tend to be thought of as existing only as a result of human intentions. Think of spears, knives, bowls, chairs, computers, robotic arms, and so on. They can't be made accidentally, as it were: they are made only intentionally for particular human purposes. Production of an artefact usually also involves intentional modification of existing natural materials, so the resulting product has characteristics it wouldn't otherwise have had: as when clay is fired, or stone is chiselled. These conditions seem to differentiate artefacts, as such, from the products of natural processes merely initiated by humans but not otherwise interfered with: wheat grown from seed, or babies grown from procreative sex, for instance. Though in a certain sense these also exist as a result of human intentions, they could equally well have been produced accidentally without deliberate intention (lots of babies are accidental); and the resulting 'product' in each case involves no intentional modification of existing characteristics.

Some philosophers have questioned this distinction. They point out there are many entities which in some sense seem 'natural' but which also involve human intentional manipulation, significantly changing the resulting product. So, although these are 'natural' they also seem like 'artefacts' too. Examples include seedless grapes, dog breeds, genetically engineered wheat, circulation systems involving artificial hearts, and artificial skin grafts. As feminist academic Donna Haraway concludes in her famous essay 'A Cyborg Manifesto', 'Late twentieth-century machines have made thoroughly ambiguous the difference between natural and artificial, mind and body, self-developing and externally designed, and many other distinctions that used to apply to organisms and machines.'[43] Similar thoughts have encouraged some, including Haraway herself, to argue that there's no clear distinction between male and female. Injected or orally-administered oestrogen can produce breasts and hip fat, and reduce upper-body musculature; testosterone can enhance biceps, cause beards to grow and make jaws squarer. Sex reassignment surgery can turn a vagina into a penis or vice versa, we are told. Does any of this present a problem for the models of the sexes we have looked at?

The short answer is 'no'. Sometimes the rhetoric of Haraway-influenced academics make it sound as though these days, humans are like chihuahuas or seedless grapes or genetically engineered wheat ears: so saturated with intentional manipulation at every stage of development that it is impossible to differentiate discrete 'natural' parts from discrete 'artificial' parts of the organism. But this isn't right. Humans can have artificial parts added via various medical means, but we can still coherently categorise the difference between them and the natural parts, by thinking about what would have been there instead, had medics not intervened. The natural parts are all, as Haraway puts it, 'self-developing', or in other words 'endogenous', meaning roughly: naturally established in the organism and not artificially put there. This point has nothing to do with health or disease. Disordered bodily aspects such as tumours can be endogenous and so natural in this sense, and artificial bodily aspects can be healthy. A surgically constructed 'neovagina' or 'neophallus' may be healthy for the individual that has it, in the sense of enriching well-being, but since it doesn't originate from within the organism unaided, it still doesn't count as endogenous.

So the distinction between natural and artificial parts of the human body remains a live one: in fact none of the features cited as essential to or otherwise relevant for sex category membership in the gamete, chromosome or cluster accounts can be artificially produced through hormone treatment or surgery or anything else. Both possession of a gamete-producing pathway and possession of a given chromosomal configuration can only be endogenous, at least given the current state of technology. Though technology allows sperm sorting and gene editing, neither technique changes sex chromosomes or alters gamete-pathway development within a single continuous human individual. The features specified as relevant to category membership in the cluster account are all endogenous too: primary sex characteristics present in the womb and at birth, and secondary sex characteristics naturally emerging at puberty, given certain internal, naturally-occurring developmental triggers.

As it happens, there are also significant qualitative differences between the characteristics added medically in the context of what is called 'sex reassignment' surgery and endogenous ones. Surgically constructed penises and vaginas look and function differently from endogenous ones in a number of ways. Breasts acquired by trans women through hormone treatment are on average very modestly sized (one study reported changes 'mainly resulting in less than an AAA cup size'[44]) and usually require silicon augmentation to reach desired proportions, making them compositionally and functionally different from endogenous ones. It's true that hormone treatment can occasionally produce qualitatively identical secondary sex characteristics of the opposite sex in a person (e.g. in the arm fat of trans women, which is reported as 'almost the same as seen in women' after twelve months), but in other cases desired changes tend to be 'approached but not achieved'.[45]

I can imagine a critic insisting: but *why* should only endogenous features count in 'natural' sex classification? Isn't that just arbitrary? The answer is that it's not arbitrary, because making a distinction between endogenous and artificial parts of a sexed body serves various legitimate explanatory purposes we can't do without. I'll look at some of these in the next chapter.

Conclusion

This chapter has established no serious challenge to the idea of two natural, pre-given sexes. There is a naturally occurrent division of humans into males and females. Over 99 per cent of humans fall unambiguously into one category or the other, including most people with DSDs. As binaries in nature go, the sex division is one of the most stable and predictable there is. In the vast majority of cases, sex is not 'assigned at birth' but detected – in most cases via observation at birth, and in a few cases later on. Despite wording of UK laws such as the Gender Recognition and Equality Acts, sex cannot be 'reassigned' through surgery or a change in legal status, nor 'changed'.[46]

Still, someone might respond: why does this distinction *matter*? After all, there are lots of pointless distinctions we can make between things. We could, say, divide all lawns up into two kinds: those that have over a million blades of grass and those that don't. It would be completely boring. So why is it important to acknowledge the distinction between males and females? What exactly does it do for us? In fact, we couldn't possibly do without it.

Why Does Sex Matter?

The most basic and obvious reason why the sexes matters is: our species would die out without them. For any species that reproduces sexually, in a way that necessarily involves one male and one female, the capacity for recognition of the opposite sex has presumably been present in most individuals for as long as the species has existed. As you would expect then, most people start reliably to differentiate the sexes early on in life, learning that, within certain ranges, distinct facial and bodily characteristics are typical for each sex, including voice and gait.[1]

Advocates of gender identity theory sometimes suggest that identifying what they call the 'assigned' sex of other people is a fraught, unreliable affair. Most of the time, this isn't true. Each sex tends to be associated with distinct ranges of observable physical characteristics, and none of the three accounts of sex looked at in Chapter 2 treat any of these characteristics as essential – still less sufficient – for being male or female. It isn't a 'gotcha' to point out that some males or females don't have a particular characteristic; or that some have characteristics typically associated with the opposite sex. Still, for most people, the generalisations are true and can be made use of in everyday identification.

To say someone can 'reliably differentiate' means only that most of the time, they get it right. Mistakes can still be made. Autistic adults sometimes struggle to reach the aptitude shown by non-autistic children in this respect.[2] Some people look markedly atypical for their sex. But even here, identification for many gets easier when a full range of information is considered: movement rather than a still photograph; vocal tone, height, musculature, extremity size, and so on. Though there are exceptions, for most people past puberty, a period of taking hormones or having surgery is required in order to look significantly unlike one's actual sex. (And even then, and especially for males, certain physical aspects strongly suggestive of one's actual sex can persist. Artificial oestrogen cannot undo jaw and hand size, for instance.)

But still, even if it's important to recognise sex for procreation, why do we need to talk about it in other contexts so much? For many like me, growing up in a culture influenced by 70s feminists, it is orthodox to think we should. There seem to be a host of obvious differences between males and females potentially affecting their respective trajectories through life. For one, females are viewed through, and so shaped by, restrictive and sometimes contradictory stereotypes of femininity ('Be pretty!', 'Be quiet!', 'Be maternal!', etc.), and males, stereotypes of masculinity ('Be tough!', 'Be loud!', 'Be self-sufficient!', etc.). These seem an uncomfortable fit for many. And apart from the direct influence of such stereotypes, there seem to be hundreds of other sex-associated trends too. Suicide is much more common in males, self-harm in females.[3] Males are more likely to have an alcohol problem.[4] Females are more likely to suffer eating disorders and depression.[5] Females outperform males in school and at university, but are less likely to be promoted in the workplace – partly because they're less likely to self-promote.[6] Females are less likely to do sport than males but more likely to do yoga.[7] Females buy 80 per cent of novels, males 20 per cent.[8] And so on.

Unfortunately, though, the listing of such trends isn't enough to demonstrate to everyone that sex should be discussed. This is partly because these days it's assumed by many – including by many feminists – that these differences are mostly or even wholly socially produced, rather than the inevitable legacy of biology. In other words, this is the re-emergence of the battleground mentioned in Chapter 1, fought between 'blank-slate' feminists and 'innatists'. In the minds of some blank-slate feminists, a belief in the social provenance of sex-associated differences provides a reason to ignore and downplay such differences, *especially* when they are thought to produce inequalities between the sexes. The background assumption seems to be that, paradoxically, by identifying and discussing socially produced inequalities, we further entrench them; whereas if we ignore them, perhaps they will go away. We see this assumption in practice on both sides of the political spectrum, from right-wing women who say they don't want any 'special treatment' as women, to left-wing parents trying to raise their children 'gender-free'. This approach finds its high point – or low point, depending on how you look at it – in academic Chloë Taylor's argument – in a feminist journal – that rape-crisis centres for women serve only to 'reinscribe gendered constructions of male sexuality as dangerous and of women's bodies as sexually vulnerable', and are 'the cause of rape', perpetuating the problem they seek to avoid.[9]

Frankly, this is mad. Attempting to alleviate a socially produced phenomenon doesn't normally 'cause' it in any way the empirically informed social sciences would recognise. But partly to bypass this stuff, in this chapter I'll focus on four areas where biology unambiguously makes at least a partial contribution to important sex-associated difference. This is not to endorse biological determinism. But what it should do, at least, is lessen any feeling in some readers that we could somehow get rid of these differences by ignoring them. Focusing on biologically informed sex differences serves another function too, for as a rule of thumb, the heavier the role biology seems to play in a given difference, the more strongly will advocates of gender identity theory seek to suppress special mention of it. Doing things this way provides an opportunity to examine the costs of this suppression.

Here, then, are four areas of human life in which sex-associated difference clearly matters (and in which advocates of gender identity theory say it doesn't).

The difference sex makes to medicine

I'll start with an easy one. The domain of medicine is the promotion of health and the curing of disease. Since health and disease can be directly affected by sex characteristics, sex is highly relevant to medicine. This is obviously true of reproductive medicine, but that is far from the only medical area in which sex is relevant. In childhood, girls are more susceptible than boys to neural tube defects, scoliosis and congenital dislocation of the hip. Boys are more susceptible to asthma, autism, stuttering and pyloric stenosis.[10] Later in life, females have greater susceptibility to multiple sclerosis, while males who get it have worse disease progression.[11] More males than females have cardiovascular disease in their lifetimes, but females get it at a higher rate than males after menopause.[12] Males are more likely than females to have haemophilia, schizophrenia, Parkinson's disease and colour-blindness. Females are more likely to have autoimmune diseases, migraines, osteoporosis, cataracts, depression, eating disorders and Alzheimer's. At the time of writing, during the 2020 COVID-19 pandemic, twice as many males as females are reported to have died.[13] In short, sex can affect disease susceptibility, progression and outcomes.

Pain sensitivity also varies between the sexes. Pain tends to be more prevalent in females than males, and females tend to display greater sensitivity to experimentally induced pain than males.[14] There are also predictable sex-based differences in responses to drugs. Some drugs are absorbed and excreted at different rates by females and males and/or require different dosages. Some drugs are more effective for one sex than another in tackling a particular disease, or have more significant side effects.[15]

None of this has anything to do with gender identity or social role. Evidence suggests most of the differences just listed are causally linked to lifelong sex chromosomes, the protective effect of endogenous sex hormones or lack of them, and other physiological factors stemming from biological fact.[16] In saying this, I don't wish to downplay the way social factors can skew the way *we think of* these sex-based medical differences, or the interest shown in them. As Caroline Criado Perez describes in her book *Invisible Women*, males have tended to be systematically treated as the default kind of body in drug trials and experimental medical studies.[17] Female-associated diseases have tended to be dismissed by some doctors as 'women's problems' associated with hysteria and neuroticism. These are social problems requiring social solutions, but they don't establish that sex itself is wholly social.

In Chapter 2 I said that characteristics relevant to maleness and femaleness are 'endogenous': i.e., self-developed within the organism and not artificially put there. In the context of medicine, we see the importance of this condition. Endogenous features count as an important baseline in specifications of human health. It's not the only baseline; as noted earlier, disease can be endogenous too. But still, by considering what features tend to self-develop in an organism at various stages and averaging them, we get one useful source of information about what's statistically 'normal' at each stage. This is then used as a source of information in working out what health for that sort of organism looks like. For instance, healthy bone density levels for twenty-year-old females can be calculated partly by appealing to the average natural (i.e. endogenous) bone density for that age group, other things being equal. What counts as cardiac health for a seventy-year-old male will differ from cardiac health for a twenty-year-old male, and these standards too can be established partly by averaging natural cardiac levels for each group. Equally, a distinction between natural and artificial bodily features is crucial to consideration of what would be reasonable or efficient to try to change in the body, and what the risks might be. Artificially altering some natural feature in an organism comes with knock-on effects for other features, bad as well as good.

In sum: sex matters in medicine. Advocates of gender identity theory cannot change that fact, but they can change how we talk about it. Efforts have mostly been focused on reframing the presentation of certain bodily parts and diseases in supposedly 'trans-friendly' ways that no longer refer directly to sex. For instance, a 2017 *Teen Vogue* article, 'Anal Sex: What you need to know', refers to females as 'non-prostate owners'.[18] A 2018 Cancer Research UK campaign urged 'everyone aged 25–64 with a cervix' to get regular smear tests.[19] Also in 2018, the word 'menstruators' was used by Planned Parenthood and the *Guardian*.[20] Interestingly, these attempts to change language seem mainly confined to female health. The American website *Healthline*'s 2018 'LGBTQIA Safe Sex Guide' refers to vaginas as 'front holes' throughout, yet terminology for penises in the document remains mostly unaltered.[21]

These language changes are supposed to protect trans people from psychological discomfort. Sometimes, though, that rationale is combined with the idea that references to biology are 'dehumanising'. In 2016, the period tracker app Clue put out a discussion piece noting that, 'Using the word "female" or "female-bodied" is offensive to some. It's seen as dehumanizing or still too gendered.'[22] But why should it seem dehumanising to refer to our sex or to our biological basis more generally? We should not confuse this with saying humans are *only* biological organisms – that is, with the idea that humans are wholly enslaved to deterministic natural instincts and drives, with no free will or 'higher' cognitive aspects. There is a philosophical tradition stretching back at least to Aristotle at pains to deny this. The most popular philosophical answer to the question of what makes humans different from (other) animal species is relatively advanced rationality. But philosophers who take this line don't deny humans are *also* biological organisms. (In any case, talking about 'non-prostate-owners' and 'menstruators', etc., is scarcely less dehumanising than talking about 'females'.)

There is no harm in naming sex in medical contexts; more importantly, there is harm in *not* doing so. For one thing, children will stop learning about it and this will cause them confusion, both in the present and later on. Equally, if you make it culturally taboo for doctors to talk about sex, they won't be as quick to see its relevance in disease, pain management and drug administration. And if you use unfamiliar words in public communications, some people won't understand you, at a potential cost to their health. 'Female' and 'male' are well-understood words for the sexes. 'Non-prostate-owner', 'cervix-haver' and 'menstruator' are not.

So: we might as well stick with 'female' and 'male'. It turns out, when you get the cervix-havers and menstruators and non-prostate owners and front-hole owners all together, there's at least one English term that applies perfectly efficiently to them, and only to them. That word is 'female'. Of course, an arguably even more accessible, familiar and useful English word is 'woman'. As intimated in Chapter 1, it has become relatively commonplace to say that 'woman' is characterised in terms of 'female gender identity' and not sex. So, for now, I'm avoiding the word 'woman', but it is worth noting here that some healthcare providers are under pressure to remove references to women from their communications. One of these is the British Pregnancy Advisory Service, the UK's largest independent abortion provider. Former Chief Executive Ann Furedi tells me, 'Trans activists seem to want an abortion-care environment that takes all reference to women out of the frame. They want literature rewritten so as not to refer to women, they want us to not describe BPAS as a women's healthcare service, or abortion as an issue that relates to women's rights and reproductive freedom.' Here too there are potentially detrimental consequences for people's understanding. Furedi goes on: '[I]t's tempting to not make it an issue and comply, until you consider the vast majority of BPAS patients are women who don't share the social, educationally privileged background of the activists ... Many patients struggle with English, and so our priority is to make communications as clear and simple as possible – gender-neutral language does not always help this.'[23] This disregard for the interests of people of lower socio-economic status or education is not unusual within modern trans activism.

The difference sex makes to sport

Sport is a second area where sex unambiguously makes a difference, and where trans activists say that it does not. It's common enough to say sporting competitors should not have an 'unfair advantage' – but what makes an advantage 'unfair'? If I were to compete at tennis against Martina Navratilova, since I'm a novice and she's a champion, she would obviously have the advantage, but it wouldn't seem unfair, or at least not intolerably so.

But another kind of advantage does seem intolerable. Two competitors would be unfairly pitted against each other if each naturally or otherwise involuntarily belongs to a particular group (e.g. juniors and seniors; visually impaired and sighted; wheelchair-users and able-bodied), and there are large systematic, statistically significant differences – e.g. on average and at peak – between relevant physical performances of members in each of those two groups. Where such differences are found, those groups are usually treated as separate categories in sport, and members of each group won't usually meet in competition.[24] Alternatively, there could be some other difference between performances justifying separate categories – for instance, a small but still potentially dangerous difference between performance levels. This sort of difference justifies distinct weight categories in boxing.

Occasionally, where a member of a group associated with lower performance levels does well enough to match or exceed performances in a group typically associated with higher levels, that person may fairly compete at the higher level. So, for instance, a junior may occasionally run and do well in a senior race without it automatically counting as unfair. But *it doesn't work the other way around*. Normally, a member of a group associated with higher performance levels (e.g. seniors) cannot compete fairly only against members of a group associated with significantly lower performance levels (e.g. juniors), *even if some individual member(s) of the second group can beat some members of the first*.

According to these criteria, for most sports, males and females should be in different competitive categories for at least two reasons. First: for most sports there are large, statistically significant differences between relevant physical performance levels for males and females. Second: in contact sports, there are also potentially dangerous differences between the two. Exceptions to these rules are either where there isn't any significant difference in performance levels, or where there is, but a female manages to meet relevant performance levels in the male group, in which case she may perhaps fairly compete against them, but not vice versa.

The superior athletic performance levels of males are accounted for by possession of a Y chromosome, associated natural differences in testosterone levels, and the irrevocable post-pubescent effects these leave on the body.[25] In terms of speed, there is a consistent 10 per cent performance gap between elite males and elite females in track and field, which also extends to swimming, cycling and rowing.[26] Research biologist Dr Emma Hilton has done a lot of work to publicise these differences. She notes that the women's world record for 100m sprinting was broken by 744 senior males in 2017 alone. In terms of strength, males are 20–25 per cent stronger than females in Olympic weightlifting.[27] Wherever speed and strength are important indicators of success in a given sport, that sport should have separate male and female categories. In contact sports, this is yet more pressing because differences in average weight combined with speed and strength make contact with male bodies particularly dangerous for female ones.

For years, none of this has looked remotely controversial. As the 2010 Equality Act says (as usual, with a confusing use of 'gender' meaning GENDER1, or sex): 'A gender-affected activity is a sport, game or other activity of a competitive nature in circumstances in which the physical strength, stamina or physique of average persons of one sex would put them at a disadvantage compared to average persons of the other sex as competitors in events involving the activity.' Lately, though, trans activism has succeeded in convincing at least some professional bodies that sex is not relevant to sporting categories.

The most extreme version of this position says that gender identity alone, not sex or even medical transition, should determine whether one competes in men's or women's categories. At the 2017 Connecticut State Championships, where athletes are explicitly allowed to compete in categories aligning with gender identity not sex, trans woman sprinter Andraya Yearwood won the women's 100- and 200-metre races without hormonal treatment or surgery.[28] Her legal right to do so is currently being supported by the American Civil Liberties Union.[29] In the UK, the current policy of Durham University states that trans students and staff are 'welcome' to train 'with the squad which best fits their gender identity, without requiring evidence of medical transition or hormone levels' – seemingly without recognising the potential effects of this on female athletes, should males start to take them up on it in serious numbers.[30]

A different and only marginally less unfair policy currently employed by the International Olympic Committee says that trans women with a misaligned gender identity can compete in women's sport, though only if their testosterone levels have been suppressed, via hormonal treatment or other means, to 10 nanomoles per litre or under for at least twelve months. This testosterone level is still six to twelve times higher than the average level observed in females, and so confers an advantage.[31] Suppression also has no effect on male features permanently and advantageously acquired at puberty, such as, on average: greater height; longer limbs; larger heart, lungs and extremities; narrower pelvis size, and advantageous cellular muscle memory.[32]

Some bad arguments have been launched to support such policies. Some have come from trans woman philosopher and amateur cyclist Veronica Ivy (who formerly raced and published under the name Rachel McKinnon). One is plainly wrong – that Ivy and other trans woman athletes are, after all, 'female'.[33] Another is that 'sport is a human right'. If so, though, it's a right for females too, without their being pushed out of qualifying, humiliated on the field or – as the BBC casually reported of one female rugby player recently – 'folded like a deckchair' during a game by a six-foot trans woman playing on the opposite team.[34] In any case, no one is stopping trans women athletes from competing in the appropriate category with fellow males. Some already do. Another strawman of which Ivy is fond is that sometimes females beat her. Yet the principle isn't 'if a few females at the top end of the female category can beat a few males in the male category, the categories are unfair and should be merged or reformed'. It's about comparing average performance levels across groups as a whole.

Sometimes comparisons are made with the situation of people with DSDs like Caster Semenya – reported as having XY chromosomes – to argue that trans women should compete with females.[35] Whatever we say about the case of competitors with DSDs and Y chromosomes, it's an important difference that their sex is (perhaps) complicated to classify, whereas the sex of trans women typically is not. And if the point is pressed that we must treat both alike, then so be it. In that case, neither should compete in female categories. For otherwise, we face nothing less than the destruction of female sport.

There is also a tendency to attribute ludicrous motives to critics. Take Australian Rules Football player Hannah Mouncey, who transitioned age twenty-six, is 6ft 2in and weighs 220lb. She complained in a *Guardian* op-ed that weight restrictions in female categories, presumably designed to exclude trans women like herself from pulverising female players on the field, could only possibly be motivated by sexist, body-shaming restrictions on what count as acceptable female shapes. 'Think about the message it sends to women and girls about their bodies,' Mouncey intoned. '[I]f you're too big, you can't play. That is incredibly dangerous and backward.'[36] Meanwhile, the *Independent*'s chief sportswriter Jonathan Liew, writing in 2019, seemed to think that any critic of trans sport policies must be worried, needlessly and neurotically, about males transitioning in great numbers in order to cheat. But that's not the worry here at all. The worry is about the intrinsic injustice of pitting one sort of sexed body, with significantly different physical capabilities, against another of a very different sort. Personal motives are irrelevant – just as they are in, for instance, doping offences.

Liew also wrote, 'Let's say transgender athletes pour into women's sport, and let's say ... they dominate everything they touch ... Why would that be bad? Really? Imagine the power of a trans child or teenager seeing a trans athlete on the top step of the Olympic podium. In a way, it would be inspiring. Sometimes we forget that there are bigger things than sport.'[37] It seems rather that sometimes Liew forgets that females have ambitions or feelings. Leaving aside what exactly is supposed to be 'inspiring' about males outperforming females in ways they couldn't hope to match, as I read this I think of Jennifer Wagner, placed 3rd to Veronica Ivy's 1st in the 2018 UCI Masters Track World Championship, tweeting afterwards that this 'definitely wasn't fair' after months of training and sacrifice. I think of Samoan female weightlifters Feagaiga Stowers and Iuniana Sipaia, beaten into silver and bronze by forty-one-year-old late-transitioning trans woman Laurel

Hubbard in the 2019 Pacific Games. I think of college athlete Selina Soule, edged out of qualifying for the finals in the 2019 Indoor Track & Field State Championships 55-metre dash by two trans women athletes, including Andraya Yearwood. I think about Mixed Martial Arts fighter Tamikka Brents, who, in a fight with trans woman Fallon Fox, suffered concussion and an orbital bone fracture in the first round. Said Brents afterwards, 'I've fought a lot of women and have never felt the strength that I felt in a fight as I did that night.'[38] I think of injuries gained, and scholarships, places and prizes lost. And all this in a context in which women's sport struggles to survive as it is. I don't see much here that's inspiring.

The difference sex makes to sexual orientation

A third area in which sex makes a difference is sexual orientation. There is commonly held to be a difference between a sexual *preference* and a sexual *orientation*. Sexual preferences include preferences for blondes over brunettes, or macho men over pretty boys. At the more exotic end, they can include predilections for cars, chandeliers and dalliances with farm animals. None of these are sexual orientations, though. Opinions differ on what makes an orientation an orientation, but my preferred explanation says that for a preference to count as an orientation, it has to be stable in individuals, widespread among the human population, and have a range of relatively important social consequences.[39]

Two such orientations are heterosexuality and homosexuality. They are defined in terms of specific patterns of attraction. You are heterosexual if you, a member of one sex, are stably sexually attracted only to members of the opposite sex to you. Alternatively, if you're stably attracted only to members of the same sex as you, then you're homosexual. If you're stably attracted to both sexes, you're bisexual. In addition to these terms, equally applicable to both males and females, the English language has words to describe homosexual orientations disaggregated by sex. 'Lesbians' are same-sex-attracted females. There are other sex-disaggregated words too, often pretty negative: 'faggots', 'dykes', etc.

Putting things this way will, I predict, raise the hackles of readers schooled in queer theory, and in particular fans of French post-structuralist Michel Foucault. It is a commonplace there that orientations are – just as biological sex categories are for Butler – socially constructed, historically contingent and culturally located. As trans scholar Jack (then non-trans Judith) Halberstam summarises approvingly: 'within a Foucauldian history of sexuality, "lesbian" constitutes a term for same-sex desire produced in the mid-to-late twentieth century within the highly politicized context of the rise of feminism ... ; if this is so, then "lesbian" cannot be the transhistorical label for all same-sex activity between women'.[40] My short answer is that, while obviously we need to acknowledge the interesting fact that throughout the ages, same-sex activity has had many different relatively local sociocultural meanings and names, it wasn't invented in the twentieth century.[41] I'm talking about distinctive, relatively ahistorical patterns of sexual relationship in individuals, and not particular cultural representations of that pattern. That's a coherent distinction to make.

Saying a sexual orientation must be 'stable' for an individual doesn't mean you can't have voluntary and even pleasurable sexual experiences at variance with it. It's fairly typical for young people to take a while to figure out what their orientation is, and sometimes it takes older people a while too. This is more likely for gay people in a culture in which heterosexuality predominates.[42] A gay person might be less willing or even able to notice relevant clues as to where the real patterns of attraction lie. Or a person can just get drunk and have opportunistic sex with whoever happens to be there, against their normal grain. They can have sex with one kind of person, fantasising wildly about another. Or they can be romantically attached to someone in a way that temporarily causes them to seem attractive but wouldn't otherwise. Strictly speaking, a sexual orientation should be understood in terms of the sex(es) you *would be* sexually attracted to under relatively self-aware, uncoerced, uninhibited circumstances, and not necessarily who you actually *are* attracted to right now. A sexual orientation is for life, not just for Christmas parties.

On most plausible models, sexual orientations develop due to factors beyond individual control. Controversy reigns about whether these are genetic or environmental or both,[43] but either way, heterosexuality and homosexuality are not conscious choices. You like sex with the sex(es) you like, and it seems to start quite early on in life.[44] On that basis, it can only be pointless and psychologically damaging to try to change someone's orientation through what is known as 'conversion therapy'. These days it is accepted by UK professional therapeutic bodies that attempting the conversion of gay people is ethically fraught.

Let's pause and look at how many times the word 'sex' occurred in the characterisations just given of heterosexuality and homosexuality, and remind ourselves, because it can get confusing with so much sex around, that this is 'sex' as in male or female and not the copulatory sense. In order to know the sexual orientation – hetero-, homo- or bi – of person A, you need to know both A's sex and the sex of the kind of person to whom A is stably attracted. In explaining why someone has the sexual orientation they have, the concept of biological sex is bound to come into the explanation.

Perhaps predictably, then – though still surprisingly, given that they started out fighting for gay rights – this conception of sexual orientation has been rejected by trans activist organisations such as Stonewall and GLAAD. In their view, it's gender identity, not sex, that makes you a woman or man. This is assumed to have consequences for sexual orientation concepts such as gay, straight, lesbian, and so on. A 'lesbian' is now understood as anyone with a female gender identity attracted to others with female gender identities. This can include biological males as lesbians, as long as they have a female gender identity. Equally, a gay man is understood as anyone with a male gender identity attracted to others with male gender identities. Being straight, meanwhile, is defined as a person with a given gender identity being attracted to someone with an opposite gender identity (albeit that talk of 'opposite' doesn't make much sense in a context in which gender identities are supposed to be multiple and non-binary). The upshot is that sex is irrelevant to sexual orientation.

There seems to me at least one glaring problem with all this: if heterosexual attraction were directed primarily towards gender identity not sex, it would be pretty inefficient in terms of the continuation of the species. If we had to work out someone's inner gender identity before we knew who to fancy, we would die out fairly quickly. In practice, people tend to insist, not that they're attracted to gender *identity* but simply to 'gender' not sex. (That is, they mean something like GENDER2.) They say they have a sexual attraction to 'Femme' people, or 'Masc' people, meaning: to people of either sex who have a stereotypically feminine presentation or masculine presentation. It is implied that assumptions about a person's sex are irrelevant to such attractions.

But for most, that can't actually be true, because what counts as a person's presenting 'Femme' or 'Masc' *changes depending on whether that person is thought of as male or female.* For instance: the female model Erika Linder looks very like a young Leonardo DiCaprio – so much so that her break-out photo shoot deliberately depicted her as Leo. But while a young DiCaprio looks relatively *feminine* for a male, Linder (at least, in that shoot) looks relatively *masculine* for a female. Even though Linder and DiCaprio have similar-looking features at the physical level, we interpret these features as differently feminine/masculine, relative to accompanying assumptions about their owner's sex. So even when you think you're attracted only to someone's feminine or masculine presentation, perceptions of sex are still playing a significant underpinning causal role in your attraction nonetheless.

This point is reinforced by the findings of a recent survey, in which 12.5 per cent of participants indicated they would consider dating a trans person.[45] For nearly half of these respondents, their stated preferences about whom exactly they would date were described by the researchers running the survey as 'incongruent'. For instance, roughly two-thirds of the self-described lesbians in the group said they would only date trans men and not trans women, or would at least date trans men as well as trans women. The researchers had assumed that, to be consistent with lesbianism understood in terms of gender identity, lesbians should exclude trans men and include only trans women. The researchers explained these findings as demonstrating 'femmephobia'. A less complicated hypothesis would be that lesbians are not stably sexually attracted to males.

In arguments about the relevance of sex to sexual ori-entation, three objections tend to come up fast. One is the familiar line: 'You can't see someone's chromosomes!' That's like saying you can't fancy brunettes because you can't see the melanocytes that create pigment in their hair. As we've seen, sex tends to be reliably connected to a variety of observable, potentially arousing physical features: look, touch, taste, scent and vocal sounds.

A second objection goes: are you really saying that a female in a relationship with a gorgeous, feminine, post-surgery trans woman isn't a lesbian, just because she's sexually attracted in this case to a male, technically speaking? Equally: are you saying that a man in lust with a hot ripped trans man, post-surgery and hormones, isn't actually gay? Actually, I'm not. Rather, I'll say what I've already had cause to say a couple of times: these sorts of relatively unusual cases stretch existing concepts to their limits. Our concepts weren't designed for them, and we just don't know *what* to say (and that's OK). There are reasons both for and against saying that this is a lesbian and a gay man, respectively. In the first case, there's female sexual attraction to a female-like body, at least on the outside, but the female-like body is artificially produced and not an endogenous phenotype. The body is actually male, no matter what it looks like. In the second, there's male attraction to a male-like body on the outside, but again it isn't endogenously produced and is a female body nonetheless.

For an objector to focus *only* on this sort of example is strange, because their own position would also classify as 'lesbians' females who habitually lust after males with absolutely standard male bodies, as long as the latter had female gender identities. And it would even count *males with standard male bodies themselves* as lesbians – as long as they too had female gender identities. They would, for instance, presumably agree that Alex Drummond – a trans woman on Stonewall's Advisory Board who has apparently had no surgery, taken no hormones, looks unambiguously male in terms of morphology, and even wears a full beard – is a 'lesbian' because of an attraction to women. In a *Buzzfeed* interview Drummond says, 'I identify as lesbian as I'm female and attracted to women ... I've been in a long-term committed relationship for a long time now so I'm spoken for, but certainly I draw out the inner lesbian in women!'[46] Yet this is surely to stretch the concept of *lesbian* to breaking point. In old money, Drummond is heterosexual, and so, presumably, are the females attracted to her.

A third objection is an accusation: why are you 'policing' sexualities? Can't consenting adults just have sex with whomever they desire? My answer is: *Of course they can* (or at least, in an ideal world, should). This objection confuses accurate categorisation for the purposes of explanation with prohibition. I'm not setting myself up as the sex police. You can go to bed with whichever consenting adult you like. What I am saying is that if you consistently have enjoyable relations with someone of the opposite sex, you're probably heterosexual/straight. That's not to stop you doing what you like. It's just to accurately describe what you're doing. No judgement, positive or negative, is implied either way. (I'm gay myself, remember.)

The long-term effects of LGBT organisations like Stonewall and GLAAD treating sexual orientation as based on gender identity have yet to be properly established, but at least two are emerging, neither good. First, it's reported by some whistleblower clinicians that significant numbers of trans-identifying children and teens are same-sex attracted.[47] Taking a cue from the prominent public messaging of LGBT organisations, they seem to be interpreting their own patterns of sexual attraction as a sign that they must have a misaligned gender identity combined with a 'straight' sexual orientation. So, for instance, same-sex attracted females are interpreting themselves to be straight boys or men. Identity exploration in children is not in itself harmful. However, it becomes a lot more serious when well-meaning parents and teachers uncritically go along with this narrative, seeking what may well turn out to be life-long medication on the minor's behalf to alter his or her body to reflect a 'real' identity. Worse, also thanks to lobbying from LGBT organisations, as we have seen, some professional therapist bodies now characterise any questioning of this self-narrative as a prohibited form of 'conversion therapy'.[48] Hence, there are significantly reduced opportunities for a child or teen to hear alternative interpretations of their sexual desires. As these children grow up, some are coming to realise that they were just gay all along. A wave of 'detransitioners' is emerging, many of whom are lesbian and gay, and many of whom now express regret about the life-altering drugs or surgery they were prescribed in the past.[49]

A second problematic effect relates specifically to young lesbians: that is, to female-attracted females. Working out your homosexual orientation in a world in which heterosexuality is the norm can be difficult. Taking the difficulties on mentally while negotiating society's expectations of you as a young female is tough. It's fairly obvious that young females tend on average to be less assertive, more anxious and keener to please than young males. Put these tendencies into a queer community in which young lesbians have sought refuge and comradeship, and in which there are also trans women self-declaring as fellow 'lesbians', and you will inevitably find lesbians – whether themselves trans-identified or not – pressured into sexual relations with members of the opposite sex, and in some case succumbing.

Recently, trans activism has given the world the fairly revolting image of the 'cotton ceiling': riffing on the idea of a glass ceiling for those women in the workplace unsuccessfully seeking promotion, but replacing glass with knickers to represent the 'ceiling' that female-attracted trans women often cannot get 'past'. Along similar lines, in 2016 Veronica Ivy tweeted, in reference to sexual relations with trans women, that sometimes 'the cis lesbian gets over her genital hang-ups and realises that she can cope just fine'. In 2019, a University of Brighton conference 'Gayness in Queer Times' asked, as part of its official call for papers: 'How can gay space be made more trans-inclusive?' and then suggested 'bedrooms' as a potential site of inclusion.[50] Also in 2019, Oxford philosopher Professor Amia Srinivasan, writing in the *London Review of Books*, described 'transphobia' as an 'oppressive system that makes its way into the bedroom through the seemingly innocuous mechanism of "personal preference"'.[51] Some legal theorists have even gone as far as to argue that the laws around 'sex by deception' should be changed, so that, for instance, a trans man or trans woman initiating a sexual encounter with someone while actively falsely claiming to be of the same sex as them cannot be treated as fraudulent.[52] Stonewall apparently agrees, arguing in 2015 that there should 'be '[j]udicial clarity of "sex by deception" cases to define the legal position on what constitutes sex by deception based on gender, and to ensure trans people's privacy is protected'.[53]

The implication of all this is that the main reason for a lesbian refusing to sleep with trans women, or a gay man with trans men, could only be bigotry and disgust for trans people. Yet this ignores a much more obvious explanation: it's the sexual orientation, stupid. With such statements coming from what seem like authoritative liberal and left-leaning voices, we get a sense of what must be the moral pressure exerted at a more local level upon younger people ill-equipped to deal with it, and especially young lesbians. A former attendee of a trans youth group recalls that 'one day, there were three MTFs over forty who were hitting on the teen FTMs, very explicitly. It was obviously making us uncomfortable, but almost no one ever said anything, only changed the topic or tried to engage them in a conversation away from us'.[54] If only those young

FTMs – that is, trans men, or 'Female To Male' people – had felt socially permitted, within queer culture, confidently to insist upon the fact of their same-sex attraction. Yet largely thanks to the LGBT organisations supposed to protect them, they weren't. And many still aren't.

The difference sex makes to the social effects of heterosexuality

There is a fourth and final way in which biological sex makes a distinctive contribution to social life. Human reproduction requires some input, as it were, from one male and one female: sperm plus egg. There is no way around it. Being heterosexual isn't essential for reproduction, but it certainly helps move things along. Being heterosexual gives you a personal motive to have sex with the opposite sex. And having sex with the opposite sex tends, if you aren't careful, to produce babies. The vast majority of births worldwide occur non-assisted as a result of sexual intercourse between males and females, and the vast majority of those couplings are between heterosexuals. In 2019, the Office for National Statistics (ONS) estimated that 1,307,000 opposite-sex cohabiting couples in the UK had dependent children, while only 3,000 same-sex cohabiting couples did.[55] Widespread heterosexuality is an adaptive trait for any sexually reproducing species, including ours.

Heterosexuality is the only sexual orientation predictably involving two people with marked physical differences between them. Same-sex couples are more likely to be evenly physically matched along a range of dimensions. This fact about heterosexuality – that it is likely to involve two very physically different humans – has specific economic and cultural effects that homosexuality doesn't tend to share, or shares only derivatively by modelling heterosexual norms. I'll focus here on two sorts of effect in particular.

The difference sex plus heterosexuality makes to work

First, the fact that only females and not males are naturally capable of pregnancy and breastfeeding partly explains, as one factor in a complicated causal story, why females tend to be less successful, in terms of pay and promotion, in the workplace. Pregnancy and breastfeeding take many females out of the workplace, at least temporarily, and also reduce their capacity to do some kinds of physical work while in it. Both these things can affect chances of career progression, either because females get pregnant or because it is anticipated by employers that they might. Many heterosexual females have disproportionate responsibility for childcare and domestic work relative to male partners, partly due to the legacy of habits and expectations formed as a result of pregnancy and breastfeeding. These factors are also relevant to why, in heterosexual couples, the career trajectory of the male tends to be prioritised over that of the female. Overall, biological differences between heterosexual males and females are part of a bigger causal story about why females tend to do more part-time, 'lower skilled', and so lower paid work than males.[56]

Those locked into culture wars about sex and gender should note that I'm *not* saying here that e.g. average differences in male and female pay are wholly explained by biology (let alone 'deserved'). You can deny this and still think that typical physical disparities between male and female bodies are one explanatory factor among many. Stable biological facts have contingent social effects in a given society in conjunction with other social aspects. A society can always choose to mitigate those effects by instigating different social arrangements and structures. In fact, that's obviously what we already do with health and medicine. So in this arena we could, for instance, try to make childcare cheaper and more widely accessible to help females into the workplace full time. Still, whether or not we choose to do that, the background biological facts about physical differences between sexes still count as part of the overall explanation for whatever present effects exist. The social consequences of sex are, as academics say, 'multi-factorial', but that doesn't negate the input of biology as one explanatory factor amongst many.

In the past, UK policymakers have tried to mitigate certain social effects of biology where they have seemed to penalise one sex in particular. Statutory maternity leave is designed to mitigate some of the economic impact of late pregnancy and early motherhood. Equality law makes it illegal to discrimi-nate on the grounds of pregnancy and maternity. In the past it has also been acknowledged that, since females typically face more challenges in career progression and promotion than males, they can be helped by dedicated resources, support and incentives: career mentoring, support groups, special award schemes, all-women shortlists, and so on. And it has been considered a social priority to collect accurate data on sex-associated differences in the workplace and home, in order to track any patterns of disadvantage for females or for males.

In recent times, however, trans activism has challenged these measures with significant success. In the workplace, resources and support formerly dedicated to females are now usually available to anyone with a female gender identity. When events at workplaces are held to protest against what is called, euphemistically, the 'gender pay gap' – more accu-rately described as the sex pay gap – they're often promoted as open to anyone with a female gender identity, male or female. The main governmental instrument for establishing 'gender' equality in Higher Education, the Athena SWAN Charter, now includes 'an inner perception of identity' as 'a key factor in the discrimination experienced predominantly by women and transgender people' without further differentiating between them.[57] Also as indicative, Labour Party all-women candidate shortlists, originally set up to increase the number of female MPs in a male-dominated House of Commons, are now explicitly open to 'all women, including self-identifying trans women'.[58] And when the *Financial Times* named its Top 100 Female Executives in 2018, presumably as a way of incentivising women's career progression in the higher echelons of blue-chip companies, the 'gender fluid' male Philip Bunce, who wears dresses and skirts and calls himself Pippa for only part of each week, was on the list.[59]

Data collection on sex has also been adversely affected. In the UK, the Census is considered by many to be the gold standard of national data collection, feeding into many academic analyses of socio-economic difference. Yet in the 2011 Census, the ONS explicitly advised respondents to answer the only question about their sex in terms of gender identity.[60] Though this advice has now been dropped by the ONS for 2021, replacing 'sex' with 'legal sex' in their guidance, at the time of writing Census authorities in Scotland and Northern Ireland apparently still plan to interpret the question about 'sex' as one about 'gender identity'. Critics say that this decision is particularly likely to affect the quality of data about younger age groups, where misaligned gender identity is more likely to be reported.[61]

Clearly, males with a female gender identity don't share the same career or socio-economic challenges as females simply by having a misaligned gender identity, because they don't share the reproductive capacity that gave rise to them (and in many cases, no one is likely even to falsely assume they do). The success of trans activism in this area has significantly reduced our collective capacity to address the original problem – *which still hasn't gone away*. To this, it's sometimes objected: 'What about infertile women? Are you saying they should be excluded from any protective measures for females in the workplace?' No, on at least two counts. The first is that females as a whole tend to be disadvantaged in the workplace in relation to their group-associated reproductive role, irrespective of whether particular individuals actually fulfil that role. The second is, in any case: that's not how protective measures for large numbers of people work. They are necessarily broad-brush. It's more efficient, in aiming a particular measure at a large group, to accept that it might not apply to a small proportion of that group, than to take the trouble of working out exactly to whom the measure applies and applying it selectively.

The difference sex plus heterosexuality makes to assault statistics

Biological differences plus heterosexuality make a social difference in assault statistics too. There are significant differences in sexual assault prevalence for males and females. In 2017 it was reported that an estimated 3.1 per cent of women (510,000) as compared to 0.8 per cent of men (138,000) aged sixteen to fifty-nine had experienced sexual assault that year.[62] Over lifetimes, 20 per cent of women as compared to 4 per cent of men experienced some type of sexual assault.[63] In 2018, twice as many women as men experienced domestic abuse at the hands of their partners.[64] Generally speaking, males are responsible for the majority of sexual and domestic assaults committed upon females. These differences seem at least partly explicable in terms of typical differences between males and females in strength, size and direct aggression.[65] That's not to say developmental and other environmental factors don't play a role too; it is just to acknowledge that things wouldn't be as they are if males were systematically smaller, weaker and less testosterone-fuelled than females.

Partly in light of these facts, for a long time there's been a social norm that spaces where females undress or sleep, and so are particularly vulnerable to sexual assault – changing rooms, bathrooms, dormitories, prisons, hostels, etc. – should be male-free. This is to minimise sexual offences against females in those spaces. Remember that sexual offences can include not just rape or other physical attacks but also exhibitionism and voyeurism. Generally, females are three times more likely than males to encounter one of these offences.[66] For females who have suffered assault by males in the past, there are rape crisis centres and domestic violence refuges. These, originally at least, were run by females for females, both to protect victims from their attackers and to allow traumatised women space to recover. Though technically all this looks like 'discrimination' on the basis of sex (since males are excluded), the Equality Act allows that it's permissible if 'a proportionate means to achieving a legitimate aim'. Up until recently, it has seemed uncontroversial that single-sex spaces and services count as such.

Recently, though, thanks to creative public reinterpretation of the Equality Act by Stonewall and other trans activist organisations, there's been an astonishingly fast reconceptualisation of the norms around such 'women-only spaces'. Previously they were clearly understood as dedicated spaces for females. Now we are told that gender identity is the only criterion for legitimate entry. Stonewall's published advice to the many organisations signed up to its paid Diversity Champions scheme is clear: 'You should allow anyone to access facilities, spaces and groups which align with their gender identity.'[67]

Diversity Champions scheme members have been quick to comply. In 2019, the City of London Corporation, responsible for governance of the financial district of London and also for maintaining over 40km^2 of London's green spaces and parks, introduced a Gender Identity Policy according to which trans people should be able to access single-sex services aligning with their gender identity. This included Kenwood Ladies Pond on Hampstead Heath, despite the existence of both a mixed and a men's pond. From 2016 onwards, it has been the policy of both HM Prison Service and the Scottish Prison Service (another Diversity Champion) to house some male prisoners professing female gender identities in the female prison estate, whether or not they have received medical intervention or Gender Recognition Certificates.[68] Most UK universities now have policies that explicitly allocate 'single-sex' facilities – bathrooms, changing rooms, showers and residences – on the basis of 'self-identification' or 'self-ID'. The Cardiff University policy says, 'You have a legal right under the Equality Act 2010 to access facilities – such as changing rooms and toilets – according to the gender with which you identify.'[69] Leeds University policy says: 'Trans people can use single-sex facilities (such as toilets and changing rooms) according to their self-identified gender.'[70] And in 2019 it was reported that posters had gone up in public toilets in the University of the West of England asking, 'Do you feel like someone is using the wrong bathroom?' Any respondents in the affirmative were instructed not to 'challenge' the person, but instead to 'respect their identity' and to 'carry on with your day'.[71] Meanwhile, most of the providers of rape crisis centres and domestic violence shelters make no distinction between trans women and women, either as clients or as employees.

These rapid, seismic policy changes are bound to have detrimental consequences for female safety as they become further entrenched. Since gender identity is not something anyone can see directly, and is supposedly potentially detached from behaviour, dress and physiognomy, practically speaking this means that any male at all can enter a space and claim, if challenged, that it aligns with his gender identity. As conveyed by the UWE poster, females are expected not to challenge but just to 'carry on' with their own business. This obviously puts them at additional risk of assault.

The full consequences of this will take a while to emerge, partly because well-established social norms take a long time to dismantle. Humans are social animals who often like to follow the lead of others. At the moment, even where a policy explicitly permits access in terms of gender identity not sex, many will be reluctant to make use of it, assuming they even know about it. Others, unaware of the policies, will continue to challenge those of the opposite sex entering a space. Both things help to preserve the genuinely single-sex norm. But this protective effect won't last for ever. As more people start to find out about the policies and to access spaces in line with gender identity, displacing the old sex-based convention, it's not hard to see how it will be easy for badly intentioned males to take advantage and so expose females to risk. Criminologists know this, as do legal and medical professionals. In 2015 the President of the British Association of Gender Identity Specialists told a Government inquiry that, 'It has been rather naïvely suggested that nobody would seek to pretend transsexual status in prison if this were not actually the case.' He goes on to talk of a case in which there was 'a plethora of prison intelligence information suggesting that the driving force was a desire to make subsequent sexual offending very much easier, females being generally perceived as low risk in this regard'.[72]

Instructive cases come from places where self-ID has been policy for longer and so where old social norms around sex are less entrenched. In 2018, it was reported that nine homeless women in a California shelter were forced to share a shower with a trans woman, 'who made lewd and sexually inappropriate comments, and leered at them while they were naked'.[73] That same year, in Canada, trans woman Jessica Yaniv launched lawsuits against several female beauticians for refusing to provide a genital wax in their own homes to Yaniv, on the grounds that Yaniv was male. The lawsuits were eventually lost, although apparently because the motive was financial gain and racism, not because female beauticians in Canada are allowed to specialise in intimate care for female bodies if they choose to.[74] In Toronto, Kristi Hanna, a female resident of a woman-only shelter for recovering addicts, was made to share a room with a pre-operative trans woman, and though the trans woman did nothing wrong, still, the experience reportedly caused Hanna and others there to have 'stress, anxiety, rape flashbacks, symptoms of post-traumatic stress disorder and sleep deprivation'.[75] The UK also had its own cases in 2018. Trans woman Katie Dolatowski was jailed for assaulting a ten-year-old girl in the women's toilets of Morrisons supermarket, Dundee, a month after filming another young girl in a supermarket toilet in Dunfermline.[76] After this conviction, Dolatowski was housed in a female-only unit for homeless offenders.[77] And trans woman Karen White, in receipt of neither surgical nor hormonal intervention nor a legal Gender Recognition Certificate, was put in a women's prison on the basis of gender identity and promptly sexually assaulted female prisoners there.[78]

Trans activist objections here tend to be of four main kinds.

The first says that predators such as White and Dolatowski aren't 'real' trans women. But why not? They say they have a misaligned gender identity, and so fit the only criterion demanded by trans activist organisations. The second response says, in outrage: Are you saying all or most trans women are predators? No, obviously not – just as to say that males generally should be excluded from woman-only public space isn't to say all or most males are predators. They aren't. To repeat: preventative measures are usually by necessity broad-brush. They aren't supposed to be a character reference for a group as a whole.

A third response is some feverish whataboutery. What about sexually predatory lesbians in women-only spaces? Aren't *they* still there? Leaving aside the fact that violent lesbians aren't anything like as pressing a documented social problem as violent heterosexual males, this response pretends that, in instigating a genuinely single-sex norm for spaces, the plan all along was to exclude *all of the* possible predators rather than just the majority of them – and that if that *wasn't* the plan, any other plan to reduce predation should be abandoned because inconsistent. This would be a preposterously stupid approach, putting logical consistency before effective practical action. Something is clearly better than nothing, especially since males continue to be the most significant cause of sexual assault on females.

A fourth and final response is to emphasise the number of times single-sex spaces give rise to humiliating episodes of 'misgendering' (aka missexing) for ambiguous-looking people. To be clear, this does happen in single-sex spaces, especially to masculine-looking women. As trans scholar Jack (then non-trans Judith) Halberstam writes: 'For a large part of my life, I have been stigmatized by a masculinity that marked me as ambiguous and illegible.'[79] Halberstam writes informatively about 'the bathroom problem' he has encountered throughout his life, including in one case someone mistaking him for a male in a public women's toilet and calling security.[80] Missexing in single-sex spaces happens, and it is a highly regrettable cost of the current system. However, that cost needs to be considered alongside the potential costs of effectively allowing any male at all into places where females are unusually vulnerable to sexual assault. On balance, I don't think the former harm outweighs the latter. The obvious solution seems to be to introduce sex-neutral 'third spaces' alongside genuinely single-sex ones for those who feel more comfortable there, rather than simply abandon the latter altogether.

It's not a competition

The four effects of sex I have discussed in this chapter – on medicine, sport and sexual orientation, and also on things like the sex pay gap and assault prevalence in combination with heterosexuality as the most commonly found sexual orientation – aren't importantly influenced by gender identities. Though every effect I discussed potentially manifests in somewhat different ways depending on cultural context, still a significant effect of some kind cuts across big differences in race, class and religion. These effects are influenced by what sex people are, what their bodies are like, which sex they are aroused by, how all this fits into a culture, and what further social effects are then produced. Even if it is successfully argued that we should recognise gender identity, there should be little doubt that we should *also* recognise, track and legally protect sex. Sex and gender identity should not be placed in competition.

4

What Is Gender Identity?

As we know, John Money and Robert Stoller first coined the concept of gender identity in the 1960s. Over fifty years later, what I'm calling 'gender identity theory' has taken off in parts of the Western popular imagination – the idea that trans people are defined, not as people who have had surgery, or taken hormones, or who dress or behave in particular ways, but as people whose gender identities are misaligned with the sex 'assigned' to them at birth. Cis people are those whose gender identities align with birth-assigned sex. And either way – whether cis or trans – gender identity is what makes you man, woman or neither.

Thanks to the advocates of gender identity theory, many institutions have moved to make gender identity a determinant of legal and political rights. In some contexts, it is treated as at least as important as sex. For instance, since 2017 legislation in several US states makes it possible to obtain new identity documents (male, female, or non-binary) on the basis of a simple declaration of misaligned gender identity, replacing any reference to actual sex.[1] This is now also true in Malta, Canada, Argentina, Chile, Denmark, Ireland and two Australian states (Victoria and Tasmania). In the UK, serious pressure is still being exerted by trans activist organisations to rewrite the Gender Recognition Act and Equality Act, and to legally recognise gender identity rather than 'gender dysphoria' or 'gender reassignment' as the significant factor in each case.

Sometimes, the thinking seems to go: whether you're a woman or man has been an important determinant of rights and protections for over forty years. It's recognised in UK laws such as the 1975 Sex Discrimination Act and the 2010 Equality Act. But: if what *actually* makes you a woman or man isn't sex but gender identity, then gender identity should be the rationale for these protections, not sex. However, the problem here is that – as we now know from the previous chapter – recognising, tracking and protecting sex is non-negotiable, whatever we end up saying about gender identity. So the status of gender identity can't get justification simply by riding on the coattails of legislation designed to protect sex. It has to earn its own keep.

I'll consider arguments that what makes someone a man or woman is gender identity, not sex, later on. I want to bracket that issue here, in order I hope to remove a lot of distracting heat from the discussion. For now, I want to work out what gender identity *is*. This should put us in a better position to see if it is as important as campaigners and some policymakers claim. I'm going to suggest having a gender identity misaligned with sex is something comprehensible, to which society should pay respectful attention – though not the degree of uncritical acceptance we currently see.

Gender identity and non-trans people

What is it, exactly, to have an 'inner' 'psychological' sense of a female or male identity? It's obviously not the same as working out, on the basis of your own body parts and reproductive processes, whether you should be characterised by others as female or male. For many trans people – and nearly all of them at first – their bodies and reproductive processes are clearly characterisable as one or other, both by others and themselves. As the well-known trans author Jan Morris writes of her childhood: 'By every standard of logic, I was patently a boy.'[2]

It seems clear that, if we want to understand what having a gender identity is like, we shouldn't ask non-trans people, for many report no particularly strong sense of one. This lack is sometimes said to be the result of 'cis privilege'– you really notice your gender identity only when you suffer as a result of it, and cis people don't. A 2017 *Vox* article suggests a thought experiment to help cis people access their gender identities. They were asked 'if a huge sum of money would get them to physically transition to the opposite gender'. Most said no. The questioner then asked them to 'lock onto' their reasons why. 'Take that sense and imagine if you had been born in the opposite body.'[3]

Yet this isn't very convincing. It seems true that most non-trans people don't have any positive desire to transition. In the above scenario, perhaps they don't fancy the thought of painful surgery or life-long drugs, and are not motivated by money. Whatever the reason, this demurral need not suggest positive possession of an inner gender identity aligned with sex.

A further complication is that lots of non-trans people *are* unhappy with their sex – but without that making them trans. In particular, lots of women don't enjoy being female. Second Wave feminist Iris Marion Young summed it up when she wrote that attitudes towards women from society 'produce in many women a greater or lesser feeling of incapacity, frustration, and self-consciousness'.[4] Less academically, the internet search term 'hate being a girl' brings up pages such as 'I hate having boobs, I don't like them at all'; '6 things I hate about myself as a woman (in science)'; 'My daughter hates being a girl, what do I do?' and '101 reasons why I hate being a girl'. None of these pieces are by trans people.

Let's ignore that problem for now. What we seem to have gathered is that there's doubt about whether non-trans people positively have something called a gender identity. Maybe, for all we know, there can only ever be misaligned gender identities, relative to sex, and no aligned ones. We shouldn't let a desire for pleasing symmetry get in the way of actual evidence. So let's focus on trans people. When we do this, several different models of gender identity emerge. The first one I'll discuss is both the most popular and the worst.

The 'stick of rock' model of gender identity

When you bite into a stick of rock you've bought for a treat at the seaside, and look at its pale insides, there's often the name of the resort printed through it in darkened sugar. On what I'll call the 'stick of rock' (SOR) model, gender identity is a persistent stable part of the self, going through it – or through you – like words in a stick of rock.

According to the SOR model, gender identity is a fundamental part of the self, and determines who you 'really are'. Recall Principle 3 of the Yogyakarta Principles, described in Chapter 1. This says gender identity is 'integral to ... personality' and 'one of the most basic aspects of self-determination, dignity and freedom'. Trans bioethicist Simona Giordano writes that gender identity is 'best understood as a fundamental element of a broader notion of who each of us is, as a segment of personal identity'.[5] Similarly, mental health counsellor Dara Hoffman Fox writes that gender identity 'is a core aspect of who we are'.[6] Says influential US trans woman Mara Keisling: 'We're among the few people who are really approaching things with full integrity and full transparency ... We're saying, "This is who I really am."'[7] A 2019 book for kids about gender identity is called *It Feels Good to Be Yourself.* And an advertisement for the American Mariposa Health clinic, which provides 'gender-affirming hormone therapy, from anywhere', exhorts prospective clients to 'Live your authentic life'.[8]

On the SOR model, gender identity is presented as 'innate'. See, for instance, Stonewall's definition of gender identity: 'A person's innate sense of their own gender, whether male, female or something else ... which may or may not correspond to the sex assigned at birth'.[9] The *Oxford English Dictionary* defines 'innate' as 'Existing in a person (or organism) from birth; belonging to the original or essential constitution (of body or mind); inborn, native, natural'. Correspondingly, many people seem to think gender identity is 'in the brain'. Also on the SOR model, the gender identity innately in you is something you become consciously aware of over time, perhaps eventually feeling compelled to express it through dress, make-up, hormones or surgery. Your strong yearning to be of a different sex, or disaffection for your own sexed body, or attempts to pass as the opposite sex, and so on, are treated as *expressions* or *evidence of* your innate gender identity. But even when you're unaware of it, it's still there, waiting to be 'discovered' or 'realised'. Model and trans woman Munroe Bergdorf writes: 'When I said "girlhood" I mean just me discovering myself. Truly discovering myself. Like understanding what it meant to be a girl, what it meant to be me.'[10]

Presumably partly because we can normally know about another person's gender identity only by asking them, SOR also has it that, if someone tells you they have a misaligned gender identity, they should be 'affirmed'. This is slightly more nuanced than 'whatever a trans person says about their gender identity is true', because it allows for the fact someone might have good reason to hide their gender identity. However, if someone says they *do* have a misaligned gender identity, we should always believe them, for they have no good reason to lie, and they can't otherwise be wrong. Eminent medic Robert Winston writes: 'No one else can tell someone else what their gender identity is.'[11] And in their *Trans Teen Survival Guide*, trans authors Fox and Owl Fisher say: 'Gender identity is ... the gender that we know ourselves to be, something no one else can feel.'[12]

Some people think children – even small children – who say they're boys or girls, in variance with their sex, must be revealing 'real' misaligned gender identities. The authors of *The Transgender Child: A Handbook for Families and Professionals* write: 'It is common for children who are transgender to try to let their parents know this when they are very very young.' The authors include testimonies from adult relatives, recounting how, at a very young age, their child spoke or behaved in a way assumed indicative of misaligned gender identity. Says one: 'He has asked how old he can be before he has his "peepee" cut off.' Says another: 'He was a little baby of about eighteen months and his first formed sentence was "Me a boy mama" ... I knew something was up. He was always wanting "boyish" type toys and I had a feeling he was different from my three older daughters.'[13] This view also finds apparent support from medical professionals. In her book for kids called *What's Gender Identity?*, Katie Kawa writes that a 'leading group of doctors who work with young people have said children often have a sense of their gender identity by the time they're four years old'.[14] Other authors put it even earlier, at between two and three.[15]

Another common aspect of SOR is a 'born in the wrong

body' narrative. Though many trans people reject this narrative, nonetheless it persists. In one recent survey, 20 out of 51 trans men used it.[16] Medical interventions are sometimes presented as an attempt to 'correct' the body or make it 'align' with gender identity. A trans man told the *Guardian*, 'The hormones and surgery is about aligning my body to what it should have been at birth. Being born with the correct parts would have made things easier.'[17] Jan Morris writes: 'I was born with the wrong body, being feminine by gender but male by sex, and I could achieve completeness only when the one was adjusted to the other.'[18]

Taken at face value, the SOR model seems to provide justification for the increasing legal and political importance of gender identity. Treating gender identity as innate and potentially emerging into consciousness early in life suggests it is something persistent and fundamental in a person, and so deserving of recognition. If your own gender identity is something only you can really know about, this would seem to require an 'affirmative' approach from professionals – after all, they are not you. And this point would also seem to legitimate self-ID for Gender Recognition Certificates, rather than professional medical gatekeeping.

So let's look at evidence for the SOR model.

Is gender identity innate?

Trans activists sometimes say that while sex is allegedly about what's 'between your legs', gender identity is about what's 'between your ears' – which is to say, in your brain. We have already seen that the former point is false: sex is about gamete-producing pathways, chromosomes or a cluster of features involving much more than genitalia. But is gender identity between the ears? Yes, in the innocuous sense that

everything psychological about you, including gender identity, is a result of brain processes. This includes features and
capacities acquired after birth partly as a result of exposure
to an environment. However, if the claim is the stronger one,
that gender identity is an innate, permanent, *structural* fact
about the brain – the lettering inside the stick of rock, if you
will – then this is far less clear.

Sometimes scientific studies make headline-grabbing claims
that look useful for SOR: for instance, that gender identity
is 'programmed into the brain' and 'irreversible'.[19] In these
studies, scientists start with some assumptions about what
'female' and 'male' brains, on average, are like. This is so they
can try to see if brains of trans women are more similar, in
some aspect of their structure, to female brains than males;
or brains of trans men more similar to male brains. There's
an important point buried here. In practice, trying to find the
neural correlates of gender identity isn't just an attempt to
correlate gender identities with structural brain aspects. It's
also, crucially, to 'justify' the identity-attribution of a person
by finding some structural aspect of their brain *more like the
opposite sex*. To see this, compare these two imaginary findings: a) 'Males with female gender identities are more likely to
be born with brain feature X!'; b) 'Males with female gender
identities are more likely to be born with brain feature X,
which most females share and most males don't!'. The latter
would look far more exciting than the former, as it appears to
justify the trans person's identity in a way the former doesn't.

Already, this takes us into contested territory, because it's
intensely disputed whether there are such things as 'female
brains' and 'male brains', in the sense of having distinctive
observable structural characteristics. Though the matter is
controversial, I'll assume for the sake of argument there are.[20]
Even so, the evidence presented about gender identity doesn't

seem very secure. A 2020 review notes that some researchers claim to have found two areas of the brain – BNST (the bed nucleus of the stria terminalis) and INAH3 (the third interstitial nucleus of the anterior hypothalamus) – more similar in trans women and non-trans women than they are in men. However, the review notes, the sample size for this study was small. Also problematically, some of the trans women in the study were long-term recipients of oestrogen, which might have affected findings. Data on other brain differences is also pronounced 'limited' and does not 'provide a reliable conclusion'. [21]

There's a more fundamental problem, though. On the SOR account, gender identity is something individuals can become consciously aware of. They have authoritative self-knowledge about it, arguably in a way in which those around them cannot. So how is, say, a male brain having a smaller and so more 'female-like' brain area BNST or INAH3 supposed to result in conscious awareness, within the individual, of a female identity? There's no obvious direct route. The BNST is said to be 'important in a range of behaviors such as: the stress response, extended duration fear states and social behavior'.[22] INAH3 is said to be implicated in sexual behaviour patterns (indeed, there's a theory that homosexual males have smaller and more 'female-like' INAH3 areas than straight males).[23]

This raises an alternative hypothesis. That is: these atypical brain areas could be producing behaviours that are on average more female-like than male-like, or, at least, are viewed as 'female-like' by society. The subject becomes conscious of this similarity, and their self-perception, reinforced perhaps by others, feeds into the contingent formation of a misaligned gender identity. For instance, if it's the case that males with a smaller 'female-like' INAH3 are more likely to be homosexual then, given still-powerful cultural associations between the stereotype of masculinity and heterosexuality, perhaps some of these males go on to form female gender identities. It's not that structural brain areas have gender identity 'programmed' into them, but rather that they influence a set of apparently female-like behaviours, the perception of which, in a given environmental context, feeds into the contingent formation of a misaligned gender identity. In that case, gender identity wouldn't be innate: being influenced by biology isn't the same as being innate.

The same sort of issue besets a different attempt to naturalise misaligned gender identity, this time connecting it to hormone exposure in the womb. In 2013 the current Director of the NHS Gender Identity Development Service for children (GIDS), Dr Polly Carmichael, told *The Times* that 'there was growing evidence that hormones in early development could have a permanent influence on gender identity and behaviour'. So far, so very SOR-friendly. In practice, as the article makes clear, this conclusion comes from looking at rare cases: females with the DSD Congenital Adrenal Hyperplasia (CAH), exposed to unusually high levels of testosterone in early development. 'Their behaviour is more boyish in terms of their choice of playmates and self identity,' Carmichael said, citing one study that 'showed that girls with CAH were more likely to prefer toys that are usually chosen by boys, such as vehicles and weapons, and have greater interest in rough-and-tumble play'.[24] A different study in a similar vein describes girls with CAH drawing 'technical objects' like 'soldiers and fighting', rather than 'women, flowers and butterflies' more typical of female children's drawings.[25]

As discussed, these are children whose bodies are significantly atypical for the female phenotype, and in several aspects more typical for the male one. Even leaving aside ambiguous genitalia, girls with CAH tend to be more muscular than girls on average, more aggressive in play and more physically active.[26] So one possible explanation of the data is that female children with CAH like being around male children more than females because of testosterone-caused physical similarities between them, and the opportunities for more vigorous play this can give rise to. Given these girls often like being around boys, it's not surprising that they then start to share interests with boys, in terms of toys, drawing or anything else. We should also note that unusual hormone exposure in the womb seems, on some studies, to be connected to later homosexual orientation.[27] For all these reasons, girls with CAH are presumably also more likely to interpret themselves as 'boyish' or 'tomboys', and even perhaps to see themselves as boys full stop. But none of this establishes it was testosterone exposure that directly produced *gender identity* in utero.

In sum, what the SOR model seems to ignore is that misaligned gender identity could be formed in a person, in a developmental context, partly as a result of their acquired map of the world and of their own place in it – of what counts as female-like or male-like, and of how they personally match up, or don't. Given available evidence, this looks more likely. When trans people say they 'know' their gender identity or have 'discovered' 'it', or that their gender identity is their 'authentic' or 'real' self, it's highly unlikely to be because they somehow gained privileged access to some prior brain fact about themselves which justifies this attribution directly.

Medical model

Like the SOR model, the medical model of gender identity uses authoritative-sounding scientific language to give the impression that gender identity is a relatively permanent feature of a brain and body. The medical model essentially sees a mis-aligned gender identity as a mental illness or disorder, the main symptom of which is a condition called 'gender dysphoria'. According to the *Diagnostic and Statistical Manual of Mental Disorders (DSM–5)*, published by the American Psychiatric Association, gender dysphoria in an adult is diagnosed via the exhibition, for at least six months, of 'clinically significant distress or impairment' plus at least two of the following (bear in mind here that, confusingly, 'experienced/ expressed gender' refers to gender identity, i.e. GENDER4, and 'other gender' refers to the opposite sex, i.e. GENDER1):

1. A marked incongruence between one's experienced/ expressed gender and primary and/or secondary sex characteristics.
2. A strong desire to be rid of one's primary and/or secondary sex characteristics because of a marked incongruence with one's experienced/expressed gender.
3. A strong desire for the primary and/or secondary sex characteristics of the other gender.
4. A strong desire to be of the other gender.
5. A strong desire to be treated as the other gender.
6. A strong conviction that one has the typical feelings and reactions of the other gender (or some alternative gender different from one's assigned gender).[28]

In practice, the presence of gender dysphoria is ascertained in adults through questionnaires such as one called the 'Gender Identity/Gender Dysphoria Questionnaire'. The 'male assigned at birth' version asks whether, in the past twelve months, a patient has felt: 'satisfied being a man', 'pressured by others to be a man, although you don't really feel like one', 'that you have to work at being a man', 'that you were not a real man' and 'that it would be better for you to live as a woman rather than as a man'. It also asks whether you have 'had the wish or desire to be a woman', 'dressed and acted as a woman', 'presented yourself as a woman' and 'had dreams in which you were a woman' and whether you have 'disliked your body because it is male', 'wished to have hormone treatment to change your body into a woman's' or 'wished to have an operation to change your body into a woman's'. [29]

As you might expect, in the medical model there's a great emphasis on 'treating' misaligned gender identity, understood as an impairment. Unusually for a psychiatric diagnosis, sanctioned treatment aims to change the body first, and not (directly) the mind. The main forms of treatment are hormones, and perhaps also surgery, either to remove sex characteristics or create new versions of them. Though this treatment removes or otherwise inhibits the function of biologically healthy tissue and reproductive systems, it is viewed as medically necessary to alleviate distress. There's often also emphasis, in medical discussion, on comorbidity with other psychiatric or psychological conditions alongside gender dysphoria: anxiety, depression, suicidal ideation, paraphilia and personality disorders, as well as histories of trauma or abuse.

The medical model has some perceived advantages for trans people. It represents the provision of surgery and hormones as a medical need (not just 'cosmetic' surgery), releasing funding for it from the NHS and other healthcare systems. It provides a narrative in which a person isn't responsible for having a misaligned gender identity. Some find this comforting in a world in which recrimination from loved ones for a transition can be high. Though it pathologises misaligned gender identity, to some extent it also culturally 'normalises' it by putting it into the medical realm with which most of us are familiar. And it presents possession of a misaligned gender identity as a disability, and as such requires society to accommodate it.

I think the medical model also has less attractive aspects, however. As with historical 'treatments' for homosexuality, there is a suspicion that in treating misaligned gender identity as a disorder, medics are effectively pathologising sex-nonconforming behaviour because of residual underlying distaste or prurience. Some have even worried that they are re-pathologising homosexuality, covertly. This impression is not lessened by the discovery that, as pointed out by academic Eve Kosofsky Sedgwick, Gender Identity Disorders were first introduced into the DSM in 1980, just at the moment when, under pressure from the gay rights movement, 'homosexuality' understood as a disorder was removed.[30]

There is often relatively little interest shown in whether psychological distress – not to mention comorbid psychiatric conditions – is connected to prevalent cultural norms about sex-nonconforming behaviour and desires. In societies where conformity to sex-based stereotypes is high, and nonconformity socially punished, it is perhaps unsurprising that trans people feel distress. But under the medical model, this is often unexplored. As one former patient of a UK Gender Identity Clinic says: 'There is a system of saying, "Okay here's your hormones, here's your surgery, off you go."'[31]

Generally, many proponents of the medical model seem relatively uninterested in the contribution made by personal interpretation of the world around one, and one's place in it. The medical model presents a neat story about a persistent, long-lasting mental problem, possibly starting in childhood or teenage years, and if not innate, then at least having an aetiology relatively detached from local environment. Again atypically for a psychiatric diagnosis, it treats misaligned gender identity more like a permanent neurodevelopmental disorder than a potentially temporary mental disorder such as depression or bulimia. Under the model, misaligned gender identity is not something relatively fluid that might emerge via personal interpretation. As Judith Butler says critically about medical 'diagnosis' (using 'gender' for gender identity, i.e. GENDER4): 'The diagnosis ... wants to establish that gender is a relatively permanent phenomenon. It won't do, for instance, to walk into a clinic and say that it was only after you read a book ... that you realized what it was you wanted to do, but that it wasn't really conscious for you til that time'.[32]

Another problem with the medical model, at least as it matches up to contemporary trans people's lives, is that some people with misaligned gender identities are stable and well functioning with 'social' transition only (i.e. non-physical behavioural changes). Equally, the 'strong desires' described in *DSM-5* diagnostic criteria – desires to be of the opposite sex or to have a differently sexed body – don't necessarily mean clinically significant distress must be an accompaniment. Indeed, the *DSM-5* effectively recognises this by making clinically significant distress a further separate condition on gender dysphoria, alongside those sorts of desires. But given the existence of these well-functioning people, it seems strange to make clinical levels of distress a condition of having a misaligned gender identity. Worse: combined with the idea trans people are defined in terms of having misaligned gender identities, it effectively says only people with a history of impairment can be trans.

Once clinically significant distress is removed as a condition of misaligned gender identity – as I think it should be – then it's no longer a medical problem. The medical model ceases to apply. Terrible distress may accompany misaligned gender identity, and medical intervention may be appropriate as a solution, but neither has to be there. And it's not a clinically significant impairment, *in itself*, strongly to want to be the opposite sex, or to wish your body were very different, as I'll discuss below. But before I do, I want to look at another influential model of gender identity, featuring a by-now familiar figure.

The queer theory model of gender identity

This model is rooted in the work of Judith Butler and other queer theorists. Before getting into it, I need to set aside a couple of distractions. We know that Butler thinks most or all categories for humans, including scientific ones, are wholly socially constructed. So, for obvious reasons, Butler is unlikely to have much truck with the idea of a gender identity 'misaligned' with sex. I also want to bracket for now the question of what makes you a 'woman' or 'man'. Here I am considering only *what gender identity is*. If we focus on that question, I think queer theorists have some interesting things to say about it.

Butler thinks that in the context of social constructionism, 'gender' – expansively meaning observable sex, the social stereotypes around sex, being women and men, and all the rest of it – can only ever be a 'performance'. Queer theory's preferred form of performance is one that breaks down or 'queers' existing power structures and hierarchies. Perhaps unsurprisingly, then, there's an emphasis on the impermanence and fluidity of gender identity. SOR-like narratives of gender identity as 'innate', 'really in' someone, 'fundamental', 'authentic', 'discovered', and so on, are all seen as misguided attempts to naturalise something fundamentally social to make it seem more legitimate. There is also a move away from the idea that gender identity must be all-or-nothing, and from a 'binary' assumption that gender identities must be male or female, towards the idea of blurred identities and of their proliferation, understood as a radical political act. This is why some aspects of current trans activism emphasise the alleged multiplicity of gender identities that I described in Chapter 1.

Particularly attractive is the emphasis on the potential influence of self-interpretation upon gender identity, and the way that attempts to naturalise gender identity can obscure that. As Butler puts it: 'Life histories are histories of becoming, and categories can sometimes act to freeze that act of becoming.'[33] Earlier in this chapter I hypothesised that a misaligned gender identity might arise as a result of interpreting a sex-nonconforming body, or sex-nonconforming behaviour, in a particular environmentally influenced way. Later on, one might come to interpret those things as indicative of something different. We see this in the phenomenon of the 'detransitioner' – someone who used to think of themselves as trans but who no longer does. 'Everybody says that gender is a social construct, but we also act like it's somehow an innate part of a person's identity,' one detransitioner told *The Stranger* magazine. 'I started to think the whole concept of transitioning was regressive.'[34] Proponents of the SOR model might dismiss detransitioners as a fundamentally different sort of phenomenon to those who 'really' have misaligned gender identity. Detransitioners were never really trans in the first place, it's sometimes said. But if identities are fundamentally attached to personal meaning-making, and if meaning-making can change over an individual's life, this can't be right.

The queer theory model has drawbacks, however. The presumed blurring and multiplicity of identities seem to have limits. Once we move definitively away from any relation – even if it is negative – to the ideas of *male* and *female* or *man* and *woman*, we lose a sense of what certain particularly complicated gender identities are supposed to be. Let's return for a moment to some of those officially protected in UK universities, as listed in Chapter 1. These included 'demifluid' (people 'whose gender identity is partially fluid whilst the other part(s) are static') and 'pangender' (people who identify 'with a multitude, and perhaps infinite ... number of genders either simultaneously, to varying degrees, or over the course of time').[35] Shorn of even an indirect connection with binary sex categories, these identities are fairly incomprehensible. It's really not clear how you would reliably know that you had one, let alone establish someone else was discriminated against on such a basis. This may not matter much to queer theorists but it should matter to policymakers.

Another concern for some is that a queer theory model seems to trivialise, or at least wholly politicise, what for many is psychologically important in a way that transcends politics. Trans woman Joy Ladin writes in her memoir: 'For me, gender is more than a performance.'[36] And as trans scholar Jay Prosser has objected, 'there are transsexuals who seek very pointedly to be nonperformative, to be constative, quite simply, to be'.[37] Equally, if adoption of a misaligned gender identity is thought beneficial only insofar as it performatively disrupts existing power hierarchies, then this seems to undermine any rationale for politically protecting it or entering it into law. On the relativistic terms set out by queer theory, to do this would just be to substitute one set of damaging power hierarchies with another.

A further problem with the queer theory model is also connected to this politicisation of gender identity. We are told insistently that all gender identities are equally valid. So, as in the SOR model, there can only be 'affirmation' – but this time, not because there *really is* some underlying innate fact of the matter that has been discovered, but rather because affirming these identities is seen as a beneficially subversive political act.

Yet this leaves no critical resources to analyse particular claims about gender identity as better founded or more conducive to individual or societal well-being than others. Where some people are making life-altering medical decisions in its name, this looks more than a bit cavalier.

This concludes my round-up of what, to my mind, are mostly unsatisfactory gender identity models. I haven't attempted to stick rigidly to the standard presentation of these models, but rather have tried to make sense of dominant models in my own way. There are some I haven't discussed. In particular, some people in Gender Studies are fond of talking of a 'Biopsychosocial' approach. As Alex Iantaffi and Meg-John Barker put it in their book *How to Understand Your Gender: A Practical Guide for Exploring Who You Are*, 'For all of us, gender experience is a complex mix of our biology, our psychology, and the social world around us.'[38] In practice, this isn't so much a theory as an initial framework for a pro-gramme of research. Iantaffi and Barker make the plausible but limited point that physical facts about sexed bodies can causally interact with individual psychological profiles, and vice versa (as when, for instance, a female with a male gender identity pursues sport and so gets a more muscular physique); and that both are influenced by current sociocultural context and possibilities. I don't disagree, but this is hardly specific to gender identity. I turn now to what I hope is a more helpful and detailed account.

An 'identification' model of misaligned gender identity

What I'll call the identification model is inspired by the British sociologist Stuart Hall. Hall, himself inspired by post-structuralist theorists like Butler, argued that cultural identities generally should be viewed as processes of active 'identification' rather than as settled, stable facts about the self. Unlike him, though, I'm interested in articulating the psychological more than the political aspects of identification.

The identification model involves the general idea of someone subconsciously and consciously 'identifying' with another. Psychoanalysts Heinz Hartmann and Rudolph Loewenstein write that although there are different ideas about identification in psychoanalytic theory: 'We all agree that the result of identification is that *the identifying person behaves in some ways like the person with whom he has identified himself* [my italics]. The likeness may refer to the characteristics, features and attitudes of the object, or to the role the object plays in reality (or to the role it plays in reality according to the fantasy of the person who makes the identification); it may mean to "take the place" of the other person. Freud ... describes it also as "moulding oneself" after the fashion of the object that has been taken as a model.'[39]

Though the talk here is of identifying with another person, you can also identify with a country (as in nationalism) or a sports team (as in sports fandom), or with a beloved pet, or even with nature as a whole. People can identify with pop stars, film stars, teachers, political and religious leaders, friends or strangers. In most psychoanalytic schools of thought, identification can be dysfunctional – especially when the subject gets lost in fantasy or harmful behaviours – but it doesn't have to be. It can be a great source of value and meaning. It is enhanced by the sense of belonging and acceptance people can find with like-minded others who share their identifications, and is part of what fuels wider social practices such as political party rallies, pop concerts, or justice movements like environmentalism and radical feminism.

Partly, identification involves affect – desire or yearning to be like, or sometimes even to merge with, another. In the words of psychiatrist David Olds, this can give rise to 'imitation, conscious and unconscious, as well as more practical aspects such as learning procedures and patterns of behavior that resemble those of the other'. Identification may also involve assuming 'the goals and values of the other', and steering 'one's life in the direction of achieving those goals'.[40] Identification also involves *already seeing yourself* as similar to the other. As Olds puts it, there is 'influence on perception – apprehending the other as similar to oneself'. Stuart Hall writes: 'Identification is constructed on the back of a recognition of some common origin or shared characteristics with another person or group, or with an ideal, and with the natural closure of solidarity and allegiance established on this foundation.' Still, perceived similarities aren't enough to make it true that you actually *are* identical to the object you identify with. As Hall writes: 'Once [identification is] secured, it does not obliterate difference.'[41]

Applied to gender identity, then, an identification model says that to have a misaligned female gender identity is to identify strongly, in this psychological sense, either with a particular female or with femaleness as a general object or ideal. (You might also say 'identify with womanhood' but I'm leaving womanhood aside for now.) To have a misaligned male identity is to identify either with a particular male or with a general object or ideal of maleness (or manhood). And to have a misaligned non-binary identity is to identify either with a particular androgynous person or with a general ideal of androgyny. Strong identification will often involve dysphoria, understood as an aversive emotional response to perceptions of one's own sexed body and to its difference with the body one longs to see.

An identification model fits well with the yearning, idealised quality of many first-hand accounts of trans experience. Trans man Lou Sullivan writes evocatively in his diary, age nineteen, prior to transition: 'My heart and soul is with the drag queens. This last week also I wanted to go and leave everything and join that world but where do I fit in? I feel so deprived and sad and lost. What can become of a girl whose real desire and passion is with male homosexuals? That I want to be one? I still yearn for that world, that world I know nothing about, a serious, threatening, sad, ferocious, stormy, lost world'.[42] Jan Morris recounts how she prayed 'Please God make me a girl' as a child, and later 'still made the same wish whenever I saw a shooting star'.[43] Jack Halberstam writes: 'If I had known the term "transgender" when I was a teenager in the 1970s, I'm sure I would have grabbed hold of it like a life jacket on rough seas, but there were no such words in my world. Changing sex for me and for many people my age was a fantasy, a dream, and because it had nothing to do with our realities, we had to work around this impossibility and create a home for ourselves in bodies that were not comfortable or right in terms of who we understood ourselves to be'.[44] And Munroe Bergdorf talks of the moment she thought about transitioning: 'It was after watching *Clueless* at a friend's house and – it was a group of girls – just seeing how they were with each other and watching the movie at the same time and seeing female interaction/friendship and how it's not a fictional thing. I think every now and then people realise that, when you haven't been exposed to something, these things actually exist. It's like a gay person going to a gay bar for the first time and realising "oh my God, this is where I fit in, this is me, these are my people".[45]

Seeing misaligned gender identity as identification also explains, in the words of American medical manual *DSM-5*, the frequent presence of a 'strong conviction that one has the typical feelings and reactions' of the opposite sex. For as just described, characteristic to identification with another person or ideal generally is the combination of *already* feeling similar to the other, while desperately wanting to be *still more* similar. When we read first-hand accounts of trans people's childhoods, it seems that gender identity is often formed partly in relation to a perception of the body, sexuality or self as atypically female-like or male-like (often with distressingly prejudiced responses from those around one). Here's Munroe Bergdorf again: 'Through high school and puberty, I battled with being told to be a "boy", and what was expected of me from a male perspective.' Paris Lees describes how her father 'humiliated' her for – in his words – 'walking like a poof' and for 'talking like a pansy'.[46] Laverne Cox recounts: 'I was bullied because I didn't act the way someone assigned male at birth was supposed to act.'[47] Though a perceived similarity with the opposite sex might be partly based on being attracted to the same sex as them, equally, other perceived similarities may be more important. Recent research suggests that gender identity and sexuality are only weakly correlated in the contemporary trans population taken as a whole.[48] Whatever the perceived similarities are exactly for an individual, in practice there need be no clear mental separation between wanting to be like another and seeing oneself as already partly like them. There is a reciprocal flow between these two psychological aspects that means they can't easily be separated.

The identification model also fits well with first-hand testimonies about experiences of gender dysphoria. According to some: 'It's a constant effort to align yourself externally with how you feel internally.' 'I would describe it as a disconnect between my mental self-image/identity and my body's physicality.' 'My gender dysphoria ignites an intense longing for my body to appear more stereotypically masculine.'[49] These descriptions convey a sense of a painful mismatch between the ideal one strongly identifies with and a perception of what one presently is. Dysphoria can fuel gender identity, and gender identity can fuel dysphoria. Psychiatrist Az Hakeem describes in his book *Trans* how he observes in clients who are developing misaligned gender identities a characteristic trajectory from 'an early sign or symptom of something not quite right' and a 'change in mood' to a 'period of searching for meaning behind the experience to change in self' and eventually an 'experienced change in self attributed to gender identity'. This is then followed by an 'increasing preoccupation with gender identity', a 'retrospective attribution of gender as cause of problems in ... life', and a 'heightened awareness of gender in everyday life in relation to self and others'.[50]

Compared to the SOR model, the identification model doesn't posit some separate fact of gender identity lying *behind* the emotions, desires, yearnings and convictions of similarity. The identification *is* the misaligned gender identity and not a symptom or 'expression' of 'it'. And although there is always a brain explanation for every psychological phenomenon including this one, there's no presumption that misaligned gender identity lies in a single neural location or particular sex-atypical brain fact. In line with the medical model, meanwhile, a gender identity isn't something you're directly consciously responsible for. Generally, we don't choose identifications, they start subconsciously, though we can have indirect influence in altering them in certain therapeutic circumstances (to be explored below). Equally, though, in common with the queer theory model and unlike the medical model, a role is allowed for personal meaning-making. Identifications may change throughout a life. There is room to acknowledge the role of contingent environmental influences on who or what we identify with.

One of the most attractive aspects of the identification model concerns its potential for variously evaluating gender identity claims. A misaligned gender identity isn't inevitably something to be fought or struggled with, for on this view, identification needn't be maladaptive. It needn't be distressing for the individual and is often compatible with a well-functioning life. Existing dysphoria can apparently lessen over time with the right interventions. Even if it did originate in childhood trauma, that doesn't mean having a misaligned gender identity is wrong for an individual, and indeed, might well be an adaptive way of coping with past or present. Most of us have aspects of our personalities forged in non-ideal circumstances, but that doesn't make them intrinsically bad for us.

There's nothing intrinsically wrong with adults exploring and expressing identifications with the opposite sex or androgyny in behaviour, dress and, in some cases, hormones and surgery. If it sometimes seems that way, it is partly because there's still such general disgust and prurience about sex-nonconforming behaviour, especially in males. My stance on this might appear odd to those feminist readers who associate misaligned gender identities with what they see as regressive social stereotypes about masculinity and femininity, in a blameworthy way. Their reasoning seems to go: for a male, for example, to say 'I have a female gender identity', or even just to say 'I feel like a woman' can only really mean, in practice, 'I feel attracted to regressive social stereotypes of femininity' – passivity, meekness, 'sissyness', and so on. Ditto for females with male gender identities. 'They said we were male chauvinist pigs, they said we were the enemy,' writes a 'he-she' character of his fellow lesbians in Leslie Feinberg's semi-autobiographical novel, *Stone Butch Blues*.[51]

I think this assumption is a mistake and will explain why further on, but in the meantime, I agree that identification with the opposite sex is likely to involve reference to social stereotypes. It's based on an ideal or fantasy, after all. But, social stereotypes are not *in principle* regressive. Arguably, stereotypes are heuristics, helping us to make rough-and-ready, fallible generalisations when we need to make decisions fast. What does seem true is that many female-associated stereotypes are *in practice* highly regressive and unhelpful. Even so, it seems strange to blame trans women for their attraction to regressive female-associated stereotypes when apparently so many non-trans women are attracted to them too. And remember, I am not talking at this point about what makes you a woman – these issues have become so entwined that it's easy to keep defaulting to that assumption.

Equally, the identification model allows that an identification with the opposite sex isn't always to be 'affirmed' without question, unlike SOR and queer theory models. Generally, our emotional connections to ideals, and associated desires and feelings, tend to fit into narratives of belief that give them sense: I value *that* because I believe it's worthwhile and admirable; I fear *that* because I believe it'll hurt me; I want *that* because I think it'll bring me *this*, etc. Changing a person's background beliefs by exposing them to new evidence can change the associated foregrounded feelings. This is particularly true with children and teens. Earlier we saw claims that children 'know' their gender identity at a very early age. Completely crazily, the *DSM-5* cites as evidence of gender dysphoria in children, a tendency to wear clothes or play with toys associated with the opposite sex.[52] But this is *nothing like enough* to show the presence of an identification of the right sort. In children who are still forming basic concepts, there can be no awareness that clothes or toys are particularly considered as being 'for' boys or girls. So a child's wearing or playing with them ordinarily reveals nothing more than the projections of adults looking on. This is even more obviously the case with pre-verbal or non-verbal children – a fact that hasn't stopped Stonewall writing, in its 2020 Schools Guide 'An Introduction to Supporting LGBT Children and Young People' that it's important, for 'pre- or non-verbal children' to '[m]ake sure that each child or young person has opportunities to express their gender identity ... and feel "heard"'.[53]

This is in my view incredibly irresponsible. A female child who says 'I'm a boy' and even who wants strongly to *be a* 'boy' could simply be playing, or just be confused about what being a boy or girl is, so that this desire doesn't outlast realisation of her error. It should concern us all that, in the words of the former Head of Psychology at GIDS, Bernadette Wren, '[a]utistic spectrum profiles are common' among her patients. In the words of another review, 'Several studies suggest that individuals with ASD [Autistic Spectrum Disorder] can successfully categorize when the task is simple or rule-based, but have difficulty when categorization is more abstract or complex'.[54] Az Hakeem writes, 'In my opinion, a great deal of gender dysphoria patients I have assessed with very rigid convictions regarding their need to pursue gender reassignment have features suggestive of Asperger Syndrome.'[55]

Alongside ASD, there are other clinically significant factors potentially relevant to children who say they are 'really' of the opposite sex, or who desperately want to be. As Wren also notes, 'a relatively high level of mental distress and developmental atypicality is ... recorded for this population ... chiefly depression, anxiety, trauma and self-harm.' She observes: 'The complex relationship of these wide-ranging difficulties to gender feelings and broader aspects of identity development is often very hard to disentangle.' Trans activist organisations tend to interpret evidence of accompanying mental health issues as somehow the fault of society for failing sufficiently to 'affirm' a child's innate gender identity, but once it's acknowledged that gender identity involves self-interpretation, it could just as easily be true that gender identity is a response to prior mental health difficulties. The founder of GIDS, Domenico Di Ceglie, has also pointed out significant statistical associations between 'atypical gender identity organisation' and 'an experience of psychological catastrophe and chaos in early infancy'.[56] Az Hakeem writes how risk factors for a misaligned gender identity include being a 'replacement baby' or undergoing 'an initial period of cross-sex rearing'.[57]

For these sorts of reasons, in my view there are no circumstances in which minors should be making fertility- and health-affecting decisions involving blockers, hormones or surgery, as is now happening in many countries. No period of therapy prior to the age of majority could be long enough to untangle all these possibly contributory strands. Yet unsurprisingly, narratives implying identity-fluidity are discouraged by groups lobbying for early social and medical transition for children, such as the UK charity Mermaids. Instead, these organisations tend to talk as if the SOR model is true. One parent featured on the Mermaids website until 2020 said of her child: 'I feel she was born trans, that it's something that happens in the womb and no one has any control over it.' Even more worryingly, as I'll cover later in more detail, these groups often use inflated statistics to suggest to alarmed parents that suicide is very likely to follow the alternative strategy of 'watchful waiting'.[58] Says one detransitioner, who had breasts, womb and ovaries removed at the age of twenty and now regrets it: 'There's a very strong narrative that if you don't transition you are going to kill yourself ... I genuinely thought it was the only option.'[59]

Being a child and teenager often involves intense but fleeting identifications: with good causes, pop stars, actors, teachers, friends, and so on. If a child is same-sex attracted, the teenage years are often an even more confusing time in which a positive, stable self-image is likely to waver in the face of perceived pressure from family, friends and wider society. When the stakes are so high, it seems that an approach of 'watchful waiting' to see whether things stay the same or change is best. Initially intense identification with an opposite-sexed or androgynous ideal can transform in many cases into something else. One detransitioner talks of how in her early twenties she began to meet other detransitioned women, and her perspective was transformed. 'Where have these women been all my life? ... It was just so normal to be a lesbian and a masculine woman and I've never felt that, ever.'[60] In light of all this, the current professional prohibition of 'conversion therapy' – i.e. prohibition of anything other than affirmative approaches to gender identity from medics and psychologists – looks profoundly misguided. What this obviously ignores is that a therapist's refusing to automatically 'affirm' a teenager's gender identity, but rather sensitively exploring her feelings with her instead, may open up space for the patient's acceptance of her own homosexuality.

Other consequences of the identification model

One consequence of the identification model is that – at least as I've characterised it – it seems reasonable to think misaligned gender identity might well have been around for millennia: that is, for as long as there have been females psychologically identifying strongly with an ideal of the male, and males psychologically identifying strongly with an ideal of the female. Different cultural and historical moments may have provided people with new ways of interpreting and expressing these feelings, but the feelings themselves look relatively ahistorical, at least potentially. Cultural historian Bernice Hausman is surely right to argue that 'developments in medical technology and practice were central to ... the emergence of the demand for sex change', but that doesn't mean the feelings underpinning it were invented in the twentieth century.[61]

Another consequence is that, in contravention of a standard commitment of gender identity theory, even people with relatively ambiguous DSDs don't all have misaligned gender identities. Cases may vary. A CAIS male who would classify herself as a girl needn't be particularly identified with being one. A CAH female who likes 'boyish' things may not be particularly intensely identified with them: she might just like them.

Is it possible for a non-trans person to have an 'aligned' gender identity, as in a strong emotional identification with an ideal *of their own sex*? Perhaps so. Some women are strongly and persistently emotionally attached to stereotypes of femininity. An ideal of femininity or womanhood has become central to their sense of self for whatever reason: for instance, women who repeatedly seek cosmetic surgery to reach feminine cultural ideals. Or think of men who seem unusually attached to masculinity: body-building Jack Reacher-loving gun-fanatic types. Maybe there's a coherent sense in which these could have 'aligned' gender identities in the way I've characterised them here. Still, clearly, most non-trans people don't feel this strongly either way, and so don't have gender identities at all: that is, most people don't have a strong psychological identification with either their own sex or the opposite one, or with androgyny.

Equally, can some *non-trans* people have misaligned gender identities? Again, I think yes.[62] For instance, if the term 'butch' is understood, as it is presented by Jack Halberstam in his book *Female Masculinity*, as a 'master signifier of lesbian masculinity' then many butch women seem to fit the criteria; as do historical figures such as the eighteenth-century diarist and landowner Anne Lister, recently vividly brought to life in the BBC series *Gentleman Jack*. Lister had sexual relationships with numerous women throughout her life, recounted in great detail in her diaries. As described by Halberstam, in several places in the diaries 'Anne refers to her gendered desires, her fantasies of having a penis, her desire to be ... [a] "husband", and her "sensitiveness of anything which reminded me of my petticoats"'.[63] But equally, Halberstam records that although 'Anne is constantly mistaken for a man or treated like one during her daily life ... she sees her gender ambiguity as neither imitative nor deficient'.[64]

This last point implies that, for law or policymaking purposes, we shouldn't define 'being trans' in terms of 'having a misaligned gender identity', because non-trans people can have them too. In light of this, if legislators want to give trans people (as opposed to say, sex-nonconforming people generally, which would include trans) protection in law, then the definition of a trans person should be someone committed to *behaving* in a certain way rather than only *feeling* a certain way, detached from behavioural expression. For instance, trans people might be defined for policy purposes as those who say, seriously and frequently, that they wish to change sex or have changed sex, and who also deliberately dress or self-adorn or alter their bodies in ways significantly atypical for their sex, or act in other culturally coded ways obviously suggestive of transness. This is broadly in the spirit of the currently protected characteristic in the Equality Act, 'gender reassignment'.[65] Equally, though, laws to protect trans people from discrimination could conceivably be subsumed under strong legislation to protect the sex-nonconforming generally:

butch lesbians, drag queens, 'camp' men, cross-dressers and even, perhaps, a 'group of men on a stag do who put on fancy dress as women' and who are then 'turned away from a restaurant'. (According to the Equality and Human Rights Commission, the latter are 'not transsexual so not protected from discrimination', but if the sole reason for excluding such men was their sex-nonconforming outfits, and not, say, the possibility of drunken behaviour, this would seem unjust.[66])

This leaves the thorny question of whether gender identity itself should also be legally recognised and protected (a question distinct from whether gender reassignment should be protected, as just indicated). As we now know, it is frequently argued that gender identity is a fundamental part of the self, or as the Yogyakarta Principles say, 'integral to ... personality', and so requires recognition in law. For people who have misaligned gender identities – understood as psychological identifications with the opposite sex or androgyny – these are indeed aspects both of self and personality, but only if 'self' and 'personality' are understood as potentially fluid and partly constituted by personal interpretation, and not in terms of innate permanent features. And equally, such identifications, whether with the opposite sex or with one's own sex, clearly aren't present for all of us. So gender identity can't also be 'fundamental' in a way that is relevant to identity documents, nor 'one of the most basic aspects of self-determination, dignity and freedom' as we saw Yogyakarta Principle 3 grandiosely claim in Chapter 1.

Meanwhile, given that possession of a misaligned gender identity is often accompanied by sex-nonconforming behaviour, and this tends to be a source of discrimination and sometimes violence, then it might look as though gender identity should be legally protected in some form, in the Equality Act or similar. However, whether it should be protected under that name or rather under the larger umbrella of sex-nonconforming behaviour needs to be considered carefully by legislators. A big risk of making an inner psychological state a ground for someone else's possible criminal conviction is that it becomes too easy to say it's a factor in any given case. Indeed, on some present formulations, the presence of a particular gender identity is in danger of looking unverifiable; as when Stonewall tells young people, 'Someone else can't tell you what your gender identity is – only you know how you feel.'[67] If it is legally protected, and infractions criminalised in its name, then professional guidelines should be formulated about how to ascertain the presence and influence of someone's gender identity in a given situation in a non-trivial way.

What Makes a Woman?

The question of whether trans women count as women, literally speaking, has become enormously toxic. A well-known slogan of Stonewall's tells us that: 'Trans women are women. Get over it!' Trans activist organisations like Stonewall present anything other than enthusiastic assent to the question as an attempted 'erasure' of trans people, strategically ignoring the fact that the question is not about trans people's existence, but about how they are correctly categorised. The direct question 'Do you believe trans women are women?' – known amongst feminists I know as 'the witch question' – is wielded like a weapon to shut dissenters up, since clearly there is something highly uncomfortable about having to answer in the negative, in full knowledge that some people have made permanent body alterations on the presumption that they can actually change sex. Non-trans people, concerned to be kind, may concede under pressure that trans women are not female, but assume, or at least hope, there is still some coherent sense in which trans women can count as women, nonetheless. So it is important to see if this is true.

What is a woman? What is a man? What membership

conditions must a human satisfy to count as either? If you have spent time reading Judith Butler or queer theory more generally, you might hear these questions in a particular way. As we know, Butler sees categories like womanhood and manhood as 'normative' and 'exclusionary'. In that context, my questions can sound sinister. Effectively, they might seem to ask: how unfeasibly perfect do you have to be to count as a woman or man? What bodily, psychological or sexual ideal do the normies require you to fit before they let you into their exclusive club?

However, this isn't what the questions inevitably mean. Questions about what a woman is, or what a man is, are at least in part questions about the public concepts WOMAN and MAN (capitalised to indicate I'm talking directly about concepts, rather than the entities they represent or refer to). Queer theory doesn't have a monopoly on accounts of concepts. A request for 'membership conditions' of a concept is a question about the conditions that already govern a concept (roughly: what an entity has to have, or be like, to count as covered by the concept), as revealed in people's use of them. These aren't decided arbitrarily by some snooty, perfectionist committee somewhere; or even by you, when you try to answer 'What is a man?' or 'What is a woman?'. When asked such questions, you aren't being invited to *stipulate* some arbitrary standard. You are not that powerful. Anyway, as I'll explain shortly, that's not how concepts work or what they are for. Instead you're being asked to reflect, at least partly, on how users actually employ the words 'woman' and 'man' in a range of contexts and see what presuppositions those uses have in common. So the right question is more like: what would you have to explain to a non-English user or a child, so they understood what the concepts WOMAN and MAN ordinarily refer to? You aren't being asked to stipulate what womanhood and manhood *should* be but describe what *they already are*.

And even this isn't the full story, because when you're trying to describe what something is, you might end up criticising the public concept of it and suggesting some adjustments. But bear in mind that in trying to answer what makes someone a woman or a man, you're more like a spy patiently doing reconnaissance work than a bouncer at a club.

Conceptual analysis

What are concepts? Philosophers argue about this, but I think of them as cognitive tools or capacities which – at least when working well – help us all to negotiate the world we live in more effectively. Concept possession helps us notice different kinds of thing and make distinctions between them, relative to interests we might have. For instance, it's not surprising most people in every culture have a concept of FOOD. Once a person has the concept of FOOD and knows how to apply it, she can distinguish potential food from non-food and help keep herself alive. Though trans scholar Jack Halberstam presents a preoccupation with concepts as a 'mania for a godlike function of naming', which 'began ... with colonial exploration',[1] in fact the capacity to name and conceptualise the world in interest-relevant ways has been with humans for as long as their higher cognitive brain functions have. We wouldn't have got very far without it.

One sign that an individual has a concept of a particular thing is an ability to identify that thing reliably using sensory information, with more hits than misses. However, we also have concepts for lots of things that can't directly be sensed at all. Most things we think about can't be sensed directly (oxygen, corruption, narratives, values, anxiety, online transactions, thoughts, energy, numbers, etc.). Whether perceptually identifiable or not, another sign of concept possession is an ability to talk coherently about that thing in a range of contexts, using special words referring to the thing that others can recognise. Names, whether individual or general, help us do the latter. If, as a language-user, you have a concept of a thing, very often you'll have acquired from others a name to refer to that thing too. Indeed, the two are linked: for our main way of getting new concepts is by being told about new kinds of things by others, using names plus definitions, explanations or examples. Using a name in the same way as other people do facilitates communication about the thing in question.

Not every division between things is interesting enough to require a concept for it. Here's a concept, albeit clumsily named: BEING OVER TWO YEARS OLD. We could think up a pithier name for this kind of thing and start to use it to classify all the objects in the world, as either satisfying it or not. But there wouldn't be much point. On the other hand, if every object in the world over two years old suddenly became lethal to touch, you can bet we'd get a pithy handle to refer to it pretty quickly. As philosopher John Dupré points out, it isn't a coincidence that most languages have many more concepts for vertebrate animals than invertebrates. We have relatively little general interest in invertebrates but many interests in vertebrates, given the multiple roles they play in human life: pack animals, pets, predators, food, and so on.[2]

So we form concepts in response to human interests. We're more interested in some things than others, given who we are. But that doesn't mean concepts don't *also* pick out already existing real divisions in the world. Concepts, when working well, pick out what's already there. Despite what

Judith Butler thinks, they don't, on their own, create particular kinds of things, though often they help spread word of those things, and in some cases, increase their popularity and number via social trends. Sometimes a concept helps us pick out something purely material: e.g. CARBON. Sometimes it helps us pick out what's arguably a purely social kind of thing: e.g. FUNNY JOKES. But either way, I would argue, the things were there before the concepts, though admittedly this claim is a harder sell about funny jokes than carbon.[3]

Sometimes it becomes clear a concept isn't working very well. In the most extreme sort of case, it is discovered that a concept refers to nothing real. That's what happened with the old concept of PHLOGISTON, formerly understood as an element released in combustion. In the eighteenth century, it became clear to scientists that there was no such thing, so the concept fell out of scientific use. Less extremely, but only just, theorists might offer a thoroughly revised understanding of an existing concept.[4] This is what has happened with the traditional concept of RACE. Theorists have proposed that the membership conditions of any given racial category aren't grounded, as previously understood, in genetics or other aspects of biology, but rather in social factors.[5]

In a third, more common case, people might notice (or think they have noticed) that a particular concept should, given the internal logic of its membership conditions, be applied to some individuals previously thought by others to be ineligible. This is what happened when animal rights activists first argued that the concept of a PERSON was applicable to higher primates like gorillas and chimpanzees as well as humans; or when art critics in the late 1990s argued that Tracey Emin's messy bed, when transported from her home into a gallery, fell under the concept ART. A fourth sort of case is where an entirely new concept is coined to help us pick out some phenomenon in the world worth paying attention to. We now have the concept COVID-19. In 2018, we didn't.

'Analytic' philosophers like me spend lots of time investigating concepts and seeing whether they're fit for purpose, which is to say, whether they actually meet the way the world is and the interests we collectively have in mapping various bits of it. That is exactly what I was doing in Chapters 2 and 3 when I reviewed the concepts of BIOLOGICAL SEX, FEMALE and MALE and argued for their continued coherent application to the world. Following standard philosopher's terminology, let's call this activity 'conceptual analysis': analysis of concepts. It shouldn't be assumed this means only recovering and recording how language-users already think of the world, in a wholly passive and conservative way. This charge is sometimes levelled at conceptual analysis, but as I mean it, it involves *both* attention to concepts and language *and* attention to the nature of things. As my examples already show, there's potentially an active element, trying to improve concepts where necessary, the better to fit the world. My conceptual analysis is concerned with how concepts *should be* and not just how they *are*. But – equally and very importantly – this admission doesn't immediately turn a conceptual analyst into the equivalent of the bouncer at the nightclub door, gatekeeping about who can get 'in' to a concept and who can't, in order to prop up power hierarchies or meet selfish interests. *Features of the world, and our collective human interests in them, are not arbitrary*, and that's what we should be trying to make concepts responsive to. We're still doing reconnaissance work, not gatekeeping – or we should be.

The function of WOMAN as a concept

A central pillar of gender identity theory is that what makes you a woman or a man isn't your sex but your gender identity. That is conceptual analysis, whether or not gender identity theorists recognise it as such. They are proposing radically revised understandings of the existing concepts WOMAN and MAN. These concepts were traditionally understood as follows: 'woman: adult human female'; 'man: adult human male'. The proposed new definitions of the associated concepts, spelled out, are: 'woman: adult human with female gender identity (whether "assigned" male or female)'; 'man: adult human with male gender identity (whether "assigned" female or male)'. Since talk of assignation makes no sense, I'll remove reference to it in what follows.

Straight away, given the arguments of the last chapter, we can see significant problems for this account of womanhood and manhood. If I'm right about the identification model, not everyone has a gender identity. This would seem to leave us requiring a different explanation for what makes those other people, *without* gender identities, count as men or women too. Whatever conditions we came up with for them, presumably they would be applicable to people with gender identities too. In that case, we'd have two competing sets of conditions for womanhood and manhood. Equally, I argued in the last chapter that some *non*-trans people have gender identities. It seems strange, even by the standards of gender identity theory, to say, for example, that Anne Lister's apparently male gender identity must make her a man when she wouldn't classify herself that way.

Still, to be fair to opponents, I'm not going to make my objections rest on the truth or otherwise of the identification model. Let's assume – for this chapter only – gender identity theorists are right about gender identity, not me. *Even so*, I'll now argue, we shouldn't define 'woman' and 'man' in terms of gender identity.

On the face of it, the proposals from gender identity theorists about the concepts WOMAN and MAN look a bit like the case of the concept of RACE mentioned earlier, which many now understand as something social rather than genetic. In that case, too, there was a proposed big revision of membership conditions. So how can we test whether a revision like this should be adopted by language-users? One way is to assess whether the traditional version of the concept, with membership conditions as originally understood, fits the way the world is, and the collective interest in mapping various bits of that world. With RACE, it's at least arguable that the traditional concept, whose membership conditions cite biological factors as determinative of race, does neither. For instance, a 2016 article in *Science*, summarised in *Scientific American*, argued that understood as 'a useful tool to elucidate human genetic diversity', the concept of RACE isn't fit for purpose, and may even be confusing people. In fact, the article argues, racial categories are 'weak proxies for genetic diversity'.[6] Hence, it continues, the traditional concept of RACE needs revising so its membership conditions are understood to refer to something purely social.

In this sort of case, where big alterations are being proposed to the common understanding of a concept, we can use a decision tree as follows (with 'C' referring to the traditional version of a concept, and 'C2' referring to the proposed new version):

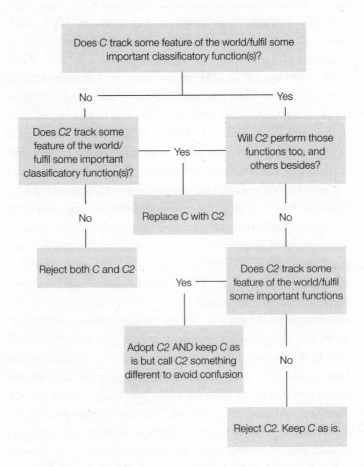

If the *Science* article is right, the decision structure with RACE seems to be: No; Yes.

What about the concepts WOMAN and MAN? For most of the histories of the English words 'woman' and 'man', they've referred, and been commonly believed to refer, to 'adult human female' and 'adult human male' respectively. It's been commonly understood that every woman is by definition an adult human female, and every adult human female a woman;

every man by definition an adult human male, and every adult human male a man. Do these concepts continue to fit the way the world is? Yes; for in Chapter 2 I argued that reports of the death of binary sex in humans had been greatly exaggerated. There are older human males and females, and younger human males and females, and no new theory has shown otherwise. So this isn't like the case of PHLOGISTON.

The next question is: is it useful to have concepts that refer to these groups? Are these concepts more like the useful concept FOOD or the currently useless concept BEING OVER 2 YEARS OLD? The answer is obvious. There's abiding public interest in having concepts to distinguish between adult human females and younger human females; and adult human males and younger human males. This is what the traditional concepts WOMAN, GIRL, MAN and BOY do. They respectively distinguish subgroups of females and males it looks important – even essential – to have concepts for.

On the gamete account of the sexes, animal species and even plant species have female and male members. So on that version of sex, we can't use the concepts FEMALE and MALE to differentiate *human* females and *human* males when we want to talk and think about them specifically. For many species that are important to human interests, we also have concepts for the female and the male of each: DUCK and DRAKE, HEN and COCK, QUEEN and DRONE, DOE and BUCK, COW and BULL. It's entirely predictable that language-users, in every human language, would develop concepts for the female and male in our own species as well.[7] Meanwhile, on the chromosome and cluster accounts, FEMALE and MALE (in many linguistic contexts, anyway) refer only to humans; but still, the concepts FEMALE and MALE don't distinguish between *adult* and *non-adult* females, or *adult* and *non-adult* males. These too are useful distinctions to be able to make, for all sorts of reasons. Though ADULT is itself a vague and historically vexed concept, with no clear boundary between adulthood and childhood, still, it's a very useful concept to have. (As repeatedly emphasised in earlier parts of the book, vagueness and lack of clear boundaries in a concept is not a problem *per se*.) It's also useful to have concepts that pick out adulthood intersecting with biological sex, because in our society so much of importance hangs on relative age: moral responsibility (as connected to sexual majority, the vote, criminal justice, and so on); different prepubescent and postpubescent health challenges; different social challenges facing different sexed age groups, and so on. If we want to explain why certain things tend to happen more often to one adult half of the population, we need a concept to refer to them, and to insert into causal explanations where relevant.

This is especially true if the aims are feminist. As Second Wave feminist Marilyn Frye put it – referring to 'woman' in the traditional sense – 'Being a woman is a major factor in my not having a better job than I do; being a woman selects me as a likely victim of sexual assault or harassment; it is my being a woman that reduces the power of my anger to a proof of my insanity. If a woman has little or no economic or political power, or achieves little of what she wants to achieve, a major causal factor in this is that she is a woman. For any woman of any race or economic class, being a woman is significantly attached to whatever disadvantages and deprivations she suffers, be they great or small.'[8] Getting rid of the concept WOMAN would mean we couldn't describe, explain, predict or manage these distinctively caused phenomena.

In sum: on all three models of sex reviewed in Chapter 2, alongside the concepts FEMALE and MALE it would seem essential, given many common purposes, to have further concepts distinguishing *adult human* females and *adult human* males in particular. This is what the concepts WOMAN and MAN give us, along with GIRL and BOY for the younger incarnations.

Another important aspect of the traditional concepts WOMAN, MAN, GIRL and BOY is that they refer to kinds of being who, most of the time, can be identified as such on the basis of perceptual cues. For instance, if I were to present you with a crowd of people, and if your senses were in full working order, normally you'd be able to make reliable assumptions about who were the adult human females and adult human males in the crowd, just by looking and listening. As we saw in Chapter 3, you might not always get it right – because you missex, mis-age or mis-human – but most of the time, most people will, and especially for people who are not at the borderline in terms of age. There are a potentially vast number of reasons why we might want to be able to perceptually distinguish the adult human females from the adult human males, and both of those from children of either sex. A few of these were reviewed in Chapter 3.

In recent years it has become clear to cognitive scientists that there's a close relationship between perception and the acquisition of some concepts. Common sense already tells us this, in fact, since one of the main ways of acquiring concepts of material entities in the world is via perception: seeing, hearing, touching, smelling and tasting things. The concepts WOMAN and MAN are ordinarily acquired partly by sight and sound. Most children get a sense of how to use these concepts partly by having women and men pointed out to them in the street, at home or in picture books.

Generally, when sighted humans look at their environment, they perceive discrete, bounded objects, not vast arrays of undifferentiated information. This is due to a brain capacity described as 'categorical perception'. As one author explains: 'Categorical perception allows us to carve up the world into the categories that are relevant to our behavior, thus allowing us to more efficiently process the visual features that are relevant to these categories. For example, when presented with a poisonous snake, it is more useful to quickly process snake-relevant features for fast categorization than to attend to the visual features that discriminate this snake from other snakes.'[9] This isn't to say some people can't visually discriminate different snakes, but only that for most people, differences between snakes and other objects will be more pronounced, and usually more quickly processed, than differences between *this* snake and *that* snake.

The cognitive process via which a child starts to be able to perceptually distinguish a particular kind of thing – say, a snake, or a dog – and so to possess its associated concept, is a pretty amazing one. The two lead investigators in UCLA's Human Perception Laboratory, Philip Kelmann and Christine Massey, write about how a child might first acquire the concept DOG, for instance. First, the child's father might point out a small white poodle, saying 'dog' as he does so. Next, he might point out a large black retriever, saying 'dog' here too. Even though each new instance encountered might look relatively different to the last in terms of things like size, colour, ear and face shape, and so on, still, relatively quickly the child starts to be able to identity breeds she has never seen before as dogs. Just as usefully, she simultaneously gains the capacity to distinguish dogs from other mammals which look somewhat similar (e.g. cats, or squirrels). 'Shape variables are often important, such as the differing jaw or body structures of dogs and cats' note Kellman and Massey. 'Shape variables are highly relational and abstract, rather than tied to particular colors, sizes, and contexts, which is what allows those who have undergone this kind of learning to effortlessly recognize a glass tabletop ornament as a dog versus a cat.'[10]

It's reasonable to think this process broadly resembles that by which children ordinarily acquire perceptual versions of concepts such as WOMAN and MAN as well. Normally a child becomes able to recognise, for example, women, by being exposed – directly or indirectly – to (images of) women with a relatively wide variety of physical characteristics, within given ranges, still eventually managing to start to identify only the relevant ones. (It's therefore an interesting question what pointing to a trans woman who has had no surgery or hormones, and telling a child 'that's a woman' and then pointing to a female and saying the same does to the child's emerging conceptual map of the world. I don't know the answer.)

WOMAN as a gender identity

As we know, gender identity theory proposes huge revisions to WOMAN and MAN, GIRL and BOY. On the new versions, some women are not adult human females (they're males), and some adult human females are not women (they're men, or non-binary). Equally, some men aren't adult human males (they're females), and some adult human males aren't men (they're women, or non-binary). Not just all this, but also: *women, men, girls and boys aren't beings you can ever directly identify by looking or listening, or by any other perceptual means.* For the thing that supposedly makes you a woman, man, girl or boy is gender identity, an inner psychological state that has no reliable correlation with outer appearances.

Fairly obviously, all this radically changes the traditional functions of the concepts in question. But – unlike the case of

RACE, perhaps – *the need for those original functions hasn't gone away*. So, if we put gender identity theory's proposal for WOMAN and MAN into the decision tree earlier, the decision structure seems to me to be: Yes; No; Yes. That is, we get an argument for retaining the original versions – how could we do without them? – but also creating new additional concepts for 'adult human (male or female) with female gender identity' and 'adult human (female or male) with male gender identity', which don't replace the originals but supplement them. Ideally, we would call these something different to avoid confusion. 'Female-identified people' would be one tentative suggestion: in which case, both men and women could be 'female-identified', where applicable, but it would be well understood that this made no difference to their original statuses as men or women either way.

In fact, the importance of retaining the original versions is even greater than I just suggested. (I'll focus on WOMAN here as my example, but similar points can be made for MAN, GIRL and BOY.) A reference to WOMAN is central to the roles of several other concepts in which it's embedded. For instance: MOTHER, which the *OED* has as 'the female parent of a human being; a woman in relation to a child or children to whom she has given birth; (also, in extended use) a woman who undertakes the responsibilities of a parent towards a child, esp. a stepmother'. WOMAN or GIRL is also embedded into ordinary concepts of GRANDMOTHER, DAUGHTER, SISTER, AUNT, WIFE and, as we have seen in Chapter 3, LESBIAN; and many other concepts too. So: if the membership conditions of WOMAN were about gender identity not sex, this would seem to mean a radical revision in our understanding of the related concepts too, to make them about gender identity as well. Some adult human males would be mothers, stepmothers, grandmothers, daughters, sisters, aunts and wives; and some adult human females would be fathers, grandfathers, sons, brothers, uncles and husbands.

Some trans activist organisations recognise these implications and welcome them. As we've seen earlier, Stonewall and GLAAD now tend to interpret the concept LESBIAN as referring to those with female gender identities attracted to others with female gender identities. In the UK courts in 2020, there was an unsuccessful attempt by trans man Freddy McConnell to be named as 'father' on the birth certificate of the child to which he gave birth, and not 'mother', even though he's an adult human female.[11] UK LGBT organisations backed him in this attempt.

But if we were to start implementing these related linguistic changes on a grand scale, as trans activists apparently want us to, we wouldn't lose our collective need of concepts to represent: the human females who give birth; or the human males whose sperm is the genetic contribution to a child; or human female offspring; or human females attracted to other adult human females; and so on. If we aren't supposed to call these 'mothers', 'fathers', 'daughters' and 'lesbians' (etc.), we'll have to come up with other terms to do the job. That is, we'll continue to need to identify and talk about these important groups of people, relative to a wide range of human interests. It's not enough for opponents to point out that, were the concepts to change in the way gender identity theorists propose, many people who count as, for example, 'mothers' now would still count as mothers under the new proposal. *For that would be an accident.* The concept wouldn't be picking out their femaleness and its connection to having given birth or raising children.

Still, I can imagine objectors insisting that, despite all this, cis people should be 'kinder', i.e. 'give up' the concepts WOMAN and MAN (as if people who argue as I do were hanging on to the words out of bitterness, like a spouse's possessions after divorce). After all, they might say, language-users collectively could just as easily develop completely new names for 'adult human female' and 'adult human male' instead. Where's the harm? Yet it seems to me this would be unlikely to satisfy the aims of gender identity theorists in the long run. Let's say we called adult human females and adult human males something else: anything will do, but as a present example let's choose, with an affectionate nod to 70s feminists, 'womyn' and 'myn'. Once bedded down among language-users, in effect this would look like a pretty superficial switch. In that scenario, we would still have clearly distinct concepts for adult human females and adult human males, with new names attached. Given their multiple important roles in human life, we would be bound to keep using those new names in all or most of the contexts in which we traditionally used 'woman' and 'man'. Trans women still would be myn and wouldn't be womyn, and trans men still would be womyn and wouldn't be myn. There would – or at least, should – still be distinct healthcare, spaces, resources, data collection and, in some cases, social arrangements for womyn and myn. That is, there would still be (as queer theorists see it) 'normative exclusion' and (as I see it) 'useful classification, and consequent rational attempts to adjust social organisation, relative to many coherent purposes'.

I conclude that, rather than changing the concepts WOMAN and MAN (etc.) to incorporate a reference to gender identity and remove sex, we should keep the original versions *and* add to our collective vocabulary further concepts that represent 'adult human with a female gender identity' and 'adult human with a male gender identity'. In case it's not clear, these concepts wouldn't be either/or. They would cross-categorise people. Women could be adult humans with male gender identities, and men could be adult humans with female gender identities. We each can, and do, fall into many categories simultaneously.

A hierarchy of interests?

My discussion so far has demonstrated the impracticality of gender identity theory's proposal for the concepts WOMAN and MAN. An important supplementary point is that women – understood as adult human females – tend as a group to exhibit certain particular social characteristics, and face certain distinctive social challenges. These vary from society to society in their precise details, but most women face certain common aspects and obstacles, broadly construed. As we know, for instance, women are significantly more likely to be sexually assaulted than men, and significantly less likely to commit sexual assaults than men. Men, not women, are also responsible for the majority of violent crimes.[12] This is an international phenomenon. We also know that, partly as a result of facts about pregnancy, women are more likely than men to occupy low-paid or part-time jobs, if they work at all. Relatedly, they are more likely to be responsible for unpaid childcare and domestic work in the home than men. For those that also work, this places consequent extra pressures on their time that men in the same position tend not to face. This affects women's capacity to work to the same level as men in the same job.

These are generalisations not universalisations, and there are many exceptions. But they don't occur randomly. They are linked in various explicable ways to prior facts about biology: women's average relative strength in relation to men, and their capacity as a group to bear children. These fairly immovable biological facts, averaged across the populations of men and women, have interacted with contingent social facts to produce the world we currently have. Many women feel it is an unjust one. They have the strong impression of living in a world set up for and run in the interests of men. Recent books like *Invisible Women* by Caroline Criado Perez and *Pain and Prejudice* by Gabrielle Jackson have emphasised how, even in supposedly progressive countries like the UK and US, there's a large data gap when it comes to understanding – or more accurately, failing properly to understand – multiple areas of women's interests, including medicine, the workplace, product design, taxation and political representation.

In this context, treating males with female gender identities as women in every possible context is a politically inflammatory act. In effect it sends a contemptuously dismissive message to women already conscious of unequal treatment of their interests. This message says: *the interests of males with female gender identities are more important than yours.* I have already described how many institutions are presently taking gender identity to determine access to spaces and resources, and to govern the gathering of data. They are also taking it to determine the reporting of information. An illustrative example is the way trans women's crimes are now reported in the press. Following news regulator IPSO's publication of guidelines on media reporting about trans people in 2016, the UK media started to report the crimes of trans women as 'women's' crimes.[13] According to the IPSO guidelines: 'An individual's gender identity ... must not be referenced unless genuinely relevant to the story.' What this seems to mean in practice is that the sex of a trans woman perpetrator shouldn't be mentioned, and instead the crime should be reported as a woman's. In a context where men – understood as adult human males – are responsible for more than three times as many violent and sexual assaults as women, headlines such as

'Woman, 41, pretended to be a boy to groom a girl' (*Metro* website, 1 October 2018),[14] 'Gang of women repeatedly stamp on man's head in 2am brawl at Leicester Square underground station' (*Daily Mirror* website, 26 June 2018), 'Sheffield woman found with over 1,000 indecent images of children hauled before the court' (*Daily Star* website, 19 July 2019), 'Woman who once shoved policeman onto Tube tracks jailed for spitting at officer' (*Daily Mirror* website, 17 February 2020) and 'Woman who "bragged about being a paedophile" approached boys at Remembrance event' (*Wales Online*, 15 May 2020) seem to demonstrate a flagrant, even provocative disregard for women's interests. The underlying message on the part of media organisations seems to be: we care more about deferring to the inner gender identities of criminally convicted males than we do about transmitting the misleading message to the public that women, as a group, have hitherto unsuspected capacities for paedophilia, sexual predation and violent assault. When the crimes in question are then recorded as 'women's' or 'female' crimes within the criminal justice system, the affront is compounded. Data we might otherwise have tried to use to combat violence against women in the original sense is now significantly compromised.[15] Again, the fact that the powers-that-be don't seem to care at all about this is infuriating to many women, me included.

Apart from the relative neglect of women's interests in relation to men's, and the negative political message sent to women about it, the discussion of this section underlines an earlier point: gender identity theory's proposed alternative to the traditional concepts WOMAN and MAN cannot possibly cover all of the still-pressing contexts in which we need to use the term 'woman', meaningfully, to refer to adult human females, and 'man' to refer to adult human males. One response to this objection might be gratefully to revert to the traditional concepts. A rival response, however, is to propose a different alternative to the traditional concepts, this time identifying women and men, not in terms of gender identity, but instead in terms of some kind of shared social role.

WOMAN as a social role

In the first chapter, I introduced an idea with a powerful attraction for many feminists over the years: the idea that WOMAN refers to those expected by society to perform a 'feminine social role'. What this means, spelled out, is usually a bit vague, but it's something like: a woman, *by definition*, is any adult human expected to occupy or perform a set of behaviours stereotypically associated with the female sex, and/or who is interpreted by society in terms of a set of female-associated stereotypes and norms. So women, by definition, are the people expected to look after children, do most of the housework, take lower paid jobs than their partners, speak more submissively, be good listeners and be caring. They are, by definition, the people who tend to be lauded as virginal or as motherly, or castigated as whores or as witches; who are easily thought of as bitches, or bossy, or slutty, or frigid, or girly, or bubbly, or feisty (etc., etc.).

In the twenty-first century this view, which I'll call 'WOMAN-as-social' or WAS for short, has become associated in some minds with a justification for the claim that 'passing' trans women are women. Passing trans women are defined as those male people who, as a result of surgery and taking hormones, eventually cannot be perceptually distinguished from adult human females by most people. Sometimes these are distinguished from other trans women by being called 'transsexuals'. If a transsexual trans woman passes, it is assumed by many that she must be subject to the same expectations and norms of femininity as are typically projected upon adult human females, and that this is what 'makes' her a woman. Passing trans men are considered to be men for similar reasons.

This sort of view is often accompanied, with an implied 'tadaah!', by the quote from Simone de Beauvoir we saw in Chapter 1: 'One is not born, but rather becomes a woman' (alternatively: 'A woman is not born but made'). The fact that in *The Second Sex* de Beauvoir was fairly obviously talking only about females and their involuntary encounters with a social system subjecting them to impossible ideals of femininity from birth seems mostly ignored. De Beauvoir wasn't talking about males who decide after puberty to radically alter their bodies artificially, and nor would she have excluded from the purview of her claims any trans man who did similar. Still, whatever the case, her quote has found new life in a modern context.

WAS and gender identity theory are competitors. Effectively, each offers a different conceptual analysis of WOMAN and MAN. According to contemporary trans activists – or at least, the consistent ones – WAS is, like the traditional versions of WOMAN and MAN, 'exclusionary', since it cannot accommodate the claims of non-passing trans women to be women, or of non-passing trans men to be men. WAS is also criticised for having nothing to say about non-binary people. Still, for many others – and in particular people familiar with, and sympathetic to, the history of twentieth-century Western feminism – WAS remains a convincing explanation of why some trans women count as women, and trans men as men.

Unfortunately, though, WAS is beset with problems. In what follows, I'll talk only about WAS as it applies to the concept of WOMAN, as befits its original historical impetus. However, my points can be altered to apply to any view arguing that the concept of MAN refers, by definition, to those expected by society to perform a masculine role.

Bad reasons given for WAS

I think WAS appeals to many people on a subconscious level. This is partly to do with cognitive factors, and partly with social ones about the way we objectify women generally. But here I'll deal only with conscious reasoning for WAS. There are two main sources of perceived support, both of them fairly underwhelming on closer inspection.

The first of these draws upon a feature of ordinary language: the fact some people tend to say things like 'she's not a *real* woman', when talking about certain adult human females. De Beauvoir has a few examples early on in *The Second Sex*. She tells us: 'They whisper, even in Russia, "*women* are still very much women".' She goes on: 'Speaking of certain women, the experts proclaim "They are not women"' even though they have a uterus like the others.' And: 'Everyone agrees there are females in the human species; today, as in the past, they make about half of humanity; and yet we are ... urged "Be women, stay women, become woman".' She concludes: 'So not every female human being is necessarily a woman; she must take part in this mysterious and endangered reality known as femininity.'[16]

Supporters of WAS take these observations to demonstrate that the concept of WOMAN refers to an expected feminine social role. What they don't apparently notice is that hundreds, if not thousands, of concepts are subject to similar temporary and rhetorical constructions in certain contexts, without us needing to propose radical alterations to those concepts generally. As was pointed out by philosopher J. L. Austin in the

1960s, whether something is counted as 'real' or not depends on what's effectively being excluded as uninteresting by way of the contrast in the current conversational context.[17] Take for instance, the concept DIAMOND, understood as a crystalline carbon allotrope. When given a huge, clear, sparkly diamond as a present, the recipient might say, 'Now, that's a *real* diamond!' Or a jeweller might say to the would-be seller of a small, dull diamond, 'Call that a *diamond*? That's not a diamond', though both know that it is. In this sort of case, there's what we might call a temporary 'escalation' or 'de-escalation', whereby concepts plus qualifiers such as 'real', 'not real' (etc.) and/or certain emphases and tones of voice are used by speakers to draw attention to particular properties of objects currently of interest, or the lack of them. So for instance: 'Now that's a *real* castle!', 'That's not a real birthday present!', etc. (Try it now with things around you: 'Call that a *sofa*?'; 'If you were a *real* husband ... ') Saying of a diamond you don't currently value that it's not a *real* diamond doesn't show that generally DIAMOND means something other than a crystalline carbon allotrope. And it definitely doesn't show that DIAMOND refers only to the socially expected or valued role of diamonds, such as being clear, sparkly and large.

Similar points, I think, apply to feminist interpretations of the activist and former slave Sojourner Truth's famous 1851 speech 'Ain't I a Woman?'. Truth points out that the white middle-class stereotypes that 'women need to be helped into carriages, and lifted over ditches, and to have the best place everywhere' don't apply to her as a former slave; yet she is still, after all, a woman.[18] This is taken by many feminists to implicitly support WAS. Yet historical statements that black women weren't women, or *real* women, were temporarily de-escalated uses of WOMAN, revelatory of the fact that racist speakers didn't value black women as they valued whites. In other contexts, the same people who made such statements would unproblematically acknowledge black women as women – not least because many slave owners instrumentalised black women's pregnancies to keep the machinery of slavery going, and were themselves responsible for some of them.

A second argument supposedly helpful to WAS brings us back, once again, to the spectre of biological determinism: the idea that females' biological status makes it 'natural' and so right for them to be in the kitchen, nursery or bedroom, but not in the boardroom or parliament. For many Second Wave feminists, WAS seemed attractive because, on the face of it, it promised to free women from accusations of biological determinism. In fact, though, as I've already argued, defining WOMAN explicitly in terms of an expected feminine social role is a truly terrible response to that problem. If – big if – it's really true that women are biologically determined to be domestic, submissive, and so on, redefining WOMAN as something nonbiological won't save them from that fate. All it will do is distractingly change the subject to a different kind of people. Meanwhile, the adult human females will still be there, working away in the kitchens and nurseries and bedrooms, subjugated by their biology. Much better instead for feminists to directly attack the idea that being female makes one naturally suited to domesticity, using available scientific evidence plus conceptual analysis to do this; or alternatively, attack the idea that what's 'natural for females' in the sense of 'found on average across the entire population of females' determines what's 'right' for all or even any of them.

These days, the old adversarial dynamic between determinists and feminists has morphed into the popular claim that, if you don't embrace WAS, but instead argue for the traditional version of WOMAN, you must be a nasty old biological determinist who wants to 'tie' women 'to their biology'. Frankly, this is bonkers. The traditional version of WOMAN whose legitimacy I'm defending says that a woman is an adult human female. In Chapter 2, I offered three models of the sexes. *Not one of them* proposed any personality traits or behaviours as essential to, or necessary for, femaleness. They don't mention personality traits or behaviours at all. They're concerned only with endogenous physical characteristics. Whether or not females are, on average, naturally suited to domesticity or any other thing is an entirely empirical matter – i.e. to do with what scientific evidence emerges, either way – and it has nothing to do with the membership conditions of BEING FEMALE. So by favouring the traditional version of WOMAN (i.e. adult human female) over WAS, there's no inevitable implication you must be committed to some view of women as naturally suited to domesticity, nor any other particular behaviour or psychological trait.

Sometimes critics of the traditional version of WOMAN get yet more confused, this time by the fact that three characteristics are being proposed as 'essential' to the membership conditions of womanhood: namely, being i) adult, ii) human and iii) female. Doesn't this fact make the view perniciously 'essentialist' in a politically suspect way? No. Or if it does, then WAS is 'essentialist' too, and so for that matter is gender identity theory! After all, both of them also propose certain membership conditions as 'essential' for (i.e. necessary to) being a woman. Is it a political problem for a definition of DIAMOND that it proposes 'being a crystalline carbon allotrope' as 'essential' to diamonds? No. Proposing certain characteristics as essential membership conditions, in this sense, is a feature of thousands of definitions of categories – that's arguably how categories work. (It's true some philosophers have argued that sometimes or always, thinking of categories as having essential or necessary conditions is a mistake. However, they think it's a philosophical mistake not a political one; and their point applies to most or all concepts. I looked at two relevant examples of this approach in Chapter 2, where I discussed cluster models of SPECIES and of MALE and FEMALE.)

Yet another strawman offered is that defenders of the traditional version of the concept WOMAN, understood as adult human female, are effectively 'reducing women to their biology'. It's as if what's really being said is that having a female biology is *all individual women can ever be good for.* But what's important to, or about, an individual can vary from context to context, depending on background interests. Arguing that the membership conditions of WOMAN as a general category essentially require being female doesn't mean that being female (or adult, or human) is a personally important feature of any given woman, let alone all she can ever be good for. Compare: the membership conditions of BANKER essentially require a person who is a banker, by definition, to be working in a bank. But that doesn't mean working in a bank is personally important to any given banker, let alone that it's all she or he can ever be good for. Being a woman doesn't cover everything individual women are or could be. It was never reasonably supposed to.

Additional points against WAS

I've just discussed arguments supposedly in favour of WAS. When it comes to looking for additional arguments against it, it seems even less promising. We can find at least three. The first applies to WAS, considered generally as a challenge to the traditional version of the concept WOMAN. The other two relate to WAS as it supposedly applies to trans women in particular.

The first challenge relates to whether, in practice, WAS was ever an adequate replacement version for the traditional version of the concept WOMAN. A big problem for WAS is that there's no single social role expected to be performed by all women that could be used to define them, practically speaking. Earlier on, I said that women tend to face similar social challenges, such as susceptibility to sexual assault, and less comparative success in the workplace relative to men – but still, this is hardly enough to define the entire category, and in any case clearly has many exceptions. This problem emerged early on in the history of WAS within feminist thought. In practice, concrete articulations of 'the feminine social role', when given by white Western heterosexual women, tended to default – surprise, surprise – to sociocultural expectations upon white Western heterosexual women. This was quickly pointed out by black and Latina feminists as well as by lesbians. Not all women are culturally expected to be passive – some matriarchal cultures value agency. Not all women are culturally expected to be refined and delicate – black feminists have argued that black women aren't viewed this way, and nor are lesbians. Incomprehensibly, once this problem was noticed, rather than concluding there was something wrong with WAS some academic feminists took the heroically ambitious route of denying there was such a thing as the unified category of women at all.[19] Others suggested we should pretend there are women for politically strategic purposes.[20]

Often missed in the interminable academic discussions that followed – as with gender identity theory earlier – was that the traditional concept of WOMAN and the version of the concept proposed by WAS obviously perform very different functions. Unlike the concepts WOMAN and GIRL taken together, WAS cannot offer an account covering 51 per cent of the population, or anything like it. We have seen that, relative to many important purposes, we continue to need concepts to distinguish adult and younger human females from everyone else, as well as from each other. Any concepts offered by WAS as putative replacements, citing only expectations of social role, cannot do this job. There is not enough overlap between the people to whom the traditional version and the WAS version actually apply. This suggests that, as with gender identity theory, the decision structure when fed into the decision tree, should be Yes; No; Yes. That is, we should retain the traditional version of the concept WOMAN, continuing to use it to refer to adult human females, and develop separate concepts to identify the various sociocultural roles women are expected to perform in different historical and social contexts.

I tend to think that this objection, like the accompanying similar one for gender identity theory, thoroughly undermines the rationale for WAS. Still, I know there will remain devotees. So I'll assume for the sake of my next bit of argument that WAS works as a general theory of womanhood, even though I don't think it does.

There are two reasons that WAS doesn't fit well with the idea that trans women are women. The first point is that women and passing trans women aren't always expected to occupy the same social role – unless you define 'social role' very narrowly as something like 'the role a stranger might expect you to fulfil, based only on what you look like to them now'. But expected social roles are much wider than that. For one thing, what social expectations and norms are projected upon you partly depend on what others know about you, and not just what a stranger would think, were they to see you from a distance in the street. If you're a passing trans woman who is 'out', then, precisely, people know you're male and that you have grown up male. In that case, in some contexts you're likely to be treated differently, and be subject to different expectations, than the average female (sometimes better, sometimes worse, and sometimes no better or worse, just different). There will be a lot of overlap, but it's unlikely to be total.

For another thing, the social role occupied by any individual extends throughout time, and isn't reducible to a single year, week or day, let alone a single moment when a stranger looks at you. Roles start early on, in childhood, and are affected by experiences. As novelist Chimamanda Ngozi Adichie said in an interview in 2017, seeming to embrace some version of WAS: 'I think the whole problem of gender in the world is about our experiences ... It's about the way the world treats us, and I think if you've lived in the world as a man with the privileges that the world accords to men and then sort of change gender, it's difficult for me to accept that then we can equate your experience with the experience of a woman who has lived from the beginning as a woman and who has not been accorded those privileges that men are.'[21] In similar vein, journalist and academic Elinor Burkett wrote of trans women: 'They haven't suffered through business meetings with men talking to their breasts or woken up after sex terrified they'd forgotten to take their birth control pills the day before. They haven't had to cope with the onset of their periods in the middle of a crowded subway, the humiliation of discovering that their male work partners' checks were far larger than theirs, or the fear of being too weak to ward off rapists.'[22] Such points would indeed suggest many passing trans women aren't women after all, even by the lights of WAS.

A separate critical point about WAS is this. As you might expect given its political origins, a frequent accompaniment to the original feminist argument that WOMAN referred to those expected to perform a feminine social role was *severe criticism of that expectation and role*. Feminists such as Catharine MacKinnon and Andrea Dworkin, apparently writing in support of something very like WAS, thought of inequality and suffering as baked into the expectations projected upon women. They wanted to smash femininity, and that's an understatement. On their view, women, as such, are socially constructed via lifelong exposure to widespread practices of sexual dominance and objectification, and men, as such, are socially constructed as sexually objectifying dominators. Wrote MacKinnon, for instance: 'To be rapable, a position that is social not biological, defines what a woman is.'[23]

So, at least as it was originally practised, thinking of WOMAN in terms of a social role was *not supposed to be a reactionary move in favour of preserving that social role.* Indeed, this is implied by a modern-day advocate of WAS, American philosopher Sally Haslanger, who basically argues that we should focus our minds on the political project of *getting rid of women.* By this she means not some bloody massacre of adult human females, but rather the elimination of restrictive and damaging social expectations upon them.[24]

To say the least, it's a bit odd, then, to see WAS co-opted in a twenty-first-century campaign to get trans women recognised as women, as if that's a progressive victory all round. If MacKinnon and Dworkin were right, no one should be encouraged to be a woman, trans or otherwise. And it's hard to see how the frequent trans activist caricature of nasty 'TERFs' zealously 'gatekeeping' womanhood in order unfairly to keep trans women out of it is compatible with the fact that many MacKinnon- and Dworkin-inspired 'TERFs', at least, spend their wider lives fighting the misogynist social stereotypes which, they believe, constitute womanhood.

If you try to believe simultaneously *both* that trans women should be categorised as women as a matter of social justice *and* that womanhood involves exposure to a regressive social

role essentially involving domination and sexual objectification, then something's got to give. In practice, what seems
to be giving these days is recognition that expected feminine
social roles might be in any way regressive or worth fighting
against. Femininity is often now presented, even by progres-
sives, as either a neutral or a positive, life-affirming choice.
It's apparently just assumed that when you act passive and
submissive, or emotional, you're being 'woman-like', or even
just being a woman – whatever your sex. For instance, trans
author Kate Bornstein writes in her memoir about a female
partner who would later transition to become a trans man:
'We had sex being boys. We had sex being girls. We were boy
and girl at random. He had as much fun on top of me as I had
fun on top of her. And we both enjoyed being on the bottom.'[25]
In other words, when on top, the partner is a 'he' and when on
the bottom, a 'her'. And trans woman Joy Ladin writes in her
memoir: 'When my wife and I discuss the destruction of our
life together, she's the one who cries. If tears start in my eyes –
and they often do – I automatically stifle them. When my wife
and I are together, she's the woman and I'm the man.'[26] The
apotheosis – or possibly, nadir – of this approach is found in
the 2019 book *Females* by trans scholar Andrea Long Chu,
which – I'm kind of hoping satirically, though I'm not entirely
sure – defines 'female' as 'any psychic operation in which the
self is sacrificed to make room for the desires of another'.[27]

When combined with WAS, this leaves a reactionary position diametrically opposed to what radical feminists could
possibly have originally meant – even if these days, they deny
this.[28] Since academic intricacies understandably tend to be
lost on the general public, were this toothless version of WAS
to become yet more popular, it would presumably leave even
more people with the impression that women are 'supposed to
be' feminine (as in: dominated, sexually submissive, emotional,

and there to do the bidding of the masculine people), and men 'supposed to be' masculine (as in: dominant, sexually demanding, unemotional, and there to have their needs met by the feminine people). It's not hard to anticipate how this cues up further agony for all concerned, and especially for those children, teens and adults who are confused and/or feel they don't fit the right mould.

Given these considerations, it's preferable, as before, to retain the original concepts of WOMAN and MAN, and then to have separate concepts for the sex-associated social roles, expectations and norms – damaging or otherwise – that we collectively have interests in tracking and critiquing. In this we might emulate a language like Swedish, in which the word for both 'woman' and 'female' is '*kvinna*', and the word for biological sex is '*kön*' (a word which, luckily for Swedish communication purposes, does not also mean the sexual act). Meanwhile, the word for the social norms and expectations associated with the sexes is '*genus*', a word that isn't applied to womanhood or manhood as such.

In the service of development of separate concepts for the distinctive social stereotypes and norms associated with each sex, English speakers could rescue the concepts MASCULINITY and FEMININITY from the current murk, and be more explicit about what they mean. In the former case, masculinity could be exclusively understood as the sets of social expectations and norms (etc.) projected upon most men and some women, and femininity those projected upon most women and some men. If we then wanted to refine these concepts further into separate sub-categories, to explicitly cover different kinds of sex-associated social expectations and norms – appearance-based, behavioural, psychological, and so on – we could do that too. We could also develop a separate concept of PEOPLE SUBJECT TO MISOGYNY (or something pithier), which could apply both to women and to some passing trans women, in virtue of what is called 'discrimination by perception'; and PEOPLE SUBJECT TO MISANDRY, which could apply to men and to some trans men. In refining existing concepts or coining new ones, we could easily develop a rich, flexible vocabulary to refer to whatever sex-associated social phenomenon we wished to describe. But: there's no reason to think that any reference to these factors can, or should be, automatically built into the concepts of WOMAN and MAN as such. Not only would this make the concepts too unwieldy, but it would also be incompatible with their original, still pressing purposes: serving as the nexus of literally thousands of intersecting discussions, explanations and predictions, of great collective importance, concerning adult human males and females.

With respect to the main topic of this chapter, then, we're left with a stark conclusion. Here's the least stark articulation of it I can muster. If trans women are women, they are not 'women' in the same sense in which adult human females are 'women'. If trans men are men, they are not 'men' in the same sense in which adult human males are 'men'. 'Trans' isn't, as we saw Julia Serano claim in Chapter 1, an adjective attached to 'woman'. There are wholly different concepts here. Ideally, we should have phonetically different terms to refer to each. But if we don't collectively develop phonetically different words, we should at least be clear that TRANS WOMAN, TRANS MAN, WOMAN and MAN are four different concepts, each with different membership conditions; and that membership of TRANS WOMAN doesn't entail membership of WOMAN or preclude membership of MAN, and nor does membership of TRANS MAN entail membership of MAN or preclude membership of WOMAN.

This conclusion may be greeted, at least initially, with shock.

I don't blame you at all, as a reader – trans or otherwise – if this is how you feel. It wasn't you personally who developed the confused idea that there were no conceivably important differences between trans women and women, or trans men and men, for which language-users might rationally want to develop separate public concepts in order to record and track them. That was the academics, lawmakers and trans activist organisations, who disseminated this narrative for various misguided intellectual or political reasons. People have built their lives around this narrative. Perhaps it feels as though I'm ripping all that away, and that causes you pain.

So straight away I want to be absolutely clear about what I'm *not* saying, before I go on to explain and justify these points in more detail in the next chapter. (I can anticipate a lot of these misunderstandings because they're frequently fired at me by critics, as assumptions about what I must really be saying.)

- I'm not saying that to physically alter oneself to look like the opposite sex, or unlike one's own sex, or both, isn't ever a reasonable thing for adults to do in response to developing a misaligned gender identity. I think it can be, and have explained why in Chapter 4.
- More generally, I'm not saying there's anything wrong with looking or being radically sex nonconforming, either naturally or artificially. Quite the opposite. Personally speaking, I value and celebrate sex non-conformity: masculine women, feminine men and androgyny. Indeed, it's partly in the service of this evaluation that I've made the arguments I have.
- I'm not underplaying the psychological relief it gives many trans people to think of themselves as members of the opposite sex. Nor, perhaps surprisingly, am I

saying that trans women and trans men, respectively, shouldn't ever *call themselves* 'women' and 'men' or be referred to that way by those around them. I'll explain why in the next chapter.

- I'm not saying trans people are 'deceivers', nor that they are 'delusional' or 'duped' – far from it. I'll explain why in the next chapter, so there can be no doubt.

Immersed in a Fiction

f, as I have argued, people can't literally change sex, what exactly did the 2004 Gender Recognition Act (GRA) make available to people that they didn't have before? My view is that the GRA, and the Gender Recognition Certificates that go with it, jointly put in place what is known as a *legal fiction* about the possibility of sex change.

A legal fiction

Between 2003 and 2004, the Gender Recognition Bill passed through several readings in the Houses of Parliament. The transcript of debates can still be read online.[1] Some contributions explored potential detriment to women's sport, women-only spaces and definitions of homosexuality and heterosexuality, should the bill be passed.[2] Others rejected those worries as overblown. The eventual result was the Gender Recognition Act, making it possible for trans people to get a Gender Recognition Certificate provided they had an official diagnosis of gender dysphoria and had 'lived in the acquired gender' for a period of two years.

'Living in the acquired gender', in practice, seemed to mean dressing in stereotypically female or male clothes, wearing make-up, or having surgery or taking hormones to look more like the opposite sex. Back then, few accompanying justifications cited gender identity. The apparent assumption of legislators was that a person's decision to alter their sexed appearance cosmetically, hormonally or surgically to look more like a member of the opposite sex made it a political requirement that the law in some sense validate or confirm those choices.

Looking at debate transcripts, it's a good question what exactly legislators thought they were doing by seeing this bill into law. At times, they talked as if granting a GRC would – impossibly, as I argued in Chapter 2 – literally change its possessor's sex. For instance, the speaker in the Lords on behalf of the Government, Lord Geoffrey Filkin, said at one point that, for GRCs to be granted to trans women, 'existing marriages' to women would have to be dissolved. This was argued for on the grounds that 'marriage is an institution for opposite-sex couples'. So Filkin seemed to be suggesting that, where a man in a heterosexual couple was to receive a GRC, this would effectively make the couple a 'same-sex' one – and hence the marriage must dissolve. In a later debate he also argued that if a trans woman previously granted a GRC were to marry a man afterwards, this wouldn't be a 'same-sex' couple but a heterosexual one.

Later on, referring to precisely this assumption of Filkin's, Lord Norman Tebbit pressed Filkin on whether he regarded 'the marriage of two persons each possessing the chromosomes and sexual organs of the same sex as being a same-sex marriage'. Filkin replied by citing earlier contributions to the debate from medics Lords Robert Winston and Leslie Turnberg, described as having shown that 'medical science on the issues is incredibly more complicated than ... Lord

Tebbit ... would have us believe'.[3] In fact, Winston's contribution turns out to have mostly been about people with DSDs
and not trans people. He referred to a person of his acquaint-
ance, Janice, describing her as: 'the most beautiful woman,
who came to my unit some time ago. She was six feet tall and
had been brought up as a woman. She had very well-developed
breasts, a perfect physique, and was actually XY. She did not
find that out until she was twenty.'[4] In other words, via this
distinctly objectifying description, Winston invoked people
with DSDs from birth – in this case, presumably, a person
with CAIS – to try to show something about trans people.
In his contribution, Turnberg did roughly the same thing.[5]
This seems to have been taken by Filkin as at least somewhat
supportive of the possibility of a literal sex change via the
granting of a GRC.

At other times, though, Filkin seemed to say something
different. When asked by Tebbit whether the Government
'attribute[s] the same meaning to the word "sex" as to the word
"gender"', Filkin answered 'No'. He continued (my italics): 'It
is ... a fundamental proposition of the Gender Recognition
Bill that, following legal recognition in their acquired gender, a
transsexual person will be regarded in UK law as being of the
acquired gender for all purposes and that in law *that acquired
gender* will be the same as *any legal definition of their sex*.
This means that, following legal recognition, if *the acquired
gender* is the male gender, the person's *sex in law* becomes that
of a man.'[6] In this piece of tortured legalese, Filkin seemed to
suggest a GRC would grant an individual only *the right to be
treated as the opposite sex is treated in law*. This is obviously
not the same thing as literally changing sex.

Given the history of misinformation sketched so far in
this book about what 'gender' means and whether binary
sex even exists, it's not surprising that in 2004 lawmakers

were confused about what having a GRC should entail. But whatever they thought they were doing at the time, it makes most sense to treat the granting of a GRC as a 'legal fiction', making it 'as if' a person has changed sex. This is certainly the interpretation that fits best with the paragraph I just quoted, though not the earlier discussion. It also fits with the wording of explanatory notes to the later 2010 Equality Act, which describe 'gender reassignment' as 'where a person has proposed, started or completed a process to change his or her sex'.[7]

A legal fiction is created when the law acts *as if* something is the case, for certain defined legal purposes, when in fact it isn't. In such cases, a fiction is involved, and not a fact. For instance, when the law treats a company as a 'person', or formally treats biological parents giving up a child for adoption as 'strangers' to the child, it creates a fiction, to be treated for legal purposes as if it is the case.[8] A legal fiction has alternatively been described as 'a legal assumption that something is true which is, or may be, false – being an assumption of an innocent and beneficial character, made to advance the interests of justice'.[9] This seems to fit with how legislators in 2004 were thinking, at least some of the time. That is, they saw creating the legal fiction that people can change sex as potentially benefiting trans people: helping them to avoid accusations of fraud, and intrusions into their privacy, for instance.[10] The final version of the GRA offered a range of possibilities to GRC possessors, in line with preservation of the fiction of a sex change. For instance, it gave possessors the possibility of changing their birth certificates, tax and pension arrangements in line with 'acquired gender'; and to have the fact of GRC possession, and information about actual sex, classed as 'protected information' by employers.[11]

However, if this is how we see possession of a GRC, we

should also recognise there are potentially occasions in which the legal status of women and men aren't respectively also transmitted to trans women and trans men simply by virtue of possession of a GRC. Indeed, the eventual published wording of the GRA acknowledges this. Despite explicitly saying that where 'a full gender recognition certificate is issued to a person, the person's gender becomes *for all purposes* the acquired gender' (my italics), it almost immediately specifies contexts in which it doesn't: including parenting definitions, hereditary succession, peerages, sport and 'gender-specific' sexual offences.[12] If it were believed that possession of a GRC really did change one's sex, these qualifications would surely seem arbitrary and unjust.

Fiction and reality

As it is with the law, so it is with many in ordinary life, I suggest. That's to say: a significant number of people, whether trans or non-trans, who would endorse – perhaps even very enthusiastically – claims that trans men are 'men' or 'male', and trans women 'women' or 'female' (etc.) are *immersed in a fiction* when they do so. They have consciously or unconsciously committed themselves to thinking – and even temporarily feeling and acting – *as if* these things are true, some or most of the time. However, I would argue that they don't believe the statements are *literally* true.

This hypothesis has its limitations. In relation to the discussion of the last chapter, I'm treating having a misaligned gender identity, and being immersed in a fiction about sex change, as separable things. You can have a misaligned gender identity and not be immersed in a fiction about sex change. You can immerse yourself in a fiction about sex change for whatever reason, and not because you have a misaligned gender identity. My hypothesis is that the two often go together, but not always. Some trans people don't believe they have changed sex, nor become 'women' or 'men' (or 'non-binary') in any coherent sense, and they don't seem immersed in a fiction either. For instance, trans woman Debbie Hayton, married to a woman, has written: 'I am not a woman nor am I LGB.'[13] Trans woman Miranda Yardley says, 'I now disavow use of the word "woman" for myself and other transgender males, preferring to use the term "transsexual" or "transsexual male".'[14] Trans woman Fionne Orlander says, 'I am a trans woman, I am a man, I can't be one without the other.'[15]

Meanwhile, some of those who make public statements like 'trans men are men' and 'trans women are women' (etc.) *believe* such statements are true, and their saying them out loud is a straightforward sign of that inner conviction. No fiction is involved. As we saw in Chapter 2, some people believe there isn't such a material thing as binary sex. Many of these people also believe it's arbitrary to which sex you're originally 'assigned at birth'. Though the interim reasoning is often hazy, they seem to think that since sex assignation is arbitrary to start with, it can't have any bearing on manhood or womanhood, so gender identity must be doing the job instead. As we saw in the last chapter, others make a distinction between sex and 'gender' understood as a masculine or feminine social role, and reason from there to the conclusion that trans men are men, and trans women are women. And then, of course, there are those who don't have any particularly complicated reasons to think these things are true, but simply accept them at face value, based on what they assume is authoritative testimony from experts. Generally, humans take on a lot of true beliefs this way, unproblematically. The only reason I believe that $E=MC^2$ or that La Paz is the capital of Bolivia is because someone told me. I've never run the proof or taken the flight. It would be far too inefficient for us to have to investigate everything for ourselves. But this also means, unfortunately, that there's plenty of room for people to accept false beliefs on this sort of basis.

Still, though, I don't think these cases cover all possible ones. Only relatively rarely will you find someone publicly denying that trans men are men and that trans women are women (etc.). On the contrary: politicians, celebrities, journalists, officials from major charities and NGOs, senior figures in the police and judiciary, and many ordinary members of the public all tend enthusiastically to repeat the same mantras that trans women are women and trans men are men, either when prompted by others or off their own bat. For many of these, it seems unlikely that they've read Judith Butler or 70s radical feminism. I don't think all of them really believe that sex is 'assigned' or that there are literally hundreds of genders. Yet neither do they seem to be going through the motions. Perhaps some are just being polite. Perhaps others are (quite reasonably, as we'll shortly see) wary of deviating from a socially sanctioned script. But still, it seems that a significant number of people who repeat these mantras – both trans and non-trans – are more emotionally involved than this, yet in a way that stops short of full belief. My hypothesis is that many are immersed in a fiction. I think this hypothesis can explain some interesting features of the current state of public discourse.

What is immersion?

Generally speaking, being immersed in a fiction is a familiar, benign and rational human behaviour. The fiction in question can be of your own or another's making. It can take years to construct – as in a great novel, film or play – or seconds, as in a self-generated daydream or a child's game of make-believe. Individuals don't always deliberately decide to get immersed in a fiction; it can just happen, given the right sort of prompt. We get immersed in a fiction of others' making every time we switch on the television and become gripped by a drama; when we laugh, cry or hide our eyes, imagining actors *are* the characters they play, or when we talk about them afterwards to friends, as if they were real. Immersion is also a character-istic state for many who go to the theatre and enter the 'world' of a play. Temporarily it can really seem to you as if you are watching events in New York, or the countryside, or on the Moon, all the while actually looking at a stage.

Novels and stories can be immersive too, as can video and role-playing games. Actors can get immersed to an even greater extent than spectators do, when they plunge themselves in a particular role. They don't just think and feel as if the fiction were real, as spectators might, but for certain periods on stage or on set they outwardly behave as if it were real, in a relatively wholesale and committed way. When immersed comprehensively in a fiction like this, you can feel things too: sadness, joy, fear or hope for yourself, or for other charac-ters in the fiction.[16] Method actors like Daniel Day-Lewis or Christian Bale go further, sometimes immersing themselves in preparation for a particular role for weeks or months, whether on- or offstage. Police working undercover also become immersed in roles for long periods of time. And for some, religious experiences can be immersive. During the Catholic mass, for instance, some worshippers immerse themselves in the fiction of transubstantiation.

Immersion is a mental state of interest to philosophers and psychologists, who tend to think of it as an intermediate state between 'bare' imaginative entertaining and full, committed belief. A key defining feature of immersion seems to be that, when you're properly immersed in a fictional scenario, *you don't think consciously about the fact the scenario is merely fictional or that it's not real* – because this would, precisely, break your immersive state. To consciously dwell on the fact that a character in a play is 'really' an actor you've seen a hundred times before would be to destroy the effect. To tell yourself the film set of a thriller in LA is actually located in Shepperton can suddenly make the action seem mundane. For as long as you're immersed, you're consciously unaware of the fact that you don't believe what you're thinking about is true or real. This feature on its own can explain a lot about the public face of trans activism.

Immersion can be individual, but it can also be collective, as for actors and audience at the theatre or cinema, or participants in a multiplayer video game. Collectively, you can passively receive the details of a fiction (as at the cinema), or actively make it up as you go along (as during a children's game). Either way, when you're immersed collectively in a scenario, normally you are incentivised to prevent others from drawing attention to its fictional nature. Both actors and audience-members tend to stare disapprovingly at people who take mobile phone calls during a performance.

Still, though, despite similarities, being immersed in a fictional scenario is not the same as simply believing it's true or real. This is because, typically in immersion, you still mentally retain *potential* cognitive access to facts about what's really the case. Though normally you aren't immediately conscious of what's really true or accurate during an episode of immersion, still, you could easily call the facts up where needed – for instance, if someone suddenly asked you, 'Who's that actor again?' You may be mentally lost in a play but you still know how to find the theatre loos when needed. The undercover policeman might spend most of every day thinking, acting and feeling as if he's somebody else, but he still reports to his bosses intermittently. Even the method actor immersed in a role still has contracts to sign and agents to talk to. Relatedly, in immersion, any action you take on that basis is usually guided only selectively by the fiction you have in mind, in a relatively controlled way, and needn't completely resemble the action you'd take if you actually believed it. When watching Shakespeare's *Hamlet* and feeling great pity – even crying – for Ophelia as she goes mad, you don't run on to the stage and try to book her into a psychiatric hospital.

As the fact that people can shed tears suggests, being immersed in a fiction – while not the same as believing it's real or true – is not simply dry or robotic. It isn't just entertaining some possibility, laboriously working out what other people watching you would expect from you given that possibility, and then deliberately acting on that basis. It's more seamless than this. Immersion involves 'throwing yourself into' or 'inhabiting' a scenario with commitment and feeling, so that your thought and even behaviour then proceeds without much conscious deliberation. As philosopher Samuel Kampa puts it, there's little 'explicit metacognition' about what to think or do next.[17]

My hypothesis is that at least some of the time many trans and non-trans people alike are immersed in a fiction: the fiction that they themselves, or others around them, have literally changed sex (to become either the opposite sex or non-binary). Apart from general behavioural indications, this is suggested by evidence that in a private, anonymous context, it seems that a majority of people would deny gender identity made any difference to whether one is a man or a woman. In a 2018 Populus survey in the UK involving 2,074 respondents (49 per cent male, 51 per cent female, weighted across a range of age groups), participants were asked 'to think about a person who was born male and has male genitalia but who identifies as a woman'. They were then asked: 'In your own personal view would you consider this person to be a woman or a man?' 19 per cent answered 'woman'; 52 per cent of respondents answered 'man', 7 per cent said 'not a man or a woman', 20 per cent said 'don't know', and 3 per cent preferred not to say.[18] One possible explanation of the fact that over half answered 'man' is that the relatively anonymous, private context of the survey, in conjunction with the question's emphasis on 'your own personal view', encouraged people to drop out of whatever immersive state they might publicly tend to be in.

Immersion in a fiction can be enhanced by props: by the movements of actors on stage or the images on screen, for instance. In the case of those immersed in a fiction about sex change, social media seems to act as a highly effective prop. It's a virtual environment where you can curate your own image day by day, throwing yourself psychically – at least for a while – into whatever stance or identity you wish to project to the world. Followers rarely get a chance to cross-check your statements in relation to other real-time information about you. It's now recognised that the rising popularity of gender identity among the young in the early twenty-first century was at least partly connected to internet culture and, specifically, to microblogging social sites like Tumblr, whose strapline tells users: 'you can express yourself, discover yourself, and bond over the stuff you love'. Parents of dysphoric teens often report that their offspring would spend hours and hours on Tumblr, absorbing and then recycling aspirational stories and memes about magical transformations that made a person seem special and cool.

From 2018 onwards, the hashtag #adulthumanfemale started circulating on Twitter, used by feminists trying to combat trans activist demands.[19] Almost immediately, though, the hashtag started to be used by trans women to refer to themselves. Saying such things with such apparent conviction initially looks hard to explain; but they are in fact what you'd expect if immersion was involved. For when you're immersed in a fiction, you needn't be constrained in what you say or do by what seems to be supported by evidence, or by what it would otherwise be rational to conclude. Accuracy isn't the point of the exercise – just as it isn't in a film drama or role play, either.

If, as I'm suggesting, many are immersed in fiction like this, what are some consequences? It's important to note right away that saying this does *not* entail such people are also 'deluded' or 'duped', or even just 'deceived'. Precisely: they're immersed, and immersion is not the same as belief. They don't actually believe trans men are men, or trans women, women. So they can't count as 'deceived' into thinking this. Theatregoers moved at the fate of the character Ophelia onstage aren't 'deluded', 'duped' or 'deceived' by the actors either.

Relatedly, it's important to stress that, on this interpretation, trans people are not automatically counted as – in the words of trans philosopher Talia Mae Bettcher – 'evil deceivers'.[20] Bettcher apparently frames any challenge to a literally true reading of 'trans women are women' as entailing this unpleasant commitment, but that's inaccurate. Ordinary trans people aren't deliberately trying to get people to *believe* falsehoods about their sex, just as actors onstage or in films aren't deliberately trying to get people to believe falsehoods about who they are either. Though very different from each other in other ways, that's what makes both actors and trans people different from undercover cops, who by definition are out to deceive others. To be immersed in a fiction is not to lie to or to deceive others. Language shouldn't be forced into a binary of 'truth' versus 'lies'; it's potentially much richer than that. Some trans people enter immersively into a fiction on the assumption it will be implicitly understood by others *as a fiction*. Others do so with no particular thoughts about what others will believe or imagine, but only the understandable and immediate desire to find relief from feelings of dysphoria. Either way, there's no automatic deceptive intent, nor eventual deceptive fact.

The benefits of immersion in a fiction

Generally speaking, immersing yourself in a fiction allows mental alleviation from whatever current mundane or stressful reality faces you. Most people already know this from their own experiences of reading novels, watching films or gaming. In Chapter 4 I characterised a misaligned gender identity as involving a strong psychological identification with an ideal of the opposite sex or androgyny. For many people with misaligned gender identities, immersing the self in a fiction of sex change is a way of managing the intense feelings of dysphoria this produces. That's valuable in its own right. But there are a range of perhaps more hidden benefits too.

Immersion can also help you experience alternative perspectives and emotions otherwise closed to you, potentially increasing empathy for others as well as better understanding of yourself. As philosopher Susanna Schellenberg writes, 'immersion allows us to occupy alter-ego points of view and practice new strategies by accessing possible spaces of action and affective responses'.[21] In light of its capacity to help people occupy alternative perspectives, counsellors often use immersive role-playing strategies with clients in a therapeutic setting.[22] In this regard, it's interesting how transitioning is frequently cited as a way of opening up a person's mind to the different ways in which the sexes tend to be treated socially. For instance, a 2016 *Time* article interviews several trans men and reports that 'Over and over again' they 'described all the ways they were treated differently as soon as the world perceived them as male'.[23]

Equally, immersion offers you beneficial opportunities for self-exploration, including aspects of yourself not prioritised or realised in everyday life. We can see this phenomenon in recreational gaming in particular. One study of immersion in video games notes that '[G]ames provide children with opportunities to experiment with different identities ... Children can choose whether to play as males or as females and can take on alternative social roles, including leadership and teaching roles.'[24] Though the context is very different, there are clear parallels here with immersion in a fiction of sex change. Also potentially relevantly, the same study notes that video games can allow individuals to immerse themselves in idealised fictions of the self, and 'experience abilities and satisfactions that are difficult to access in everyday life'.

So immersion in a fiction can be personally helpful, at least for a while, and for some people longer-term. In this regard, I think particularly of some young trans men and non-binary people. Therapists working with young women with male or non-binary gender identities report that often the onset of gender dysphoria is puberty. Everyone knows puberty can be hellish, and for young women today it can be particularly so: suddenly confronted with highly sexualised role models in the media, complicated and intense social hierarchies round about you, the onset of often aggressive male sexual attention, and a familiar body that's changing fast in ways one can't control. In her book *Irreversible Damage*, about the recent rapid rise of trans-identification among young women in the US (mirroring a simultaneous trend in the UK), author Abigail Shrier interviews Sasha Ayad, a therapist whose practice is mostly with trans adolescents. Says Ayad, 'A common response I get from female clients is something along these lines: "I don't know exactly that I want to be a guy. I just know that I don't want to be a girl."'[25]

Puberty is particularly punishing on so-called 'tomboy' girls. As trans scholar Jack (then Judith) Halberstam wrote in 1998: 'Female adolescence represents the crisis of coming of age as a girl in a male-dominated society. If adolescence for boys represents a rite of passage ... and an ascension to some version (however attenuated) of social power, for girls, adolescence is a lesson in restraint, punishment, and repression. It is in the context of female adolescence that the tomboy instincts of millions of girls are remodeled into compliant forms of femininity.'[26] Faced with remodelling as the only apparent choice, it's not surprising that some tomboys choose to mentally opt out. Although opting out isn't confined to tomboys. As Shrier reports, these days many trans men or non-binary adolescent females don't want to 'pass' and, she writes, 'make little effort to adopt the stereotypical habits of men: They rarely buy a weight-set, watch football, or ogle girls. If they cover themselves with tattoos, they prefer feminine ones – flowers or cartoon animals, the kind that mark them as something besides stereotypically male: "queer" and definitely not "cis men". They flee womanhood like a house on fire, their minds fixed on escape, not on any particular destination.'[27]

In this context, immersing yourself in a fiction that you're male or non-binary can be understood as a useful mental refuge for a younger woman from social pressures, a creative reframing of a dissatisfying reality, and an attempted shield from the kinds of attention that young women characteristically attract. It can also bring social recognition from peers, membership of a supportive community, and a growing sense of autonomy and individuation from one's family of origin, all of which can be beneficial too.

Getting immersed in a fiction about sex change isn't just of potential benefit to individual trans people, though. Those around them can also get immersed in the same fiction at least some of the time, and many do. This can help establish immersion for the trans person, which can be good for the reasons just stated. And it can reduce potentially distressing mismatches between how the trans person is seeing things and how those around them are seeing things, so facilitating interpersonal relations. Generally, being able to get immersed in the fictions of others is a socially productive skill, allowing individuals to integrate well into different social worlds, and to smooth over potential cognitive and emotional differences between the self and others.

In sum: from the perspectives of trans people and those who care about them, there's often a rational point to immersing yourself in a fiction that people can change sex. That said, we also need to name, recognise and try to manage a range of risks associated with the practice. Some of these risks occur at the personal level. The main ones, however, emerge at the institutional level, once powerful figures become immersed in a fiction and seek to compel the same attitude in others.

Personal risks of immersion

At a personal level, one risk of immersion for trans people is losing your capacity to admit, even completely privately to yourself, the facts about your sex in some relevant contexts. In that case, what starts as therapeutic can end up as harmful denial. This is a particular risk where the immersed subject strongly desires that the fictional scenario in which they're immersed be true or real. As a result of misaligned gender identity, a lot of trans people really do wish they were of the opposite sex or androgynous, and/or feel strongly averse to the sexed reality that faces them.

A useful – though of course only partial – comparison is the relation some researchers have found between problematic and disordered video-gaming habits, sometimes known as Internet Gaming Disorder (IGD), and professed motives for gaming like 'escape' and 'fantasy'.[28] IGD can involve, for instance, compulsive preoccupation with gaming, withdrawal symptoms when not gaming, depression, interruption of other ordinary activities, and disturbances of relationships with others. Other cases of immersion aren't usually like this. When you see a film, read a novel, watch a play, usually you aren't that mentally invested in the fictional scenario represented, and it's easy enough to 'come out' of the immersive state and remind yourself of what's really true.

Earlier I mentioned social media, and its potential as a prop: you're the playwright, controlling what you disclose about yourself, while your favoured audience is there to uncritically support and applaud. A general risk of supplementing your personal fiction with social media use is that doing so can detach you from reality in maladaptive ways. One way is that the experienced relative reward of virtual life can enhance aversion to the actual facts about your body, increasing your dysphoria. You can become averse to any evidence of sexed facts about yourself, or even of any reference to sex whatsoever, for fear of breaking the immersive state. It's widely acknowledged by psychologists that avoidance of an unpleasant thought often makes feelings worse. Says one detransitioner: 'Don't get me wrong, I still love Tumblr, but spending too much time online and not moving enough makes me feel more disconnected from my body.'[29] Again, an instructive partial parallel can be made with gaming; this time, with psychological identification with a game avatar, and how positive feedback from the virtual world increases psychological reliance on the game. Researcher Sasha Sioni describes how 'Vicarious interactions through a gaming avatar may fulfill ... needs [for social connection and approval], reinforcing stronger self-identification with the avatar, which in turn can offer players a stronger and more positive sense of self. Such influences may work synergistically to motivate increasing intensity of and preoccupation with gameplay.'[30]

A related risk is starting to try to control the speech and thoughts of those around you so they too never refer to or think of your sex, in any context. These attempts might include your parents, your spouse and your children, and can be very destructive of interpersonal relationships. Shrier's *Irreversible Damage* contains testimonies of parents, describing how newly adult children have cut them off for alleged 'toxic' or 'problematic' comments referencing their sex. Yet it isn't reasonable to expect the person who gave birth to you, or the person who married you, or your own children, to permanently relate to you mentally as of a different sex when they know that you are not. If relatives and friends successfully manage to immerse themselves in this fiction quasi-permanently for your sake, then that's great; but not everyone has the capacity to do it, and it's not a moral failing on their part.[31] A differently damaging attempt to control your environment might involve isolating yourself from others, and so becoming avoidant of many ordinary interpersonal situations. This too can be destructive, both of current family relationships and of the possibility of a resilient, fulfilled self with lots of different experiences under your belt in the future.

With or without the help of props, being in complete denial

about the facts about your sex is a problem, not least because there will be times when you need to come out of the fiction and disclose it to others, as discussed earlier. One obvious one is seeking medical care. Another is playing fairly in sport. If your sex isn't already obvious to others, you will also need to disclose it whenever you enter into sexual encounters with other people. Despite what's now argued by some trans activists, a person's right to privacy doesn't beat another person's right to choose sexual partners in line with their basic sexual orientation.[32] And when it comes to data collection explicitly about the sexes, data robustness is compromised when answers are in line with gender identity not sex.

Getting 'lost' in immersion is potentially problematic where it closes off valuable future possibilities, whether as a child or as an adult. In Chapter 4 I talked about how a misaligned gender identity emerges in response to personal meaning-making. For some people it's permanent, and for others it's relatively temporary. If, despite your membership of the female sex, you mentally lose yourself in the fiction that you are *really* a boy or man, or *really* non-binary (etc.), you can easily calcify this particular narrative about yourself into a fixed story, at the expense of other possible ones. Depending on your particular situation, this story might not ultimately be right for you. The risk is particularly acute in early youth. As Bernadette Wren, former Head of Psychology at the NHS Gender Identity Development Service for children, writes: 'Although it may be argued that the confident and sure knowledge of the lasting value of physical transition can be established unequivocally in early or mid-childhood, there is as yet little or no research evidence to underpin this claim.'[33]

In this regard, we need to bear in mind that immersion in a fiction about sex change can be later accompanied by permanent alterations to the body. In turn, these physical alterations can foreclose other possibilities later. For instance, for both sexes they can remove the possibility of having children, and for women, make breastfeeding impossible. It should also be recognised that surgically or hormonally altering your body to resemble the opposite sex, or to resemble your own sex less strongly, exposes you to a range of permanent, non-negligible and sometimes painful accompanying side effects.[34] This needs to be seriously considered. It's conceivable that being totally immersed in a fiction interferes with this serious consideration.

We can see, then, that though there can be genuine personal benefits to immersion, there can also be costs. Many of the most pressing dangers around immersion are wider ranging than this, however. Individual histories remain just that – individual. Large-scale problems also emerge when institutions coercively make it a social norm that *everyone* immerses themselves in the fiction that certain people have changed sex, or are non-binary, on pain of social sanction if not.

Coercing people into immersion

In early parts of this book, I described how, within many UK organisations, gender identity is being prioritised as a significant element of life, and reference to sex suppressed. Actually, it's worse than this: in my opinion, immersion in a fiction about sex change is being coercively required of people. To give a flavour of the sort of coercive institutional environment I have in mind, I'll now quote some extracts from Stonewall literature aimed at organisations applying for paid membership in its Diversity Champions scheme. Several other LGBT organisations have similar ambitions to Stonewall, in terms of changing public language around gender identity and sex. However, given its progressive history, wealth, influential connections to politicians and public reach, it's a good one to focus on.

The Stonewall Diversity Champions scheme gives organisations access to PR-friendly branding in exchange for their instigating – to put it frankly – certain measures of social control. Current members of the scheme include blue-chip companies, political parties, local authorities, government departments such as the Department for Education, schools, most universities, newspapers and broadcasters, police and armed forces, arts organisations, the Crown Prosecution Service, the Equality and Human Rights Commission, and many other major national bodies. Effectively, Stonewall seems to be aiming at the removal from member organisations of any public reference whatsoever to sex that might offend a trans person, by anyone. For instance, as already described, it explicitly advises: 'You should allow anyone to access facilities, spaces and groups which align with their gender identity.'[35] More generally, though, there's a heavy emphasis on controlling language and behaviour even when it comes to issues that have nothing to do with space allocation.

Stonewall defines 'transphobia' as (my italics): 'The fear or dislike of someone based on the fact they are trans, *including denying their gender identity or refusing to accept* it.'[36] And of course, Stonewall also famously says that trans women are women, and trans men are men. The implication is that if you 'refuse to accept' that, say, having a female gender identity makes you a woman, or make any other difference in your speech or behaviour because of the sex of a trans person, you're 'transphobic'. Examples listed in Stonewall's 2017 report 'LGBT in Britain: Hate Crime and Discrimination' include, alongside genuinely distressing anecdotal accounts of violence and bullying, the following rather more mundane example: 'I was asked if I was a boy or girl in a clothing shop as I wanted to try on male clothes. The woman said "you know they're boy's clothes. Are you a girl or boy?"' Also included: 'A female security guard refused to search me when I was waiting in line to get into an event. She made a fool of me in front of the entire line. She said I wasn't a female and made me stand in the men's line.'[37] Note that neither of these incidents involves violence or intentional disrespect, nor even a plausible indication of dislike on the part of the speakers. They simply involve a reference to sex, and a difference in behaviour on the basis of it.

Elsewhere, Stonewall offers as 'examples of transphobia to include within your policies': 'Speculating about someone's gender "Is that a man or a woman?"'; and 'Purposefully ignoring someone's preferred pronoun'.[38] It's implied there are few circumstances in which it would be appropriate to refer to, or even ask about, someone's sex. On pronouns, meanwhile – which, we're told, should represent gender identity not sex – Stonewall's stated advice, for everyone and not just trans people, is: 'When you introduce yourself, also introduce your pronoun ... Put your pronouns in your email signature and/or social media profile. Try to avoid addressing groups or people with gendered language ... If you're not sure what someone's pronouns are, ask them. If you accidentally misgender someone, just apologise to them and then move on using their correct pronoun.'[39]

In a different Stonewall document, universities specifically are advised to 'review your course curriculum' to equip 'lecturers and teachers to use inclusive language, avoid gender stereotyping, and cover LGBT topics sensitively and accurately'.[40] With respect to academic events, they advise: 'Speakers who hold strongly anti-LGBT views, such as ... denying that trans people exist as the gender they say they are, cause LGBT people to feel deeply unsafe.' (This misleading use of 'exist' is ubiquitous in trans activist literature, suggesting to the unwary, usually falsely, that critics of gender identity must be saying trans people don't 'exist' – or even that they shouldn't.) The document continues: 'When assessing the risks associated with hosting external guest speakers at events, we encourage you to think of ... gender identity in the same way you would other key aspects of someone's identity, such as race or faith.' On student enrolment, Stonewall suggests: 'Students should have the ability to change their personal details, including their name, title and gender, at any time on your systems.' University sports clubs are told: 'Where clubs and opportunities are already inclusive of all genders, consider renaming them as explicitly mixed (for example, changing "judo" to "'mixed judo").' And as with other policies, there is a heavily punitive flavour to any perceived infractions. The same document tells universities to: 'Ensure your discrimination, bullying and harassment policies are explicitly inclusive of ... gender identity', and to: 'Proactively encourage and communicate routes for reporting discrimination, bullying and harassment'. It goes on: 'Ensure that each point of contact for reporting discrimination, bullying and harassment is also equipped to identify hate incidents and crimes, so they can provide students with support in reporting these to the police.'

Effectively, Stonewall's objective seems to be to incentivise organisations, either via rewards (branding, prizes, public approval) or punishment (accusations of transphobia, public disapproval) to get its members immersed in the fiction that those with female gender identities are women and those with male gender identities are men. This completely immersive 'institutionalisation' of a fiction that people can change sex is profoundly dangerous for several reasons. The first and most obvious one is that, as I argued in Chapters 3 and 5, sex continues to exist, as do the many circumstances in which it's appropriate to mention or respond to it, either with regard to specific individuals or as a general fact. Indeed, one such circumstance was cited just now in the 2017 Stonewall 'hate crime' report. Despite what this report suggests, it might be perfectly appropriate for a female security guard to refuse to search a male person and to ask a male to do it instead.

A second problem is the cost to freedom of speech. An individual's choice to get immersed in a fiction or not is precisely that: a choice, falling into the realm of autonomy and individual conscience. Even if we sometimes automatically get immersed in fictions given exposure to the right sort of prompts or props, we can usually choose to pull ourselves out of them. Non-hateful speech shouldn't be compelled. It's not hateful in itself to refuse to immerse yourself in a given fiction and to choose instead to refer to facts. It is perhaps considered rude to refuse in some cases, just as it can be rude to point out facts about someone's weight, or that they've gone grey, or look aged – but 'hateful' it is not. And when trans women like Debbie Hayton, Miranda Yardley and Fionne Orlander refuse to enter into the fiction that they are women, and state that they are men, they are not being 'self-hating'.

In recent years, there have been several notable cases of UK institutions compelling people to adopt the language of gender identity. I've talked about one of them, involving guidelines for media crime reporting, in the last chapter. Another example was during the 2018 criminal trial of trans woman Tara Wolf, for the assault on a sixty-year-old radical feminist Maria MacLachlan. Wolf did not have a Gender Recognition Certificate at the time of the trial. Prior to the assault, Wolf had written on social media of the wish to 'fuck some terfs up'. The traumatic assault upon MacLachlan was captured on video, and the trial resulted in a conviction for Wolf. Yet despite this, and despite MacLachlan being there as a *victim* to testify about her assault, in the course of the trial District

Judge Kenneth Grant told MacLachan, 'The defendant wished to be referred to as a woman, so perhaps you could refer to her as "she" for the purpose of the proceedings.'[41]

In a different case from 2019, tax researcher Maya Forstater lost her position at the Centre for Global Development think tank on the grounds of using alleged 'offensive and exclusionary' language in tweets. Her tweets were in opposition to the Government's move to reform the Gender Recognition Act in favour of gender identity. In her tweets, Forstater stated her belief in binary sex, and her belief that 'men cannot change into women'. When she later took the Centre to an employment tribunal, the judge found in the Centre's favour, ruling that Forstater's stated belief that there are two sexes could not count as a protected philosophical belief under the terms of the 2010 Equality Act. The judge's incredible ruling was that Forstater's refusal to – as I would call it – immerse herself in a fiction about sex change, and instead to state facts, was 'not worthy of respect in a democratic society'. [42]

In these cases, the judges' pronouncements didn't come from nowhere. The Crown Prosecution Service – as already mentioned, another Stonewall Diversity Champions scheme member – currently advises that gender identity should determine the naming and pronouns of defendants.[43] The *Equal Treatment Bench Book*, issued to the judiciary by the Judicial College in 2018 and heavily citing Stonewall throughout, states: 'It is important to respect a person's gender identity by using appropriate terms of address, names and pronouns. Everyone is entitled to respect for their gender identity, private life and personal dignity.'[44] The personal dignity of women who have been assaulted, or who wish to freely speak their mind on matters of political importance to them, apparently doesn't figure as a consideration.

A third risk to society of compelled immersion is to

knowledge production. As noted earlier, when people are collectively coerced into immersing themselves in a fiction, it simultaneously becomes important not to make any second-order reference to the presence of the fiction. Any such reference will tend to destroy first-order immersion, just as an actor saying 'I'm an actor!' or 'This gun isn't real!' on stage will destroy an audience's immersion in a play. A taboo then arises around naming reality. This is particularly bad in contexts such as universities, whose main point is to produce and disseminate socially useful knowledge, broadly speaking.

I find it particularly telling that academics who are strongly critical of views like mine, as expressed in this book, tend not to address them with argument or evidence – as would be expected, given disciplinary norms – but often instead resort, relatively unusually for such norms, to complaints about my presumed motives or personal failings. They also tend rhetorically to collapse criticism of the intellectual tenets of trans *activism* into moral criticism of trans *people*. Here's a particularly good example from the preface of Helga Varden's 2020 book *Sex, Gender and Love*. Varden writes (my italics): 'I want clearly to distance myself and my theory from those who, in the name of feminism, write *to undermine the reality of and/or to criticize people who are trans* ... it greatly saddens me to see what I consider to be the thoughtlessness with which many feminist (and other) philosophers relate to trans lives.'[45] Such moralising rhetoric upfront is a clue that truth-pursuit is not the aim here, but something more like the propping up of a fiction. Another interesting academic phenomenon that looks like grist to my mill is what philosopher Mary Leng has called the 'Reverse Voltaire': 'I agree with what you have to say, but will fight to the death to prevent you from saying it.'[46] That is, some academics will admit, when pressed, that sex exists, and is distinct from 'gender', but will insist that it shouldn't be mentioned wherever it conceivably might offend trans people. This makes it look as though immersion is in play for them too, a lot of the time.

In 2019, having experienced unusually virulent and personalised attempts to smother my public writing on sex and gender, I put out a call to fellow academics to send me accounts of any similar experiences. I was inundated. Correspondents told me of their journal submissions and grant applications being rejected on the grounds of 'transphobia'; of editorial positions withdrawn on similar grounds; of academic publishers bullied into delays or retractions; of official university complaints of harassment and bullying against them; of informal chats from departmental heads indicating the likelihood of threat to promotion prospects, and so on.[47] The result is that academics have largely been cowed into silence. The social effects of recent changes in favour of gender identity within UK institutions cannot properly be explored, precisely because UK universities have instigated similar policies themselves. Interesting phenomena such as the recent rapid rise in the numbers of younger girls and women with misaligned gender identities cannot be properly analysed. When one researcher at Brown University in Rhode Island, Lisa Littman, tried to investigate this academically, publishing an article on 'Rapid Onset Gender Dysphoria', trans activists immediately pronounced it 'deeply flawed' (presumably because it counteracted the popular SOR model discussed in Chapter 4), after which both the publisher and her own institution disassociated themselves from the work.[48] In 2016 an entire Gender Identity Service in Canada was closed at the behest of trans activists, for alleged 'conversion therapy' of young people with misaligned gender identities – that is, of actively questioning their origins rather than 'affirming' them.[49] Such close and overtly politicised policing of academic and therapeutic work around trans children and teens in particular means that potential relations between factors such as autism, homosexuality, a history of trauma and the possession of a misaligned gender identity in that population are arguably not being properly explored.[50] Perhaps most worryingly of all, it seems an adequate medical understanding of the long-term effects of drugs such as puberty blockers and hormone courses, dispensed to many young people with misaligned gender identities, might also have been hampered.[51] None of this is in the genuine interests of trans people – in fact, it positively works against them.

When you show a child a film, sometimes they don't understand it's a fiction and think it's real. Yet another risk in the currently coercive environment many find themselves in is of onlookers – of whatever age – failing to fully understand what the true facts about biological sex are. For, as is predictable, some are taking others' unacknowledged immersion in a fiction that trans women are women, and trans men are men, etc., to indicate that these things are literally true. As described earlier, humans take on a lot of beliefs on trust, simply by listening to others and copying them. This is a reasonable general practice – indispensable, in fact. However, where someone has taken on beliefs in this way, having unwittingly gained them from watching others immersed in a fiction rather than reality, the result can be a kind of dogmatic faith-based stance: 'It must be true, but I can't say why – all I know is it would be very bad to deny it.' (Not for nothing have commentators noticed that the mantra 'Trans women are women! Trans men are men!' can sound like a religious incantation.) In effect, the psychological effect captured so well in the fairy tale 'The Emperor's New Clothes' seems to be present. The tale's famous denouement details how 'Everyone in the streets and the windows said, "Oh, how fine are the Emperor's new clothes! Don't they fit him to perfection? And see his long train!" Nobody would confess that he couldn't see anything, for that would prove him either unfit for his position, or a fool.'[52]

The risks of sex-incongruent language

There's another potential cost to all this which, if eventually established to be a genuine phenomenon, needs serious consideration. In a pseudonymous blog post from 2019 called 'Pronouns are Rohypnol', 'Barra Kerr' argued that measures to coerce people into calling trans women 'women' and trans men 'men', and to use sex-incongruent pronouns for them, slow both speakers and listeners down cognitively, as their brains struggle to process the relatively unusual sex-incongruent language choices. Kerr makes a comparison with the Stroop Test, a psychological experiment in which participants are asked to list the colours of a set of differently coloured words, but where the words themselves are names of colours, distributed in an 'incongruent' non-matching way so that, for example, the word 'RED' is coloured yellow, and 'GREEN' is coloured blue. When psychologists run the Stroop Test, they find participants' processing of the colours of the words to be significantly delayed, compared to when colours and words are congruent. The Stroop Effect has been explained as a result of what is called 'semantic interference', understood as the result of competing messages being simultaneously sent to the part of the brain responsible for the retrieval of declarative facts.[53] Similarly, Kerr argues, trying to use preferred sex-incongruent pronouns for a person – e.g. 'woman' or 'she' or 'her' for someone whose appearance strongly suggests they are male – results in Stroop-like effects of its own.[54]

To this, we might add a point introduced in the last chapter, when I observed that WOMAN and MAN are perceptual concepts, usually first acquired as a child by being shown a number of examples in the world around the child or in picture books ('Look, that's a lady!', 'What's the man in the shop doing?', and so on), from which the child's brain starts to be able to extrapolate the relevant concept and apply it to new and different cases. Remember also that, in the vernacular, a 'passing' trans woman is defined as someone who has had sufficient medical intervention to come to look visually indiscernible from a woman. When a viewer (any viewer, including trans viewers) who has the perceptual concept WOMAN sees a 'passing' trans woman, the very same perceptual systems initially are recruited as are also recruited in visual recognition of women generally. That's implied, precisely, by the fact the trans woman 'passes'. In the absence of any confounding information about the trans woman's sex, the viewer will automatically visually classify the trans woman 'as a woman'. And even *with* simultaneous access to confounding information about a passing trans woman's actual sex, via some other informational route (say, because she has told you she is trans), there's a sense in which a viewer will still automatically see the trans woman 'as' a woman, even if that viewer simultaneously ultimately concludes she isn't one. This automatic tendency of human brains to see objects 'as' other objects, based on shared visual or other perceptual profiles, is also employed in going to the cinema and seeing screen images 'as' the things they depict, or seeing certain shaped clouds in the sky 'as' animals or trees, or the shadow in the corner 'as' a ghost. It's automatic. It's consistent with knowing what you are seeing isn't really there, or not really as you are seeing it. In that case the brain is, in effect, sending simultaneously conflicting messages.

This also has consequences for how the visual system deals with automatically categorising trans people who are *not* 'passing'. Based on available numbers, it seems that these currently greatly outnumber passing trans people in the UK. This is partly because surgery is relatively expensive, waiting lists are long, and hormone courses on their own often can't remove evidence of post-pubertal aspects distinctive of sexed anatomy, particularly for males. Where, for instance, a trans woman is physically unlike a woman in ways relevant to ordinary recognition, no amount of berating your internal visual processing system will convince it to start seeing her – in the relevant sense – 'as' a woman. The visual recognition process precisely precludes this.

One obvious consequence of this is that trans activism's attempts to socially sanction or even criminalise what they call 'misgendering' and I call 'accurately sexing' within institutions look even more illiberal, especially in environments where young people are only just getting to grips with the original concepts in the first place (e.g. schools). People can't help seeing what they see. With children, we usually encourage them to say what they see, so it's bizarre to change the game and start punishing them for it. Another consequence is that Barra Kerr's hypothesis looks supported, at least with respect to attempts to use sex-incongruent pronouns and other language for non-passing trans people. Effectively, the brain is automatically visually classifying as 'not-a-woman', while trying to label as 'woman'. With passing trans people, presumably, Stroop-like effects are lower.

Part of Kerr's thesis seems to be that Stroop-like effects are deliberately provoked by trans women to lower the defences of women to their aggressive sexual attention. This seems to me to be fearmongering. However, that particular disagreement can be left aside, because if Kerr is right, it doesn't matter what the particular intentions of trans women are: either way, the cognitive disadvantage for those who try to comply with preferred pronouns will be the same. This certainly seems worth investigating, given facts discussed in Chapter 3 about how strength and sexual aggression are differently averaged across male and female populations respectively, and how men are responsible for the majority of assaults upon women. In this context, something that slows down the cognitive processes of women with respect to potential aggressors may turn out to have very serious personal ramifications for them.

A related point concerns how the use of preferred pronouns and sex-incongruent language can influence public discussion, in the physical absence of the trans person in question. In Chapter 5, I described how newspaper articles now tend to refer even to convicted criminal trans women as 'women' and use 'she' and 'her' pronouns for them. Public commentators often do the same, moving seamlessly between 'woman' and 'trans woman', 'she' and 'her'. For viewers or readers who don't fully grasp what a trans woman is, this can be confusing (I can't be the only person who regularly has to explain to my parents that a 'trans woman' isn't a female who has transitioned to live as a man). But even for those who do understand, the use of sex-incongruent language can send a misleading set of impressions to a reader's subconscious. We are set up to have certain expectations about the people called 'she' or 'her': for instance, that they will on average be more physically vulnerable and less sexually aggressive than the people called 'he' or 'him'. The psychological effect of these expectations really becomes obvious only where an exception proves the rule: that is, where, unusually, expectations are set up and then flagrantly flouted within a single piece of prose. A good example comes from the reporting of the trial of trans woman Karen White, eventually convicted for sexual assaults on female prisoners while placed in a female jail. The prosecutor was reported in newspapers as having said, of the defendant: 'Her penis was erect and sticking out of the top of her trousers.'[55] This memorable sentence spells out in stark detail a fact often figuratively concealed by the use of 'woman', 'she' and 'her'. More often in the written medium, though, expectations unconsciously generated in readers by an author's sex-incongruent language choices are left intact, to the potential detriment of clear communication.

My own use of pronouns

In this book, I've argued that, when speaking literally and not immersed in a fiction, 'woman' and 'man' should be used in line with sex. Equally, though, so far I've been using pronouns in a way that, I assume, tracks what most individual trans people would prefer. That is, I normally use 'he' and 'him' for trans men, 'she' and 'her' for trans women, and 'they' and 'them' for non-binary people, where preferred. Most of the time, I choose to immerse myself in a fiction about sex change for trans people, where it seems they would wish me to. (I choose to make an exception for trans women who assault or aggress women. So, for instance, I will not call Karen White 'she' nor 'her'.)

The discussion of the last section has revealed this choice is not an uncomplicated one. Though I've made it, I remain genuinely conflicted by the issue. At the very least, it's clear the decision to use sex-incongruent language of any sort should normally be a free choice. It's not acceptable on the part of any organisation to coercively require this on pain of sanction. Trying to encourage social norms of politeness in a company or institution, including encouraging people to use preferred pronouns where sex isn't relevant, is one thing; having HR departments threaten people with accusations of 'transphobia' and 'hate speech' if they don't is quite another. As a trans person, having your preferred pronouns or other sex-incongruent terms used by others is a courtesy on their part and not a right on yours.

When trying to work out what to do for the best in this area in everyday interactions, we should probably remember that the available options for referring to trans women and trans men are not, as commonly presented, *only* 'woman'/ 'she'/ 'her' *or* 'man'/ 'he'/ 'him'. For one thing, if something isn't relevant it doesn't need to be mentioned. There are plenty of potentially awkward facts we don't mention in everyday discourse, in order to keep interpersonal relations ticking along. For another thing, where sex isn't relevant to a particular conversation, sex-neutral pronouns such as 'they' can be used for trans women and trans men if 'she' and 'he' are personally impossible. That is, we don't necessarily have to choose *either* sex-congruent ones *or* sex-incongruent ones. This may not seem ideal to either 'side' – not to mention, to some grammarians – but it's a compromise, and that's probably the most we can hope for. For centuries, the rich resources of the English language have provided opportunities for the diplomatic finessing of psychologically uncomfortable facts where possible, without denying them completely. We should try to use those resources creatively where we can. Equally, though, we need to remember messages from earlier chapters as well as parts of this one. In every organisation, there will be circumstances where glossing isn't appropriate, and where those facts need to be referred to – not out of spite or rudeness, but for the rational and equitable functioning of the organisation.

You might be wondering: how have we collectively lost sight of the availability of this sort of compromise? In the next two chapters, I'll propose some explanations, both historical and psychological.

7

How Did We Get Here?

Let's go back for a moment, to 2014. By then, Stonewall had arguably won its last major objective for gay rights – bringing same-sex marriage into law – and was ready to take on a new mission, thereby finding itself a new income stream in the process. With its launch of the 2015 'A Vision for Change: Acceptance without Exception for Trans People' campaign, it found one. Many of the ambitions expressed in the accompanying 'A Vision for Change' document will by now be familiar. Trans people should be able to access services and resources 'that align with their gender identity'. The 2004 Gender Recognition Act (GRA) should be changed because it 'denies trans people the ability to determine their own gender', and the spousal veto should be removed. The Equality Act should rename the protected characteristic of 'gender reassignment' as 'gender identity'. Non-binary people should be able to alter their passports to reflect this allegedly fundamental fact about them. There should also be '[j]udicial clarity of "sex by deception" cases to define the legal position on what constitutes sex by deception based on gender, and to ensure trans people's privacy is protected'. [1]

Partly as a result of A Vision for Change and the lobbying that went with it, in 2016 the cross-party Women and

Equalities Select Committee initiated a public inquiry, the 'Transgender Equality Inquiry'. In Chapter 1, I mentioned the background influence of an intellectual position popular in activist academia, 'standpoint epistemology'. This says that, as members of an oppressed minority, the views of trans people should be deferred to when it comes to anything to do with transness, and those of non-trans people mostly ignored as irrelevant. Whether those involved noticed it or not, this certainly seems to have been a guiding principle in the Trans Inquiry. Twenty people were called as witnesses to the inquiry, excluding MPs. Eleven of these represented trans activist organisations or causes, nine of whom were trans themselves and two of whom were parents of trans people. Nine other witnesses were there as relatively neutral experts, though some of these were also trans. No representatives for other interested parties with competing interests were called as witnesses: no representatives of women-only groups and services, and no therapists or parents with concerns about transitioning children, for instance.

Many of the trans representatives made recommendations, then repeated in the Final Inquiry Report, based only on putative connections to trans lived experiences rather than any independent expertise. So for instance, Susie Green, chair of the charity Mermaids and mother of a trans child, was there as a witness and was extensively quoted throughout the report. Green is an IT consultant with no medical expertise. Mermaids' written submission was quoted as recommending that 'pubertal-postponement treatments should be made available to older children (aged 16 and 17) as well as younger ones'. Anna Lee, a representative of Lancaster Students Union with a recent degree in Mathematics and with no obvious connection to sporting matters, was cited as recommending that national governing bodies for sport should relax their requirements around trans

athletes. Jess Bradley, a young representative for Edinburgh
Action for Trans Health, was heavily cited throughout the
report, making recommendations about the NHS for reasons
that are unclear. Action for Trans Health's publicly stated political objectives at the time included the immediate release and
pardon of all trans prisoners, an end to all birth certificates,
and for hormones to be prescribed, free and upon request, by
the NHS. On their website they described the history of trans
medicine as 'a history of colonial and fascist abuse'.

In the report summarising the Inquiry's findings, the
Women and Equalities Committee made a host of recommendations that could have been taken straight from Stonewall's
original Vision for Change. Many of these were then endorsed
in the Conservative government's later response to that report.[2]
For instance: the Government committed itself to review the
GRA 'to determine whether changes can be made to improve
it in order to streamline and de-medicalise the gender recognition process'. The very highest bar was set for single-sex
exemptions under the Equality Act, with the Government
noting 'it is very unlikely that any exceptions will apply in
ordinary "high street" service provision situations'. It further
noted 'there are likely to be few occasions in sport where
exclusions are justified to ensure fair competition or the safety
of competitors'. It was approvingly reported that, already at
that point, 'equality guidance provided to the judiciary ...
provides advice on how to prevent transgender people from
being "outed" in court proceedings'. (We saw some of the
effects of this guidance in Chapter 6.) Later, in 2018, Prime
Minister Theresa May was the face of the launch of an LGBT
Action Plan, in which the Conservative government restated
its intention to remove 'bureaucratic and intrusive' obstacles
to legally acquiring a Gender Recognition Certificate, and to
move to a 'more streamlined and de-medicalised' process.[3] A

public consultation on GRA reform was eventually delivered, launched with an apparently confident assumption it would be warmly received by the public with the minimum of opposition. (As it turns out, they were wrong about that.)

By any measure, Stonewall's 'A Vision for Change' was staggeringly successful – at least, until it came up against grassroots public test. My question for this chapter is: why? More generally: how did so many prominent figures and public institutions become receptive to the conclusions of gender identity theory? Why has ideologically driven policy-capture been, apparently, so easy? Of course, the explanation is bound to be complex, and I can cover only part of it. One significant factor is the intellectual story I've tried to trace, disseminated through university departments and beyond. Another factor concerns various commitments and tensions within current feminism, which I'll discuss in my final chapter. But here, in some detail, are three other salient factors as I see them.

A history of prejudice against gay, trans and other sex-nonconforming people

One important factor, I think, is public awareness of a history of prejudice against sex-nonconforming people, plus a commendable desire to be (seen to be) on the other side of it. Very often, this prejudice has been directed towards gay people in particular. It still is in various parts of the world. Gay people are counted by others as sex nonconforming, in the sense that they occupy what's perceived to be a female-associated sexual role (men) or a male-associated sexual role (women). Heterosexual disgust about same-sex activity as 'unnatural' and 'deviant' speaks to an implied relation to the heterosexual norm.

Sex between men was a capital offence in England and Wales until 1861– the last men to be hung for 'buggery' were executed in 1835 – and was criminalised until 1967.[4] The conviction and sentence of Oscar Wilde to hard labour in Pentonville Prison serves as salutary reminder of the potential dangers of living even semi-openly as a gay man in the nineteenth century and for most of the twentieth. During the post-war period, in line with a general renewed concern about public morals, there was a repressive public clampdown on gay sex. As historian Dominic Janes describes, 'the police manufactured evidence, intimidated witnesses, entrapped homosexual men, and ensured that careers and relationships were ruined'.[5] Then, after a period of relative progress for gay people in the 60s and 70s including decriminalisation, in the 1980s public attitudes were set back by the advent of HIV AIDS. According to authors of the British Social Attitudes survey (BSA), this period 'saw frequent (and often incorrect) scares about how the HIV virus could be transmitted ... as well as a frequent distinction being made between those who were "innocent" victims (for example, contracting the HIV virus through blood transfusions) and those, like gay men or intravenous drug-users, who were seen to have "chosen" to place themselves at risk'. As the BSA records, a belief that same-sex relations are 'always wrong' increased during this time.[6] Also in the 1980s, the Tory government introduced Section 28 of the Local Government Act 1988, stating local government 'shall not intentionally promote homosexuality or publish material with the intention of promoting homosexuality' or 'promote the teaching in state schools of the acceptability of homosexuality as a pretended family relationship'. This slur upon gay adults, children, and their families indirectly prompted the formation of Stonewall, who boldly and brilliantly fought Section 28 alongside other gay rights lobbying organisations until an official repeal in the early 2000s.

The more recent trans activist incarnation of Stonewall has been keen to draw parallels between current attempts to reform the law in favour of gender identity and the historical campaign it waged in the 1980s against Section 28. It now frames Section 28 as legislation that banned 'discussion of identities in schools'.[7] Yet Section 28 was nothing to do with 'identities', in the contemporary sense of internal psychological representations of the self, which may or may not correspond to reality. It wasn't a ban on positive representations of people who 'identified as gay'. Rather, it was a ban on positive representations of gay people: gay in the sense they had sexual orientations towards people of the same sex as them and acted on them.

As the attempted comparison implies, though, historical events such as Section 28 have now become touchstones for progressive-minded people in the twenty-first century. They are recollected with shame as times when the heterosexual majority failed in its responsibilities towards the homosexual minority. Feelings are further heightened by memories of violent attacks on gay people like the nail-bombing in 1999 of the Admiral Duncan gay pub in Soho, which killed three and wounded seventy, following previous nail-bomb attacks on Black and Bangladeshi communities by the same neo-Nazi perpetrator. In the 2019 version of the British Social Attitudes survey, two-thirds of those polled said same-sex sexual activity was 'not wrong at all': 'an increase of almost 50 percentage points since the question was first asked in 1983'.[8] The public's journey towards a more understanding and empathic stance in the twenty-first century is symbolised for some in the apparently heartfelt personal journey of former Tory Prime Minister David Cameron. In 2009 he publicly apologised for having personally supported Section 28, and in 2013 his government introduced the same-sex marriage bill under his stewardship.[9]

Alongside concern to do the right thing by gay people, there continues to be public confusion about the relation between gay and trans people. This isn't new. As well as appearing sex nonconforming in virtue of their perceived sex-incongruent 'sexual roles', many gay people are also genuinely sex nonconforming in that they fail to match sex-associated physical or behavioural stereotypes. Many lesbians look or act masculine, and many gay men feminine, relative to averages or norms for their peers. Either way, there has long been confusion about whether being gay somehow changes your sex. In Ancient Greece the passive partner in sexual activity between men was often referred to as a 'woman' or 'womanly'. In the nineteenth century, Karl Heinrich Ulrichs popularised his 'third sex' theory, according to which a gay man is a 'feminine soul confined by a masculine body'.[10] Around the same time, the idea of gay people as 'sexual inverts' was promoted by authors like Havelock Ellis. Richard von Krafft-Ebing described lesbianism as 'the masculine soul, heaving in the female bosom'.[11] In Radclyffe Hall's infamous novel about female 'inversion', *The Well of Loneliness* (1928), the main female character, Stephen, is described as occupying the 'no-man's land of sex'. And in 1952 Alan Turing, a gay mathematician whose work made an incalculable contribution to artificial intelligence and code-breaking, was involuntarily administered female hormones after a conviction for gross indecency.

Perhaps unsurprisingly, then, there is residual confusion in the public mind about the precise relationship between being gay and being trans – perhaps especially for heterosexual onlookers, trying hard to be sympathetic from the sidelines. Confusion is increased by the long history of drag queens, drag kings and other forms of transvestism within gay culture, and by practices such as gay men calling drag queens 'she'. As earlier discussion indicates, the mere fact of being same-sex attracted or otherwise sex nonconforming is nothing like enough to establish either possession of a misaligned gender identity or being trans. Equally, many trans people are heterosexual: stably attracted to members of the opposite sex. Still, for public figures and organisations wary of being on the wrong side of history (again), when Stonewall and other prestigious gay rights organisations started adding a 'T' to 'LGB', nearly all were happy to go along with it.

More recently, an increasingly polarised political climate has strongly contributed to the desire to be especially sympathetic to trans people, especially during the time of Trump. Given the degree of social interplay between American and British left-wing outlets and commentators, US concerns tend to influence British ones. The fury and despair felt by many Democrat voters towards Trump produced a flattening of political discourse, as complex issues came to be treated as simple 'good versus bad' ones. This included trans issues. In the US, the picture for trans rights is much more mixed than in the UK, and some reasonable and deserved protections are genuinely lacking. At federal level, there is no legally protected characteristic of gender reassignment (or, indeed, sexual orientation), as in the UK Equality Act. There is also no NHS, which UK trans people are entitled to use for their healthcare needs, as is everyone else, and which normally removes the possibility of huge bills.[12] In 2020, Trump's government removed healthcare protections for pregnant women, and gay and trans people that had been in place since 2016. The year before, he banned transgender personnel from serving in the military.[13] Even though inapplicable to the UK situation, genuinely discriminatory actions like these against trans people produced a reactionary bounce in UK progressive minds towards support for whatever looked even vaguely like the opposite approach. They were also leveraged by UK trans activists and sympathetic journalists as evidence of a generally worsening situation for trans people, including in the UK, without explicit consideration of how the background context might relevantly differ.

But capitalising on public sympathy for sex-nonconforming people is not the only way in which trans activist organisations have exerted influence. Another relevant factor is the use of propaganda. I'll look at three notable examples.

Trans activist propaganda and its effect

Transgender Remembrance Day

In the words of US organisation GLAAD: 'Transgender Day of Remembrance (TDOR) was started in 1999 by trans-gender advocate Gwendolyn Ann Smith as a vigil to honor the memory of Rita Hester, a transgender woman who was killed in 1998. The vigil commemorated all the transgender people lost to violence since Rita Hester's death, and began an important tradition.' What started as a spontaneous grassroots commemoration of a violent and senseless act in the US has in recent years become a corporate fixture for many UK institutions. On 20 November every year, companies, public sector organisations and universities hold ceremonies to commemorate TDOR, often with senior management figures present. At many of these ceremonies, candles are lit and the names of all the trans people murdered in the previous year are read out, one by one. As John Lucy Muir writes on the Stonewall website, 'Each year we pause in memory of those murdered or who've taken their own life as a result of transphobia.

Sometimes we gather with friends and attend services, reflecting on those lost to hatred and bigotry. We read through the list of names and the horrifying details of the manner in which their lives were lost: "Cause of death; throat cut"; "Cause of death; shot at point-blank range"; "Cause of death; blunt force trauma, set on fire". Each year the list continues, on and on.'[14]

The list of names for each year is recorded on a dedicated website with a printable list of names to be read at ceremonies.[15] Stonewall strongly encourages members of its Diversity Champions scheme to get involved, citing, among other organisations, De Montfort University's participation as exemplary. In its 'Communicating an Inclusive Service' document, Stonewall approvingly describes how, at De Montfort, '[m]essaging centres around significant days like Transgender Day of Remembrance ... with rainbow flags flying ... The visible commitment of De Montfort University's Vice-Chancellor ... is key to its success in this area.'[16] High-profile UK politicians are also keen to show solidarity with the trans community on 20 November, issuing supportive tweets on the day or public statements, like the one made by Labour leader Jeremy Corbyn in 2017. On TDOR in 2019, Labour's Shadow Women and Equalities Minister Dawn Butler published an emotive public statement in the LGBT publication *Pink News*, simultaneously expressing solidarity with trans people and pledging Labour's commitment to reforming the GRA.[17] Generally, TDOR is used as a key reference point for the general picture of transphobic violence and hate crime against trans people painted by UK LGBT organisations, which is also sometimes used to back up the claim that trans women should have access to women-only spaces like changing rooms and bathrooms (the apparent implication being this will be safer for them, as it will protect them from violent transphobic men).[18]

And yet, for a list doing so much political heavy lifting in the UK, when we examine it we find something odd. Most of the names, by a large margin, are from the Americas. According to the Trans Murder Monitoring Project, which also monitors trans murders worldwide, in 2019 there were 331 murders of trans and 'gender-diverse' people overall, with 160 of them (48 per cent) occurring in Brazil, 63 (19 per cent) in Mexico, 31 (9 per cent) in the US, 14 in Colombia, and 13 in Argentina. Nine occurred in Europe as a whole, including one in the UK.[19] In 2018 meanwhile, of 369 murders, 167 (45 per cent) were recorded in Brazil, 71 (19 per cent) in Mexico, 28 in the US, 21 in Colombia, and 9 in Argentina. Sixteen were recorded in Europe as a whole, again including one in the UK.[20]

To put this into some context: in 2017 there were 63,880 homicides in Brazil, and in 2018 this dropped to a still staggering 51,000.[21] The 2020 World Population Review classed Brazil as the seventh most murderous country in the world, with an average of 30.5 murders per 100,000 people.[22] Mexico was sixteenth with 19.27.[23] Another fact worthy of note is that, according to the Trans Murder Monitoring Project, 61 per cent of trans people murdered in 2019 were in the sex trade. In 2018 the figure was 62 per cent. Entry into the sex trade for many trans people might well be an indirect result of inequality: that is, of career options being discriminatorily restricted due to being trans. One report on violence against those in the sex trade details how, for many, 'choosing sex work is a reflection of limited livelihood options and limited economic resources' especially where the trans person is an economic migrant.[24] Still, as trans scholar Talia Mae Bettcher notes: 'Not all acts of violence against trans people need be transphobic in nature. A trans woman might be targeted not because of her trans status but because she is simply viewed as a sex worker.'[25] It's well established that prostitution puts you at unusually high risk of violence, from clients, co-workers, police and others, especially in Latin America.[26] It also seems relevant that, in the words of one study, though trans people overall in the US don't face a higher risk than average of being murdered, 'young transgender women of color almost certainly' do. This too looks potentially partly connected to the disproportionate presence of Black and Latina trans women in the US sex trade.[27]

This complex context isn't conveyed by those pushing for the commemoration of TDOR within UK institutions. Instead, the murders are presented as produced from a single cause: 'transphobia'. Let no one misunderstand me – the increased susceptibility of those in the sex trade to death and violence (and poverty, and drug misuse) is a horrific fact, to which any society should pay urgent sympathetic attention. But using the murders of trans prostitutes overseas to make political points in the UK by shoehorning them into a formless rhetorical void, in which all such deaths are treated as the same, explained vaguely as a result of transphobia, is precisely *not* to pay attention to the full picture. And the victims deserve better than being instrumentalised to make simplistic political points.

When we look at the murder rate of trans people in the UK over a decade it turns out it is, on average, around one a year as an absolute value. No trans people have been murdered in the UK in the last two years. Generally speaking, roughly 1 per 100,000 people are murdered on average in the UK every year.[28] As indicated in my introduction, according to Stonewall, their 'best estimate' of how many trans people there are in the UK is 'about 600,000 trans and non-binary people in Britain, out of a population of over 60 million'.[29] If that's right, this means the murder rate for trans people is lower than for the general population as a whole. Needless to say, this isn't a message you're ever likely to get from attending a TDOR event in the UK.

Misrepresentation of suicide statistics

My next example is from Mermaids, the UK organisation that self-identifies its mission as 'helping gender-diverse kids, young people and their families since 1995'. At the time of writing, Stonewall is partnered with Mermaids and several other trans activist organisations in a five-year project, funded by the National Lottery Community Fund, to 'improve trans people's access to health and justice systems'.[30] Part of Mermaids' aim for several years has been to lobby for increased and earlier access to puberty blockers and cross-sex hormones for children with misaligned gender identities, and to lower the age at which Gender Recognition Certificates can be given to them.

In pursuit of this aim, Mermaids habitually invokes the possible suicides of trans children. In its 'Media Guidelines for Reporting Suicide', published in 2013, the UK Charity Samaritans warned against implying a single event could have been the only cause of a suicide, writing that this can be 'misleading and is unlikely to reflect accurately the complexity of suicide'. It also noted: 'Approximately 90 per cent of people who die by suicide have a diagnosed or undiagnosed mental health problem at the time of death'; and that 'Young people are particularly vulnerable to "imitative" suicides. Research shows they are the group most likely to be influenced by the media.'[31] Undeterred by such considerations, on World Suicide Prevention Day in 2019, Mermaids published an 'open letter' citing the suicides of trans children as a reason to reform the law to allow children to acquire Gender Recognition Certificates.

This letter opened dramatically (their bold): '**Change now to save transgender children from suicide** ... We know that there is nothing more devastating than the loss of a child or young person to suicide. We see, first hand, the terrible psychological trauma suffered by some of our service users because they live in a society that seems unable or unwilling to understand and accept them. Overall, the number of suicides in the UK fell between 2017–2018 but the number of under 19's taking their own lives in that period rose by 15% ... Meanwhile, research from the charity Stonewall shows that nearly half of young trans people have attempted suicide.' It continued: **'We know that by failing to support trans children and young people, we are losing them to suicide** ... It is nothing short of a national scandal that the current system is leading smart, talented, creative, motivated, kind and loved young people to consider ending their lives. It is time the Gender Recognition Act 2004 was changed to allow transgender people of all ages to self-identify. **We are at the forefront of one of the greatest civil rights challenges of our time. Young transgender people are losing their lives. Our society must stop failing them.'**[32]

Looking more closely, the first statistic cited by Mermaids in this hyperbolic letter is a general one concerning all UK people under nineteen, and so of course can show nothing about trans people specifically. The letter states that in 2017–18, suicides in this age group rose by 15 per cent. The reference given in the footnotes is to an Office for National Statistics document for 2017 which in fact records nothing at all for this age group in particular, but records *decreases* in the suicide rate for the age group ten to twenty-four years.[33] Being maximally charitable, perhaps Mermaids intended instead to reference ONS data from 2018, which indeed records an upward trend in suicide for this age group of around 36 per cent. This looks worrying, though, again, nothing to do with being trans – but it's surely also important to note that *generally*, across all age ranges, there was an 11.8 per cent increase in the suicide rate in 2018.

The accompanying ONS interpretation warns: 'Suicide rates tend to fluctuate on a year-to-year basis. It is therefore too early to say whether the latest increase represents a change in the recent trend.' It also notes that the standard of proof for suicide was officially lowered halfway through 2018, which may well have affected results.

Following their next claim up – that 'research from the charity Stonewall shows that nearly half of young trans people have attempted suicide' – we find a reference to a Stonewall 2017 publication that does indeed say: 'More than two in five trans young people (45 per cent) have at some point attempted to take their own life.' Looking more closely, we find that these findings were drawn from an online questionnaire polling 3,713 children aged eleven to nineteen, 16 per cent (roughly 594) of whom said they were trans.[34] A non-probability sampling method was used.[35] It's widely agreed among statisticians that this is an inadequate method with which to extrapolate to a population as a whole, because the sample isn't random.

When we turn to actual suicide statistics, GIDS themselves report that 'suicide is extremely rare' in patients.[36] Oxford sociologist Dr Michael Biggs has discovered via Freedom of Information requests that between 2016 and 2018 one patient of GIDS committed suicide and two attempted it. 'In addition,' he writes, 'two patients on the waiting list committed suicide (in 2016 and 2017) and two attempted suicide. This makes a total of three suicides in two and a half years.' Biggs also notes for comparison that 'anorexia multiplies the risk of suicide by 18 or 31 times (depending on the method of estimation), while depression multiplies it by 20.'[37] As we saw in Chapter 4, a 'high level' of depression is documented as present in GIDS patients, as noted by the Head of Psychology working there. Anecdotally, some detransitioners report they were anorexic before or during developing a misaligned gender identity.[38]

In short, there's little solid evidence to justify Mermaids' emotive rhetoric in their open letter, let alone the spurious causal connections they make with an absence of GRA reform as a relevant factor, or otherwise with an absence of early access to medical intervention.[39] This claim that trans-identifying children are at particular risk of suicide has been repeated over and over again by Susie Green in order to lobby for her organisation's aims. It is hugely irresponsible given the Samaritans' guidance. Green told the *Daily Mail* in 2014: 'The self-harm and suicide rate among transgender teens is extremely high, so offering blockers saves lives. It's quite simple.' She told the *Daily Mirror* in 2015: 'Those who feel they don't have their parents' support are much more likely to self-harm and attempt suicide.' She told the *Guardian* in 2015: 'If they feel their body is changing against their will, that's when we get a lot of suicidality.'[40] Time and again Green has used propaganda, based on distortions and in some cases outright falsehoods, to lobby for faster access to life-changing drugs and surgery for minors. Slowly the misrepresentations have spread across the public sector and become received as truth. For instance, a 2017 education resource pack produced for teachers by the 'Schools and Teachers Team' at the prestigious Tate art organisation stated, without any reference to further evidence, that: 'There is an extremely high rate of suicide amongst transgender children in schools.'[41]

Hate crime

My final example of propaganda is the use of rhetoric about hate crime. In October 2019 the *Telegraph* reported the apparently shocking information that 'Hate crimes double in six years with transphobic abuse recording biggest rise, police figures show'.[42] An article drawing the same conclusion appeared in the *Guardian*.[43] Apparently keen to draw a link between public discussion of women's rights in relation to trans rights and a rise in transphobic violence, Stonewall's spokesperson told the *Guardian*: 'We have long been concerned about the impact debates on LGBT-inclusive education and trans equality in the media, online and in the streets would have in our community. The significant rise in hate crimes against trans people shows the consequences of a society where transphobia is everywhere.'

Yet what these reports crucially failed to explain is that the data listed referred not to convicted crimes but only to 'hate crime incidents' recorded as such at the scene by attending police officers, or by other case officers later. The definition of a 'hate crime incident' used by the Crown Prosecution Service is 'any incident/criminal offence ... *perceived*, by the victim or any other person, to be motivated by a hostility or prejudice against a person who is transgender or perceived to be transgender'. In other words, a hate crime incident isn't equivalent to a crime; it is equivalent to a perception of it. College of Police guidelines make clear that: 'The victim does not have to justify or provide evidence of their belief for the purposes of reporting, and police officers or staff should not directly challenge this perception.'[44] The incident is 'recorded', in the sense of being 'flagged' in police systems, but as the CPS itself notes: 'Flagging is a subjective question ... For a conviction to receive enhanced sentencing in court the police need to provide sufficient evidence to prove the hostility element, however this is not required for flagging purposes.'[45]

In other words: these reports, and Stonewall's opportunistic response to them, are completely misleading. It's also surely relevant to note that, as we've seen earlier in this book, Stonewall's definition of 'transphobia', disseminated throughout Diversity Champions member organisations including many police forces and the CPS, includes 'denying' someone's gender identity 'or refusing to accept it'. With this being the Stonewall line, and given their public reach, it's perhaps not surprising that recorded 'hate crime incidents' went up in 2019 so significantly. But this shows nothing about levels of actual hate crime. In fact, in 2019 it was reported that less than one in ten of 'reported hate crimes' were actually being prosecuted, which suggests that in many cases there wasn't sufficient evidence to proceed.[46]

To be clear, transphobic violence does happen in the UK. In 2018–19, 1,475 convictions for 'homophobic and transphobic crime' were recorded by the CPS, compared to 8,416 racist convictions in the same year.[47] Assuming – perhaps wrongly – that the courts haven't been influenced by Stonewall's definition of transphobia, this suggests a genuine social problem of aggression towards trans people (though it also suggests racism is a much bigger problem, at least in terms of absolute numbers of crimes). Beyond information about criminal convictions, to get a true picture of the extent to which violence towards trans people is a social problem in the UK, what we really need is data that isn't produced by trans activist organisations for the purposes of lobbying. We need data that conforms with (gold) standard academic norms for knowledge production. Whether we can get this in a climate in which most universities are also Stonewall Diversity Champions is another matter.

Such instances of propaganda by trans activist organisations encourage non-trans and trans people alike to think of trans people as unusually and extremely vulnerable to being murdered, attacked or dying by suicide. The propaganda is aimed at non-trans people in particular, and is designed to get them on board with the activist agenda. The telling of emotionally compelling stories of violence and victimhood, easily vividly pictured both during the reading of them and afterwards, doubtless encourages many of those who take the stories at face value to throw themselves into a fiction about sex change in the name of doing good. It presumably also makes people – as philosophers might say – less 'epistemically vigilant' to intellectual inconsistencies within their own stance. After all, if the stakes for trans people are *this* high, we should presumably do everything in our power to help and support them – including ignoring any nagging doubts we might have about how it's all supposed to add up, or who else might be affected by it.

Objectification and 'trans women are women'

A different influence upon public opinion that I think should be implicated in any explanation of the current climate, is the extent to which women in particular are objectified, sexually or otherwise, in Western culture. Given this culture, it isn't surprising that many people – including many women themselves – relate, consciously or unconsciously, to womanhood as something like a set of outward appearances. Though this thought doesn't rationally fit with gender identity theory – which after all is concerned with inner life, not outward bodies – in my view it significantly prepares the ground for a positive attitude towards gender identity theory's politicised conclusions, at least. For it can foster the thought that some men (because they look like sexualised feminine objects) can be 'women'.

What is objectification? From Simone de Beauvoir to Martha Nussbaum to Catharine MacKinnon, feminist philosophers have long been interested in analysing the concept.

Broadly speaking, to objectify a woman is to treat or represent her as a partly or wholly dehumanised, de-mentalised object.[48] There are various ways to do that. Fashion and advertising offer several possibilities for doing so visually. You can represent her as a dazed, passive thing to be fucked, with a vacant expression and glazed eyes, as in many high-end fashion advertising campaigns. Extending this, you can represent her as sexually dominated, with her personal autonomy diminished or removed: bound or gagged, for instance. You can dress her up in animal skins or leopard print and represent her as a kind of wild, highly sexualised animal, something the fashion industry has been particularly fond of doing to black women over the years. You can dress and pose her as a stereotype: the Capable Housewife (in domestic setting, comfortable clothes, tolerant rueful smile), the Brainy Scientist (white coat, stern expression, glasses on end of nose), the Little Girl (kneesocks, pigtails, blowing bubblegum), the Sexy Vamp (cleavage, tongue on front teeth, wink). You can place her in a row with other similarly shaped, similarly adorned women, visually emphasising what they all have in common in looks and dress, so that individuality is rhetorically diminished, and one woman looks replaceable with any other. You can make her just a pair of legs, or breasts, or an arse, focusing the camera on body parts and even omitting the head and face. In all such cases, the thinking mind, personality, autonomy or particular individuality of the woman in the image is downplayed, diminished and ignored, to a greater or lesser extent. She's 'objectified' in the sense she's made more like an object and less like a fully individuated human being: less rational, less individual, less present, less important for who she actually is. In extreme cases, she can even be used as if or pictured as an inanimate object: a 'table' for men's feet, or as a 'plate' for food – as in the Japanese practice of

Nyotaimori, using a woman's naked body as a receptacle for sushi in restaurants.

Throughout various cultures, a similar story can be found. Women are represented as generic, idealised outward forms, whose mental life is diminished or irrelevant; or else their bodies are used to convey archetypal stories, symbols and ideas. Rarely are they represented as themselves, in their full, particular individuality. The female nude dominates Western visual culture: female bodies presented as objects to be studied, lasciviously examined and displayed for others' enjoyment. As academic Lynda Nead put it: 'Within the history of art, the female nude is not simply one subject among others, one form among many, it is *the* subject, *the* form.'[49]

The way women are habitually objectified in Western visual culture looks connected to the predominance of men in the art world, and the relative absence of women. Among other things, the absence of women painters from galleries has meant far fewer self-portraits, where self-portraits in painting have traditionally been a medium for close studies of individual psychology and personality. More generally, just in terms of sheer numbers, the visual representation of women is controlled by men at every stage of production, and so predictably reflects male interests in, and emotions towards, women. As feminist art activists The Guerrilla Girls pointed out in the 1980s, in the Metropolitan Museum: 'Less than 5% of the artists in the Modern Art Sections are women, but 85% of the nudes are female.'[50] In the National Gallery there are currently 'around ten' oil paintings by women among the 2,300 in the permanent collection.[51] In the contemporary art market, women's paintings comprise around 2 per cent of sales.[52] Returning to fashion and advertising we find a similarly depressing story: in 2017, only 13.7 per cent of US fashion magazine covers were shot by women photographers, and some women's magazines hired no women photographers for cover shoots at all.[53] In the advertising industry, 29 per cent of staff are women, and only 12 per cent of creative directors are women.[54]

All this contributes to a world in which, from an early age, girls and boys alike are confronted with images of women that sexualise, depersonalise, dehumanise or de-individualise them: on newsagent shelves, in tabloids, on the television, in galleries and on the internet. Woman, as a visual ideal, is perpetually represented as a collection of outward surfaces, exchangeable for any similar-looking set of surfaces, but whose inner life is of negligible importance. This then narrows the field of psychological possibilities for women as they enter the cultural environment. Women start to *see themselves* as objects: to 'self-objectify', in a way that has demonstrable negative effects on confidence, happiness and even attention spans.[55] As art critic John Berger famously wrote in *Ways of Seeing*, echoing points made by Simone de Beauvoir decades earlier: 'Men act and women appear. Men look at women. Women watch themselves being looked at. This determines not only most relations between men and women but also the relation of women to themselves. The surveyor of woman in herself is male: the surveyed is female. Thus she turns herself into an object of vision: a sight.'[56]

No better confirmation of this could be found than on Instagram, where the selfies of women have been found to outnumber those of men by a significant margin.[57] A 2015 survey found the average sixteen- to twenty-five-year-old woman spends over five hours a week taking selfies. A large proportion of women's Instagram selfies follow very narrow visual 'rules', and in the words of one study 'replicate normative feminine cues popularised through mass media'.[58] For unconfident beginners, influencers explain how to take 'the perfect selfie'. Reports the same study: 'YouTuber Huda Beauty ... endorses a selfie-taking technique that she calls "T-Rex Hands," which involves draping a bent hand on one's hair, chin, or forehead. She also demonstrates a pose called "the looking down giggle" and a subtle lip pucker.'

These days, another significant dimension to cultural representation of women is online pornography. As one recent study puts it: 'internet pornography use is a common phenomenon ... Various reports have placed internet pornography as the largest single category of electronic media both in terms of total bandwidth and total traffic ... In short, the consumption of internet pornography is a common activity for many adults and adolescents worldwide.'[59] Hardcore and violent pornography dominates the output of pornographic websites, and relentlessly depicts women and girls as objects to be manipulated, fucked, dominated, humiliated and hurt. What's happening in the minds of women during pornographic sex is of interest to the camera or director only insofar as it will be arousing to viewers: passivity, pain and humiliation being dominant themes.

It would be the work of several years properly to explore the effects this sort of culture has on developing minds, and on the way all of us who come into contact with it tend to mentally represent and relate to women as a result. I think it reasonable to suppose it also has a bearing on how we unconsciously think of trans women in relation to women, especially if trans women draw upon highly sexualised and objectifying stereotypes of womanhood in constructing their public images, as they sometimes do. A person (male or female) who unconsciously relates to women as dehumanised objects, or as mere sets of sexualised outer appearances, is presumably less likely to mind when trans women with the right sexualised look get classed as women by wider society. I was once personally assured by a trans woman that she really *was* a woman because, as she said, 'men want to have sex with me'.

Objectification and autogynephilia

Objectifying cultural images of women also seem to play a further, often unrecognised background role in the current situation. Namely, it's reasonable to think they contribute to conditions under which some men develop misaligned gender identities in the first place. The phenomenon of men sexually fantasising about wearing women's clothes or having a woman's body is well documented, both academically and anecdotally. The figure of the 'transvestite' or 'cross-dresser', a man who dresses in women's clothing either privately or publicly for sexual pleasure, was a familiar concept to most people in the twentieth century. These days it has been sub-sumed under what is sometimes called the 'trans umbrella' and is heard about much less. Stonewall's published definition of 'transgender' now includes 'cross-dresser' as a possible form.

The male condition of sexually fantasising about dressing as or being a woman was christened 'autogynephilia' by sexol-ogist Ray Blanchard in 1989. There's a documented tendency for those who have autogynephilia to deny it – presumably because of the associated and, in my view, undeserved social stigma.[60] Professional therapists and academics who have studied it, including Blanchard, have been subjected to intense pushback from trans activists for doing so.[61] Nonetheless, that autogynephilia exists as a psychosexual phenomenon seems secure, not least from the self-reports of some trans women themselves. Self-described autogynephilic trans woman and academic Anne Lawrence describes it, following Blanchard, as 'the propensity to be sexually aroused by the thought or image of oneself as a woman'. In his controversial 2003 book *The Man Who Would Be Queen*, psychologist J. Michael Bailey of Northwestern University sympathetically documents the fact that a number of men, from teenage years onward, secretly dress up in women's clothes, look at themselves in the mirror, and masturbate. Fantasies sometimes develop of having breasts and a vagina. Often there is intense guilt and shame attached to autogynephilia, and there is a documented tendency for sufferers vehemently to deny the 'erotic component' of their cross-dressing.[62] Both Bailey and Anne Lawrence note that autogynephilia can lead to a misaligned gender identity, which can then lead to transitioning. Those men who have it, Lawrence writes, 'are sexually aroused by imagining themselves as female but also idealize the idea of being female, derive feelings of security and comfort from their autogynephilic fantasies and enactments, and typically want to embody their feminine identities in an enduring way (i.e., by undergoing sex reassignment).'[63]

Blanchard, Bailey, and Lawrence stress that not all trans women are autogynephilic: many are not. Autogynephilia seems most common in heterosexuals or bisexuals, not homosexual males who transition for different reasons.[64] These clinicians also are keen to promote acceptance and understanding for those who have the condition. Still, in response to their work in this area, there has been enormous, furious controversy – controversy also inherited by historian Alice Dreger when she wrote a book, *Galileo's Middle Finger*, which was partly about the pushback Bailey's book had received.

A relatively common and fairly bizarre protest response to the hypothesis that autogynephilia exists as a significant or interesting phenomenon is that 'women have it too'. This has been argued by, among others, Julia Serano, trans scholar Andrea Long Chu (who, never shy of testing a concept to breaking point, goes further and calls autogynephilia 'the basic structure of all human sexuality'[65]) and sexologist Charles Moser. By adapting Blanchard's original questionnaire used to identify autogynephilia in men, Moser published research purporting to show that 93 per cent of women respondents to his version of the questionnaire 'would be classified as autogynephilic'.[66] Bizarrely, though, Moser apparently assumes a man answering 'yes' to the question 'Have you ever become sexually aroused while picturing yourself having a nude female body?' and a woman answering 'yes' to the statement 'I have been erotically aroused by contemplating myself in the nude' are both providing evidence of the same kind of sexual preference: an autogynephilic one. This ignores some crucial disanalogies in their respective mental states. For the autogynephilic man, there is a) an underlying belief he is *male not female* and b) a positive fantasy of being female, both apparently crucial to underpinning the thrilling transgression of the fantasy. In contrast, for the woman, there is no underlying belief she is male not female (so no transgression there); and any positive awareness of her own femaleness doesn't need to feature as part of the active content of her sexual fantasy or desire. Arousal at the thought of being female is certainly not made inevitable simply by the fact a woman is aroused at the thought of 'herself'.[67] She may also be blonde, but being aroused by 'herself' doesn't necessarily mean she has a thing for blondes.

In contrast, what does seem true is that many women are turned on by explicit objectification, passivity and humiliation. The popularity of the erotic novel *50 Shades of Grey* among women readers establishes this beyond doubt. I assume these sexual desires are inherited from and shaped by an objectifying culture. To this extent these women share a sexual preference for humiliation with some males: namely, those autogynephiles with preferences for 'forced feminization' and 'sissification'. As an article in *Vice* magazine from 2016 vividly relates: 'In the BDSM community, "sissies" are men who cross-dress, often for sexual pleasure. Many of these men engage in "sissification" or "forced feminization," where a female dominatrix will switch her male submissive's gender role ... [T]he common denominator is usually the forced cross-dressing of the male submissive – anything from lingerie to evening gowns.'[68] Andrea Long Chu writes in her book *Females* of 'sissy porn' and its 'central conceit that the women it depicts (some cis, some trans) are in fact former men who have been feminized ... by being forced to wear make up, wear lingerie, and perform acts of sexual submission'. Chu goes on to describe a further component of sissification whose 'technical term' is 'bimbofication', and involves 'hypnosis, brainwashing, brain-melting, dumbing down, and other techniques for scooping out intelligence'. She relates how, in sissy porn: 'The gestures ... almost always register the evacuation of will: wilting faces, trembling legs, eyes rolled back into heads.' Chu takes these kinds of represented gestures as a 'centrifuge for distilling ... femaleness to its barest essentials: an open mouth, an expectant asshole, blank, blank eyes'.[69] This construction of femaleness as mindlessness, humiliation and passivity, both by Chu and by the pornographers she describes, exaggerates familiar tropes from a visual culture that objectifies women generally.

For most sexual desires, including desires to be sexually humiliated, I don't think there's any point stigmatising them when they are pursued safely in private with consenting adult others; though there is always room for questioning whether acting out such desires is in the best interests of the individual, and to what extent. The lack of point in stigmatising is especially the case given that many sexual desires are unconsciously inherited from a particular cultural environment, probably during development. The sexual desires of a man to be humiliated or forced aren't 'worse' than those of a woman to experience the very same thing. The fact that our culture seems to treat the former as abhorrent and the latter as more 'natural' is yet more proof of the sexist way we tend to construe women as sexually submissive in the first place. If we were able to collectively recognise this, perhaps we could allow more space for autogynephiles to admit the erotic component of their feelings to themselves instead of furiously denying it and constructing alternative narratives involving 'innate' gender identity instead.

I also reject the oversimplification of the radical feminist academic Sheila Jeffreys, when she says autogynephilia and sissification give us insight into 'the transgender perspective ... on femininity'.[70] Apart from the fact Jeffreys is here apparently ignoring trans men, this looks like focusing on the wrong causal explanation. Some autogynephiles don't transition, and many trans women aren't autogynephiles. Being an autogynephile isn't a 'worse' reason to transition than any other: it's part of an individual's history, and may be, in particular cases, what is needed for them to live a happy life. Instead, what autogynephilia and associated sissification practices give us, I suggest, is another source of insight into the general way our culture reprehensibly objectifies and dehumanises women – with inadvertent consequences for the sexual development of *both* girls and boys growing up within it.

Many radical feminists who have spent the last decade stigmatising and overemphasising the connections between autogynephilia and transness will, I assume, be outraged by such thoughts. Still, I think of these points as wholly compatible with the evidence-based feminism I prefer. In the next and final chapter, I continue my feminist line, this time taking issue with modern activism, and in particular with certain trends within feminism itself.

A Better Activism in Future

In this book, I've rejected gender identity theory. Since current trans activism enthusiastically embraces gender identity theory, it follows that I don't believe ordinary trans people are well served by current trans activism. Trans people are trans people. We should get over it. They deserve to be safe, to be visible throughout society without shame or stigma, and to have exactly the life opportunities non-trans people do. Their transness makes no difference to any of this. What trans people don't deserve, however, is to be publicly misrepresented in philosophical terms that make no sense; nor to have their everyday struggles instrumentalised in the name of political initiatives most didn't ask for, and which alienate other groups by rigidly encroaching on *their* hard-won rights. Nor do trans people deserve to be terrified by activist propaganda into thinking themselves more vulnerable to violence than they actually are.

Current trans activism needs a different vision and agenda. Equally, I think, ordinary women haven't been well served by recent mainstream feminism. In this chapter, by way of a conclusion, I'll outline four opinionated guidelines for a better activism in future.

Be more non-binary

We are living through a time of online outrage and increasing irrationalism, and the combination has not been a happy one for public discussion. Generally, shallow emotion seems to be in the driving seat for many keyboard warriors: not the slow burn of genuine anger that fuels the prolonged, difficult pursuit of a worthwhile goal, but rather a feel-good performative outrage whose main expression is typing furious snark on to a computer screen before switching over to Netflix. In this febrile atmosphere, and where most interactions take place in front of a virtual audience, there's an increased emphasis on 'winning' arguments, in the sense of getting others to back down or look humiliated, rather than in the sense of getting things right. People often define their own positions on a given issue in reaction to some other position, mentally treated as the antagonist it's important to reject (and be seen to reject) at all costs. Many then seem psychologically incapable of making common cause with those at the 'other' envisaged pole, partly because it might be interpreted by onlookers as a defeat or a climbdown. Critical thinking seems to be receding as the will to (be seen to) win surges. Things are no different in arguments about how to arrange society for the mutual benefit of trans people and women. On the one side are trans activists, whose views have been discussed throughout this book. On the other are groups of feminists: some radical, and some of them known as 'gender-critical'. Both groups contain trans and non-trans members.

This book is at least partly a feminist one, broadly speaking. At various points, I've made what I hope is a strong case for the interests of women in particular. So far, though, I haven't gone into much detail about the views of feminists who tend to oppose trans activism. I'll do so briefly now.

Radical feminism has roots in the Second Wave of feminism, from roughly the 1960s onwards. Broadly speaking, radical feminists think that sexism and misogyny – i.e. ingrained contempt for women – permeate all social and institutional structures, so that a radical restructuring is ultimately needed for women's 'liberation'. Women and girls' oppression is thought of as grounded in something called 'the patriarchy' – a systematic set of social relations that acts to disadvantage and immobilise females relative to males, and (on many accounts) to use them for their reproductive labour. The patriarchy operates not just in the public sphere (in workplaces, law, economics and politics) but also in the private one (family, the home, sexual relations and love). It permeates academia, culture and even language itself. It's particularly evident in sexual-assault statistics, prostitution and sex trafficking, surrogacy tourism in the Global South, pornography, domestic violence, femicide, sexual objectification, stalking and other social problems adversely affecting women in particular, which laws and wider societies seem mostly incapable of resolving, and to which sometimes they seem indifferent. The patriarchy also operates in women's heads, internalised developmentally as a set of restrictive stereotypes about what women and girls are permitted to be or do; and the feeling women and girls are automatically 'less than' or 'other than' the central presence in the world: men.

For radical feminists, attempts on the part of trans activist organisations to change women's legal rights, and to alter their spaces, resources and language – while in practice largely leaving men's intact – is just the patriarchy doing its business as usual. The fact that, technically, females with misaligned gender identities are now explicitly permitted by many institutional policies to enter male bathrooms, changing rooms, sports teams and clubs, and have access to male resources, has made negligible difference to men in practice. It's still mostly trans women who are pushing for entry into the opposite sex's spaces and resources. Given average biological differences between the sexes discussed in Chapter 3, it's still mostly women who are adversely affected by their successes. For radical feminists, this isn't a coincidence. Nor is it a coincidence that, for instance, recent changes in law and policy have taken away female-only facilities and female-only sports but have left, for instance, the laws of primogeniture and inheritance for a first-born aristocratic male – trans woman or otherwise – untouched. When secret fraternal society the Freemasons recently announced they would henceforth accept trans women and trans men as members, but continue to exclude 'cis' women, this is roughly what radical feminists would have predicted.[1]

Alongside the radical feminists fighting trans activist demands are gender-critical feminists. These tend to be critically focused on 'gender' understood as a set of restrictive social stereotypes (GENDER2 from Chapter 1). They share this preoccupation with radical feminists but tend to be less focused on patriarchy as an overarching explanatory factor, and less attracted to the separatism to which some radical feminists aspire. Many gender-critical feminists are also blank-slate feminists, holding that all behavioural and psychological average differences are developmentally acquired, and that none are structured into sexed brains in the womb or at puberty. Their utopia is sometimes described as a 'gender-free' world. But to be gender critical doesn't necessitate this extreme a position; it means just that you hold that many behavioural and psychological differences between men and women are developmentally acquired, damaging and could (and should) have been different. Gender-critical feminists particularly rebel against the idea, implicit in gender identity theory, that what makes you a woman or man is a feeling. As far as they are concerned, this feeling could only be, deep down, about the applicability of restrictive and damaging sex-associated stereotypes to yourself. To call a boy a 'girl' because he says he feels like a girl – where in practice this boils down to his liking make-up, Barbie dolls and sewing, and not liking sport or war games – is to capitulate to society's restrictive expectation that these are inherently female activities and preferences.

Not all feminists are against trans activism or gender identity theory, however. Many 'Third Wave' feminists are for it. Third Wave feminism is defined mostly in reaction to Second Wave feminism, and its favoured axioms are discussed at various points in this book. Knowingly or not, Third Wave feminism is strongly influenced by postmodernism and post-structuralism.[2] So, for instance, many Third Wave feminists seem to think, like Judith Butler and Thomas Laqueur, both discussed in Chapter 2, that sex is a social construct. Their political focus is a disparate 'gender', understood as a kind of performance, and untethered to the supposedly illusory idea of natural biological sex. Third Wave feminists also tend to think, as mentioned in Chapter 5, that neither 'females' nor 'women' can function as a coherent politically relevant category, and so conclude that feminism needs to recalibrate its political objects (I'll return to this in the next section). And in a liberal vein, many are firmly focused on notions like 'choice' and 'identity': for if biology is dead, or more accurately never lived, then who you are as a woman seems to be up to you. As we have also had cause to notice in this book in several places, there's a big emphasis in Third Wave feminism on 'inclusion'. As academic R. Claire Snyder puts it, Third Wave feminists 'depict their version of feminism as more inclusive and racially diverse than the second wave', even going so far as to define Third Wave feminism as 'a form of inclusiveness'.[3] Radical and gender-critical feminists are often criticised by Third Wave feminists as 'exclusionary': as overly focused on promoting a white, middle-class perspective, and of excluding women who don't share this perspective – including trans women.

These then are the two entrenched 'sides' thrashing it out in public about whether trans women are women and what that means. On one side are trans activists and Third Wave feminists; on the other, radical and gender-critical feminists. In the race to (be seen to) 'win', a number of less than ideal argumentative strategies are employed. One constant is arguments about which group gets to count as the 'real' feminists. Rather than actually arguing about substantive points, energy is strategically diverted into arguments between feminist factions as to who are the true keepers of the feminist flame, mirroring a dynamic within other political movements – who is 'really' on the Left or on the Right, for instance. Effectively what each is doing is arguing for their own preferred version of doctrine. When pursued in a spirit of genuinely curious inquiry, this is an activity that can help keep a movement invigorated and self-critical. When used strategically to get another activist to shut up about a substantive conclusion you disagree with her about, it's a very different phenomenon.

In order to be seen to win, there's also a frequent appeal to strawmen: that is, the noisy attacking of flimsy positions held by no serious opponent, rather than critical engagement with the more complex and nuanced positions opponents actually *do* hold. The latter are harder to attack successfully. In the row about whether trans women are women, and whether women-only spaces should be open to all those with female gender identities, this shows up in the presentation by trans activists, as supposed 'gotchas', of facile points like 'not all women have uteruses', 'some women have beards', 'some lesbians are violent too', and the stunningly casual 'women will get raped in changing rooms anyway'. These are observations no one reasonably well informed would disagree with, but which make no difference either way to the better versions of the arguments they purport to discredit.

A third destructive presence is the ubiquitous use of *ad hominems*: the unsubtle mention of supposed features of a person's character, identity or motives in order to try to discredit the conclusions of their argument. In some limited circumstances these factors are relevant to the success or otherwise of arguments, I think, but if so, the relevance has to be carefully – even forensically – established. They are not automatically relevant, and certainly not when selectively picked up on the flimsiest evidence, and used as rhetorical cudgels against some people, but not against identical others. Often the phenomenon seems particularly marked within fights among feminists. A case in point is the way Third Wave feminists – often themselves white, middle class, and 'cis' – complain that the arguments of opponents cannot be sound because their authors are white, middle class and cis. The concept of privilege is also weaponised by all sides, used not so much as a serious tool of analysis but as a playground insult, and often producing the amusing spectacle of one group of people castigating another group of identical background, education and financial means for their 'privilege'. Meanwhile, 'transphobe!' and 'misogynist!' are chucked about liberally.

The frequent insult-strewn denigration of the motives, characters and physical looks of so-called 'TERFs' – by trans activists and even by some Third Wave feminists – tells its own familiar sexist, ageist story. While professing to stand against restrictive feminine stereotypes for women generally, certain feminists still apparently don't mind very quickly representing women they disagree with – but somehow not the men – as failing to be 'kind', so revealing themselves to be happy to invoke a restrictive maternal stereotype when it suits them. Those who dare to argue in public against so-called kind and inclusive positions are accused of bad faith and even of dogwhistling to the far right – as if they couldn't possibly be addressing the mainstream majority straightforwardly, in good faith, and for rational purposes.

But radical and gender-critical feminists bear their share of responsibility too. From this side, there is frequent casual denigration of trans women's characters, and also the commonplace suggestion, without evidence, that any trans woman's reasons for transition are likely to be malign. The phenomenon of autogynephilia is played up, hyperbolised and stigmatised, and other possible motives for MTF transition ignored. While many critics of gender identity theory emphasise – as I have also done in this book – that their points are not predicated on the idea all or most trans women are potentially predatory, some radical feminists apparently proceed explicitly on this inflammatory and unevidenced assumption. Some radical feminists are apparently so averse to trans women that they would verbally attack even those trans women arguing *against* current trans activism, and *against* gender identity theory and its consequences. So, for instance, radical feminist academic Julia Long has written contemptuously of the trans women who are critical of gender identity theory, and who 'ingratiate themselves' into public meetings about the GRA through 'linguistic manoeuvres which involve making claims to their legitimate and customary accommodation within the social group "women" whilst simultaneously acknowledging that they are male'. She writes: 'This combination appears to entirely bamboozle audiences, causing them to lose their critical faculties and instead endorse the men's utterances with rapturous applause and approving... comments.'[4] This is severe polarisation indeed. A less patronising way of looking at audience responses might be that those attending these meetings are not so blinded with animosity towards the male sex that they can't recognise a mutually beneficial common cause when they see it.

There is also, within radical and gender-critical feminism, a regrettable tendency to talk about trans men and detransitioned women who have had medical intervention in the past as 'ruined', 'mutilated' or having 'wrecked their lives'. If these feminists seriously want to reach out to younger generations in future, and especially to the increasing numbers of women detransitioners, talking dehumanisingly and crudely about them in the instrumental pursuit of political goals is not the way to do it.

Some within radical feminism are also responsible for a perversely literal, selectively uncharitable approach to language choices. Again according to Long, nobody should use the words 'transsexual' or 'trans woman' *at all*, because these words imply it's possible to change sex, when actually it's not. She writes of people like me, who 'correctly insist that it is not possible to change sex' but nonetheless 'breezily continue to use the term "transsexual" or "transwoman" as if such a change were possible and as if such individuals exist'.[5] Presumably, then, Long doesn't use the term 'healthy food' (because food can't literally be in good health); never talks about the 'Overton Window' (because after all, it's not literally a window); and insists slow worms don't exist (because they aren't actually worms). This line of Long's and of other radical feminists gives succour to the otherwise unmerited narrative of trans activists that their critics 'want trans people not to exist'. The truth is that, while the surface forms of wholly unknown words can be misleading to the unwary, good communication about their meanings can remove lingering misunderstandings and so make surface forms practically irrelevant. As long as it's clearly understood, as I have explained in this book, that transsexuals and trans women don't literally change sex, the words 'transsexual' and 'trans woman' are powerless to mean otherwise.

Despite this polarisation, there are areas in which common cause might still be found. In particular, many people in trans activism are, like radical and gender-critical feminists, strongly motivated to reduce the cultural stigma of sex nonconformity. Although there are robust disagreements about the best means to achieve this, and the language used and background commitments differ, in a broad sense all sides want to break down oppressive sex-associated stereotypes in their own way. That's a good starting point, at least. Meanwhile, non-binary and 'agender' people in particular could conceivably unite with gender-critical feminists to try to loosen the grip of the many stereotypes to do with masculinity and femininity, which each group tends to see as inapplicable to themselves.

Generally speaking, I think, all sides should be more non-binary, as it were; each should move away from 'either with us or against us' narratives and look for compromise where there is some to be found. An example was explored in Chapter 5, where I talked about the limited role for personal immersion in fiction about sex change. Effectively, trans people are stuck in between those trans activists who say their sex should *never* be referred to, and those feminists who say it *always* should. The argument of Chapter 5 was that, if people are conscious and thoughtful about it, they can, if they choose, find an interim position involving immersion in a fiction at least some of the time; and if not that, then at least, omit mentioning sex in interpersonal contexts where it isn't relevant. And it's unhelpful and conceptually inadequate to insist, as Julia Long does, that we don't use any word to refer to trans women other than 'men'. We clearly need more fine-grained descriptive concepts, in addition to a completely generic 'men', to refer to what is a coherent and interesting group of people within the wider category. Trans women and trans men each deserve non-inflammatory vocabulary which articulates their particular experiences, and which can be fed into political and legal discussion of their particular needs.

My final example of being more non-binary is in the currently apparently intractable row about sex-separated spaces such as bathrooms, changing rooms and hostel dormitories. Until recently, these were sex-segregated as a social norm for women's protection, and the norm was mostly applied on the basis of ordinary visual inspection from fellow users. People who looked like men in women's spaces could be challenged with confidence by women there. People who looked like women in men's spaces could be challenged with confidence there too, if users so wished, though the need was less urgent. As discussed in Chapter 3, these norms pose problems for any women in those spaces who look like the opposite sex. However, they are also a valuable form of protection for most women, who, after all, are getting undressed or sleeping in these spaces, and so who – given facts outlined in Chapter 2 – are more vulnerable to sexual assault, voyeurism and exhibitionism from men than usual.

These days, trans activist organisations like Stonewall are attempting to change the social norms for women-only facilities in many institutions nationally so that men can access them solely on the basis of an inner feeling of misaligned gender identity. So now, on the explicit terms of current institutional policies, women in those spaces cannot reasonably challenge people who look like men in those spaces, because, for all the women know, they might permissibly be there ('respect their identity', 'carry on with your day').

This isn't directly a problem about 'passing' trans women

entering such spaces, because they, precisely, pass, and so – as well as being practically impossible to control – their presence in the spaces is unnoticed, so doing nothing to disrupt the social norm. (In this sense it's true, as trans activists sometimes say, that 'trans women have been using women-only spaces unproblematically for years'. They mean passing trans women, and in that sense, they are right.) However, encouraging trans women who are *not* passing – and even, potentially, those who have made no real alteration to their physical appearance whatsoever – to be in a women's changing room, by virtue of a misaligned gender identity, is a completely different matter, for it disrupts the general social norm significantly. It effectively makes it permissible for *any man* – trans woman or not, mis-aligned gender identity or not – to enter, because the criterion is an inner, invisible feeling, undetectable to the naked eye, and so impossible for other users to gainsay.

By exactly the same token, though, the permissible presence of passing trans *men* – by definition, women visibly indistin-guishable from men – in women-only bathrooms and changing rooms, *also* disrupts the social norms that normally make it reasonable for women to challenge people who look like men there. It also looks unreasonable to expect passing trans men to shoulder the psychological stress of entering such spaces with the misunderstandings that can then entail. So, insofar as radical and gender-critical feminists should – by dint of being concerned with female interests – also be concerned with the political interests of trans men, the obvious thing for *all* sides to do is lobby for 'third' spaces, where women and men who either look or feel unlike their own sex can use facilities and feel more comfortable. Effectively, public discussion has become polarised, into 'trans people should always use their own sex's spaces' and 'trans people should always use the opposite sex's spaces' (or the even more extreme: 'all spaces should be gender-neutral'), but *these are not the only options*. If Stonewall had put its considerable financial resources and influence into joining with feminists to lobby for third spaces within institutions, a huge amount of animosity and vitriol could have been avoided.

Stop changing the subject

It's a notable feature of recent mainstream feminist and gay activism that each has expanded its original remit significantly. Third Wave feminism is now widely conceived of as for 'all women, including trans women'. Sometimes it's even described as 'for everybody', rather than for just those two groups in particular. This isn't the reasonable idea that a world free of sexism is better for both women and men. It's the idea that feminism as a political project *should no longer just be about sexism*. As the website *Everyday Feminism* puts it: 'Feminism strives to end the discrimination, exploitation, and oppression of people due to their gender, sexual orientation, race, class, and other differences and supports people in being free to determine their own lives for themselves.'[6] In other words, feminism is now supposed to be everybody's mum.

Meanwhile, gay activism has, relatively recently, become 'LGBT' activism and so has merged with – and arguably been taken over by – trans activism. In some parts of the culture, this has expanded yet further into 'LGBTQIA+' activism, standing for 'Lesbian, Gay, Bisexual, Transsexual, Queer, Intersex, Asexual' 'plus' any other sexual identities not covered explicitly in that abbreviation, like being polyamorous or 'aromantic' ('having no desire for romantic relationships'). Either way, LGBT activism double-counts heterosexual trans people as a new political focus: first for being trans, and second, for also being 'gay' or 'lesbian', understood in terms of their gender identities (see Chapter 3).

There are different background reasons for the expansion of the remit in each case, but the net effect is the same: a dilution of political focus, increasing vagueness as to what the goals are supposed to be, and conflict as various new and some-times competing interests have to be balanced – or more likely pitted – against each other. In particular, with the admission of trans women into the remits of both feminism and LGBT activism, old habits of male socialisation have apparently died hard. In many cases trans women are now at the forefront of feminism and LGBT activism respectively, with dissenting women ignored or demoted to the back.

In the case of mainstream feminism, one effect of this has been feeble paralysis where there should have been vigorous action. Energy has been poured into carefully avoiding the word 'woman' in potentially inflammatory contexts, rather than mounting firm resistance to the multiple encroachments on sex-based rights, spaces and resources that LGBT activist organisations simultaneously have been pursuing. The failure of mainstream feminist organisations to provide effective resistance to these challenges, on behalf of the women and girls they still purport to represent, has been marked. For instance, during the Government's public consultation in 2018 – about whether 'self-ID' should be the only criterion for granting a Gender Recognition Certificate, and about whether single-sex exemptions in the Equality Act should be retained, to allow genuinely women-only services – the official responses of major feminist organisations like the Fawcett Society, the Women's Equality Party and Women's Aid were, at best, indecipherably bland and timid, and at worst, missing in action. It was left to individuals and grassroots organisations like Woman's Place UK, Fair Play for Women, Transgender

Trend, For Women Scotland, Scottish Women, Women and Girls Scotland and We Need To Talk to take up the slack in fighting the proposed changes to the GRA. These groups held meetings, made websites and wrote blog posts, marshalling their tiny resources highly effectively against well-embedded organisations like Stonewall, Mermaids and the Scottish Trans Alliance, each of which receive hundreds of thousands or even millions of pounds every year, in some cases from government bodies themselves. For their pains, organisers and supporters of these grassroots groups have been repeatedly slandered and vilified, while many mainstream feminist organisations studiously look the other way.

In a similar fashion, LGBT activist organisations putatively fighting on behalf of same-sex attracted people have effectively become toothless, wherever the interests of same-sex attracted people and heterosexual trans people have clashed. For instance, Stonewall has had absolutely nothing critical to say about emerging reports that there is a disproportionately high presence of same-sex attracted children and teens in gender identity clinics. Worse, it has actively forged alliances with Mermaids, the organisation that propagates a SOR model of gender identity for children, and which as we have seen apparently weaponises false suicide statistics which may well frighten parents into acceding to social and medical transition. Stonewall has also co-sponsored the 'Memorandum of Understanding on Conversion Therapy', which prohibits professional UK therapists from doing anything other than 'affirm' a misaligned gender identity, whether found in a same-sex-attracted minor or otherwise. Again, it has been left to grassroots organisations such as the LGB Alliance to take up the interests of gay people where they conflict with those of trans people.

In both feminism and LGBT activism, the dilution of

energies brought about by an expansion of political focus has been exacerbated by the fact that the types of people now assumed to be able to participate, as central actors speaking 'for' those in the movement generally, has also been expanded. A new phenomenon has arisen, which I think of as 'The Emperor's New Dress': namely, a trans woman being asked to participate in some role, for or on behalf of women, for which they have little relevant expertise other than being trans. This has produced sometimes breathtakingly surreal juxtapositions: for one, the platforming of trans woman dominatrix Hailey Heartless as a speaker at the Vancouver Women's March in 2018.[7] Heartless makes videos, including at least one where she imagines humiliating a 'little TERF' sexually.[8] In the UK, trans woman and journalist Jane Fae – who before her transition at fifty campaigned extensively against the censorship of extreme pornography, including sadism, bestiality and necrophilia – now self-describes as a feminist and writes for the *Guardian* under that description. In academic events on feminism, it's now common to include, as a platformed speaker, at least one trans woman, sometimes with no relevant research whatsoever – as in, for instance, 'The Future of Feminism' event run at the LSE in 2016, whose headline speaker was a trans woman philosophy professor with no record of feminist publications at the time, and who had transitioned only the previous year.[9] In 2017, a nineteen-year-old trans woman, Lily Madigan, was voted in as Women's Officer of the Rochester and Strood Constituency Labour Party. And at the British Film Institute in 2018, trans woman Munroe Bergdorf – not a filmmaker – was invited to be the keynote speaker at 'Woman With A Movie Camera' summit, ostensibly for women in the already intensely male-dominated movie business.[10]

As new demographics are brought into the fold, so too are new interests, unlike the old ones and in some cases directly opposed to them. A good example of mission creep is found in Stonewall's lobbying to alter laws pertaining to 'sex by deception', wherever those laws would criminalise trans people initiating sexual relations with others but not announcing their biological sex. In their 2015 'A Vision for Change' document, Stonewall presented this as an infringement of trans people's 'privacy'.[11] Changing the laws around sex by deception is also taken up in several academic articles by Professor Alex Sharpe, a legal scholar at the University of Warwick and member of the Trans Equality Legal Initiative (TELI). In a blog post, Sharpe seems to imply that any person duped into sexual relations with another person while being positively misled about their biological sex must still somehow 'know', for according to Sharpe, 'ignorance is a form of knowledge'. Though Sharpe's discussion is directly about the Gayle Newland criminal case – in which (non-trans) female Newland was convicted for having sex with a woman while pretending to be man – it's not hard to see the potential relevance to trans people (like Sharpe herself, who self-describes as lesbian). In poetic vein, Sharpe takes us into the mind of Newland's victim and asks: do 'we' (i.e. does she) 'not see our lover's face, do we not sense her in other ways? Do we not breathe her in, feel her touch, experience the contours of her body, feel her breath upon our skin, the timbre of her voice? And are we not undone in such moments, irrespective of the eyes? Is it right in such circumstances to disown our desires because we are retrospectively disappointed?'[12] In other words, despite the criminal conviction of Newland for deception, this law professor is apparently arguing that Newland's victim must have wanted sex with Newland all along. Given the relatively high proportion of self-identified 'lesbians' among trans women, it's also not hard, from a perhaps less poetic perspective, to see the potential costs to lesbians, should Sharpe's favoured legislative changes go ahead.

With the expansion of LGBT activism, relatively suddenly the people referred to as 'intersex' have also found themselves a political focus alongside trans people, so explaining their presence in the extended 'LGBTQIA+' grouping. This is seen to further validate the inclusion of trans people as a political focus. As we've seen in Chapter 4, having a DSD doesn't entail having a misaligned gender identity, and nor does it entail any non-standard sexual identity either. That is, the existence of people with DSDs is used by LGBT activist organisations instrumentally to argue (as we have seen, wrongly) that 'sex is a spectrum' in a way that benefits public perception of trans people, because it tends to distract from the fact nearly all trans people are born with standard chromosomal configurations and morphologies. The inclusion does not appear to properly recognise the separate plight of people with DSDs, many of whom suffer debilitating symptoms, have undergone traumatic surgeries, and sometimes struggle to come to terms with their conditions. They deserve better than to be shoehorned into a narrative that isn't theirs, and to have their genuine political needs obscured.

Why have these activist movements expanded recently in this way? In feminism, the reason is partly ideological. It proceeds from the true, common-sense observation that women's experiences and social situations differ across the world – including differences in particular challenges or disadvantages faced, and advantages won – to the bizarre conclusion, encountered in Chapter 5 and popularised in Third Wave feminism from the 1990s onwards, that women cannot function as a unit for a coherent political focus at all. The philosopher Elizabeth Spelman takes this line in her influential 1988 book *Inessential Woman: Problems of Exclusion in Feminist Thought*. In doing so, she apparently forgets the existence and function of abstract concepts: or, more strictly, the existence of one abstract concept in particular – WOMAN – since strangely she doesn't apply the same arguments to the concepts of MAN or WORKING-CLASS PERSON or BLACK PERSON or GAY PERSON, etc., and yet exactly the same spurious moves could be made there too. For instance, as legal scholar Kimberlé Crenshaw (of whom more in the next section) points out, the anti-racism movement is not similarly affected by the obvious fact not all members of a given racial group have suffered equally under racism. Crenshaw writes: 'The fact that some sectors of a population might have suffered more under a particular racial regime due to cofactors such as class or age or disability has generally not been seen as evidence that the initial frame of group-based harm is itself problematic.'[13]

Abstract concepts help us pick out general classes or groups of things, for certain explanatory purposes, independently of local differences at the level of particulars. The concept of a TREE, for instance, covers oaks, ashes, rowans, redwoods, etc., as well as covering differences between particular oaks, ashes, rowans, redwoods, etc. We need the concept TREE for some important explanatory purposes: for instance, trees, as opposed to other plants, are more likely to be hit by lightning, in virtue of their relative height. So too does WOMAN (understood as adult human female) feature in many important explanations, as we have seen. For instance: women, as opposed to men, can get pregnant, and are more likely to have certain health challenges, attain distinctive performance levels in sport, face certain distinctive socio-economic challenges and be vulnerable to sexual assault, and so on. It was never the claim these things happen to *all* women, just as the comparable claim about trees wasn't that all trees get hit by lightning. The fact women differ greatly in their local experiences and social circumstances – as do, of course, men, working-class people, black people, trans people (and so on, for any human grouping) – shows only that the concepts WOMAN, MAN, WORKING-CLASS PERSON, BLACK PERSON, TRANS PERSON (etc.) can't explain everything about social situations on their own. As has so often been the message in this book, we need more concepts to cover the important sub-groupings and variations. But that doesn't make the original concepts worthless.

The move from 'feminism is for women' to 'feminism is for everyone' has other less intellectual origins too, shared by gay activism's move from 'LGB' to 'LGBTQIA+'. One of these, I suggest, is a desire for novelty and reinvention in the public mind. Another is a kind of unconscious mental capitulation to the social forces which made feminism and gay activism so important to pursue, in their original senses, in the first place: the abiding dislike for women and gay people which still exists as significant oppressive forces in society, and which causes people to discount their interests or even positively act against them. If your one job is to fight, fairly hopelessly, against the persistent tides of denigration, interest-relegation and mockery faced by women and gays, it's probably not surprising you eventually end up altering your own job description.

Another influence, at least in the case of feminism and lesbian activism – fairly ironically – is that women and girls tend to be socially valued for qualities associated with the maternal: excessive kindness, the self-sacrifice of your own needs in relation to others, a lack of firm boundaries, and an enhanced sense of moral responsibility for putting things right. This stereotype often informs women and girls' own self-conceptions and so makes them more susceptible to complaints they should be centring the needs of others who are not 'themselves'.

Yet another generally salient factor is the current cultural mania for 'diversity and inclusion', taken as some kind of mindless mantra without genuine thought being given to what it actually means or should be doing. Diversity and inclusion sound good but are not coherent goals unless located in a wider explanation of why they bring value. They are best understood as indirect signs that a system is working fairly; signs that minority groups have unfettered access to institutions at every level, without their minority group membership counting against them. A diverse and inclusive organisation is one where – unfashionable phrase – equal opportunity genuinely happens. To this extent, our institutions and organisations should be diverse and inclusive as an indirect sign of their good health. These days, though, we see diversity and inclusion pursued as vague goals in their own right, sometimes in areas in which they are completely inappropriate. So, for instance, earlier in this book we saw the Butlerian idea that our very *concepts* should be 'inclusive': WOMAN should 'include' trans women, and LESBIAN should 'include' trans women attracted to women, or else 'marginalise' them. But, as I argued in Chapter 5, the whole point of concepts is to be *exclusive*, not in an ethically suspect sense, but in the reasonable sense of providing a working cognitive tool to help us pick out a distinctive kind of entity in the world, in which we have important explanatory interests. In contemporary culture, the idea has now taken hold that our political movements should be diverse and inclusive, not just in who gets to participate, but also *in their political projects*. Yet this is to dilute their point. As many feminists have pointed out, it's the equivalent of moving from 'Black lives matter' to 'All lives matter': it significantly changes the subject, and so is to the detriment of the people who were the original political focus, yet without the material changes in their circumstances that would justify this diversion.

Feminism is only for women and girls, in the sense that women and girls should be its exclusive political project.

Post-structuralist and Third Wave arguments have provided no convincing reason to deny this. Similarly, gay and bisexual people should be the exclusive political project of gay activism, with separate campaigns for lesbians and gay men where their interests differ. Trans people should be the exclusive political project of a separate trans activism. If there is capital to be gained by separate movements sometimes deliberately uniting for well-defined ends, then that is one thing, but merging permanently is quite another. Sometimes this simple point is confused with the claim that feminists, gay activists and trans activists, as individuals, cannot care about other groups, or organise in their interests. Of course they can. The claims just made about feminism, gay and trans activism are claims about coherent political projects, not about the people that undertake them. Still: with a professional feminist (pussy) hat on, your job is to argue for women; what you do in your own time is up to you. When the distinctive social challenges of being a woman and a girl cease, feminism will no longer be needed. In the meantime, there is enough to do without taking on the struggles of others *under the guise of feminism*. By exactly the same token, professional gay activism is for – in the sense of directed towards, by definition – only those people who have homosexual or bisexual orientations, and who tend to face distinctive challenges because of this. Trans activism is only for trans people, who face distinctive challenges because of being trans. The people in charge of the organisations that purport to represent these groups need to stop changing the subject.

Be more intersectional

Equally, though, the people in those organisations need to be more intersectional. For those readers who would place the

cause of intersectionality squarely on the side of current mainstream feminism and trans activism, this suggestion may come
as a surprise. That's because current mainstream feminism
and trans activism tend to misrepresent the valuable lessons
of intersectionality. These days, it's often argued trans women
must be women, because feminism should be 'intersectional'
and so should be for 'all women', including those kinds of
women excluded from consideration as women in the historical past. 'People used to think black women weren't women'
so the argument goes. 'So trans women must be women.' In
fact, this argument has nothing to do with intersectionality:
you could take the word 'intersectional' out, and you'd still
have the basic form. That form is: 'if a particular group has
been wrongly excluded from a given category in the past, then,
where a completely different group is presently being excluded
from that same category, this exclusion must be wrong too'.
Obviously, though, that a mistaken inference has been made in
the past about category membership doesn't mean every similarly structured inference made now about the same category
is a mistake. People used to think whales weren't mammals;
this doesn't mean mackerel are mammals now. That this line
has looked even slightly attractive to anyone is presumably
because it implicitly relies upon a Butlerian view of concepts
as 'exclusionary' weapons of dominance and hierarchy, and
not the view of concepts I argued for in Chapter 5: concepts as
cognitive tools, responding to the world, and to non-arbitrary
shared interests in it, and used in the services of reference,
explanation and prediction.

Another prominent recent critic of intersectionality is
Douglas Murray. In his popular book *The Madness of
Crowds*, Murray lays many current ills at the door of intersectionality, describing it as 'the invitation to spend the rest
of our lives attempting to work out each and every identity

and vulnerability claim in ourselves and others and then organize along whichever system of justice emerges from the perpetually moving hierarchy which we uncover'.[14] I think Murray is confusing intersectionality as an analytic tool with its wider popular subsumption into identity politics. You can be against popular identity politics – I am – and still think the concept of intersectionality, as originally presented, is a useful tool for analysing systems of discrimination. Properly understood, intersectionality is the point that, in the words of the black feminist Combahee River Collective, writing in 1977, 'the major systems of oppression are interlocking'; so that, for instance, 'there is such a thing as racial-sexual oppression which is neither solely racial nor solely sexual'.[15] Or, as the legal scholar mentioned earlier who coined the term and who has done most to promote the concept, Kimberlé Crenshaw, puts it: 'Black women can experience discrimination in ways that are both similar to and different from those experienced by white women and Black men. Black women sometimes experience discrimination in ways similar to white women's experiences; sometimes they share very similar experiences with Black men. Yet often they experience double-discrimination – the combined effects of practices which discriminate on the basis of race, and on the basis of sex. And sometimes, they experience discrimination as Black women – not the sum of race and sex discrimination, but as Black women.'[16] Despite the picture painted by Murray, there is no automatic implication here that being oppressed as a black woman is the most interesting thing about you as a black woman; nor that presenting some other arbitrary feature of yourself as a putative grounds for discrimination would be equally interesting, as Murray implies. If only traditional grounds for discrimination against others – race, socio-economic class, sex, sexual orientation – *were* 'perpetually moving'. From where I stand, they seem depressingly static, even if present culture tries to ignore them.

Crenshaw's work is full of concrete, patiently evidenced examples of how intersecting discrimination works in practice within legal systems and employment contexts. Black women are often treated as the same as white women for the purposes of feminism, and the same as black men for the purposes of anti-racism. In both cases, they tend to be treated as subject to exactly the same forms of discrimination, and it's assumed their problems are subject to identical remedies. Yet this unfairly ignores important differences from both situations, partly because of the double inflection of two forms of discrimination at once.[17] Equally, being subject to two major forms of discrimination at once makes it hard to use current legal systems to establish the presence of either in an individual case, because models are set up to recognise the causal influence of one form of discrimination at a time.[18] This too has discriminatory effects.

Part of what Crenshaw shows in her writing is that feminism cannot take 'being a woman or girl' as the only relevant criterion in formulating political action in the name of women and girls. Feminism also needs to get concrete information about how being a woman or girl causally feeds into patterns of discrimination in particular social and cultural contexts. This will differ from context to context. Being an Afghan woman in Afghanistan will differ from being an Afro-American woman in the US, and both will differ from being a white woman in the UK. Additionally, between white women in the UK (for instance) there will be relevant local class-based and socio-economic differences.

For me, this is what being intersectional essentially demands: close, patient scrutiny of the multiple background factors systematically involved in a person's undeserved plight, and an examination of how they interact. Feminism needs to be responsive where necessary to these local differences. It also needs constantly to monitor its practice for bias towards the interests of a particular conception of what women and girls need or want, based on an illegitimately narrow perspective, inapplicable to others. So, for instance, when some Second Wave white feminists argued in the 70s and 80s that unpaid domestic labour in the home was a source of oppressive restriction for all women, black radical feminist scholar bell hooks pointed out that, perhaps unlike white women, being in the home was a source of safety and affirmation for black women: 'Historically, black women have identified work in the context of family as humanizing labor, work that affirms their identity as women, as human beings showing love and care, the very gestures of humanity white supremacist ideology claimed black people were incapable of expressing. In contrast to labor done in a caring environment inside the home, labor outside the home was most often seen as stressful, degrading, and dehumanizing.'[19]

Mainstream feminist organisations in the UK have embraced the conclusions of gender identity theory enthusiastically. In doing so, they have failed to properly demonstrate, on behalf of women and girls, the ethos of intersectionality to which nearly all pay lip service. They have prioritised too narrow a perspective of (trans) women's interests, and have failed to notice when the consequences of their political choices have impacted disproportionately on women falling into two or more vulnerable groups simultaneously. Take, for instance, the demand that trans women should be housed in the female prison estate, and the failure of mainstream feminist organisations to object, or apparently even to consider how this might affect women prisoners. 20 per cent of the UK women's prison population is BAME, as compared to 11.9 per cent of the population generally. In 2018, 3,262 out of 7,745 women entering women's prisons were recorded as being of no fixed abode on arrival. Seven in ten women in prison report being victims of domestic violence in the past, and 31 per cent have spent time in local authority care as children. 53 per cent report having experienced emotional, physical or sexual abuse during childhood. Half of the women entering prison report needing help with a drug problem. And 80 per cent are in prison for non-violent offences.[20] Yet in 2015 the mainstream feminist establishment turned a blind eye to the admission of trans women with convictions for violence, some without any medical intervention or GRCs, into the female prison estate alongside these intensely vulnerable women. It continues to turn a blind eye today.

The two women prisoners sexually assaulted in 2018 by trans woman Karen White, a convicted paedophile on remand in a woman's prison for GBH and rape, are examples of the way women from particularly vulnerable societal groups have been treated as collateral in the service of nominal 'inclusivity'. Another instructive example is the way that, in the rearrangement of general social space to accommodate the perceived needs of trans people, women and girls of relatively lower socio-economic means have been almost completely ignored. One 1999 study looking at data within a decade suggested that 'places where women's average levels of income are higher also tend to be places with lower levels of rape'. It goes on: 'Residing in places where incomes are higher apparently enables women to afford a more safe and secure living environment, that is, to live in better, more crime-free neighborhoods, rely more on private versus public transportation, and the like.'[21] One might also add: it also allows them to rely more on private versus public organisations, such as, for instance, private sports clubs and health spas, instead of council-owned sports centres, public swimming pools and soft play areas. *The Times* in 2018 reported there had been 134 complaints of sexual misconduct in council-owned sports centre and swimming pool changing rooms the previous year, and of those, '120 related to incidents that took place in unisex changing rooms and 14 to incidents in single-sex changing rooms'.[22] These relevant facts seem to be ignored by organisations, including local government organisations, rushing to instigate self-identification as the official means of entry into women-only spaces on their premises. They also seem to be ignored by the often well-off and well-educated people arguing that organisations are right to do so.

Less well-off women and women in prison – who of course intersect – are not the only groups of women recently abandoned by the mainstream feminist establishment in their enthusiastic embrace of the conclusions of gender identity theory. They have been equally unconcerned with the potential (or in Scotland, the actual) effects of removing the so-called 'spousal veto' within the GRA upon 'trans widows' – the significant number of women whose husbands or partners suddenly come out as trans, relatively late-on in life. Depending on circumstance, this may leave some of them in marriages in which they don't wish to stay, unable to pay for a divorce, or in a religious community that forbids them to seek one.[23] Relatedly, mainstream feminists also seem indifferent to the disproportionate effects that policies making women-only spaces open to people with female gender identities have on those of strict religious observance such as orthodox Jewish people or Muslims, for whom genuine sex-segregation in social settings is particularly important. In their haste to adopt obscurantist terms like 'menstruators' to avoid mentioning the dreaded 'W' or 'F' words, they have effectively abandoned women for whom English is a second language, or those who haven't been to university and are less familiar with Gender Studies arcana. In their failure to challenge school policies that make toilets 'gender neutral' (unisex), they have shown little thought for the girls in tough schools for whom single-sex spaces used to be a welcome relief from bullying or sexual harassment by boys. And perhaps most awkwardly, they have been left unable properly to explain why, internationally, half the population in a given culture might be disproportionately subject to specific experiences like rape, sexual slavery, female genital mutilation, honour killing, female infanticide, banishment to menstrual huts, surrogacy tourism or death by stoning for the act of adultery. Clue: it's not possession of a female gender identity.

Mainstream feminism has also abandoned trans men. As the cultural paradigm of a trans women has increasingly moved away from permanent physical alteration – as indicated by the recent advent into cultural vocabulary of the 'girldick' – the paradigm of a trans man or non-binary female is apparently moving somewhat towards surgery and bodily modification.[24] One study tells us that trans men self-report what they call 'gender confirming surgery' at much higher rates than trans women: 42–54 per cent versus 28 per cent. The majority of this is radical mastectomy, known as 'top surgery', but still, the prevalence rates for genital surgery is estimated at 25–50 per cent for transgender men yet only 5–10 per cent for transgender women.[25] Mainstream feminism – a political project supposedly aimed, at least some of the time, at women and girls – has had very little to say about the possible reasons for this cultural difference, and its potential connections to a more general culture of self-improvement, purity narratives and masochism, as traceable more widely in female body modification practices like dieting and cosmetic surgery.

Gay and trans activism are also failing their intersectional briefs. Since adding the 'T' to the 'LGB', gay activism has apparently abandoned the political representation of lesbians wherever lesbian interests vary from, or clash with, those of gay men and trans women.

Sociologist Michael Biggs has tracked, over fifteen years, the occurrence of the word 'lesbian' in the annual reports of major LGBT advocacy organisations such as Stonewall, the Equality Network and the US organisation HRC, and found it shifting from an early position of relative infrequency to markedly even lower frequency in recent years, sometimes not appearing in a given year's report at all. Meanwhile, the frequency of the word 'trans' has leapt ahead, particularly in the last decade.[26] The fact that some LGBT organisations are fronted by a lesbian CEO is no substitute for the systematic failure to properly represent lesbian interests on equal terms, within the organisations' operations.

As documented in Chapter 3, the insistent demands from sometimes prominent trans women that lesbians consider them to be potential sexual partners are studiously ignored by LGBT organisations, while the critics of such demands are demonised. When grassroots lesbian organisation Get the L Out protested at the 2018 London Pride parade, carrying banners that said 'lesbian=female homosexual' and 'trans activism erases lesbians', mainstream LGBT organisations attacked them hard.[27] Stonewall's chief executive Ruth Hunt, herself a lesbian, immediately put out a press release entitled 'Transphobia at Pride in London', accusing Get the L Out of demonstrating 'hatred towards trans people' and condemning the London Pride organisers for letting the peaceful, brief protest happen 'unhindered'.[28]

To add insult to injury, in 2018 the *Sunday Times* revealed that Stonewall had recently financially sponsored Canadian trans woman Morgan Page, as part of their 'Empowering trans leaders and organizations in England' programme.[29] It was already on record that in 2012, Page had organised a workshop for Planned Parenthood, entitled: 'Overcoming the Cotton Ceiling: Breaking Down Sexual Barriers for Queer Transwomen'. According to the workshop description, participants would 'explore the sexual barriers queer transwomen face within the broader queer women's communities' and 'work together to identify barriers [and] strategize ways to overcome them'[30]. Put in plainer language, the workshop would strategise about how to get same-sex-attracted lesbians to sleep with people of the opposite sex. In former times, gay activist organisations used to criticise those males seeking to erode the sexual boundaries of lesbians; it didn't fund them.

LGBT activism also fails on intersectionality for trans people themselves. It has no interest in acknowledging the somewhat different political and social situations of trans men and trans women respectively, but insists on treating both as identical for the purposes of lobbying. As far as trans activism is apparently concerned, there is no relevant difference in the situations of a fourteen-year-old trans-identifying teenage female, attracted to other females, who is crowdfunding 'top surgery' and self-harming in the meantime, and a forty-one-year-old late-transitioning autogynephilic heterosexual male with no intention of divorcing the wife. Equally, trans activism does not appear to attend to the particular needs of the relatively high proportion of people with autistic spectrum disorder in the trans community, which surely differ from the neurotypical. As we saw in the last chapter, it has also failed to seriously investigate the differences in the way trans women of colour and trans women in the sex trade are disproportionately affected by violence, treating any infraction as a result of vague 'transphobia' without recognising or investigating other causal factors.

Finally, modern LGBT activism also ignores the particular interests of transsexuals, in the sense of trans people who have medically transitioned. Many transsexuals object to the political demands ostensibly made in their name, and especially at the idea of gender identity, which they don't tend to acknowledge as the thing that makes them trans. Instead they emphasise the experience of dysphoria and the often painful and physically demanding personal journeys they have taken to overcome it. Many are also reasonably comfortable in acknowledging their sex: after all, if it wasn't for their sex, they wouldn't be trans. Says transsexual trans man Buck Angel: 'I was born biologically female. I use testosterone to masculinize myself so I feel more like me. I had a legal sex change and now live as a male. All male pronouns. I am a transsexual and will never be biologically male. But I do live as a male.'[31] Yet within grassroots trans activism, transsexuals with views like Angel's are often derided as 'truscum': 'scum' who think of themselves as 'true' trans. At official level, their views tend to be ignored or denigrated.

Use less academic (high) theory, more academic data

Perhaps surprisingly for a philosopher, my final suggestion can be summed up as: less theory, more data. The message of the previous section was that if feminism and LGBT activism want to function effectively and fairly in future, they need to pay proper attention to the local experiences of particular groups within the demographics they purport to speak for. They need to look at the interests and challenges each face, which may well differ significantly from those in the wider group. In order to do this, activist organisations need robust, accurate data.

In the area of trans experience, academics have largely failed to provide this.

Somewhat stunningly given the political demands made in the name of trans people by trans activists, here are some of the basic things we still don't know enough about:

- How many trans women, men and non-binary people there are in the UK, with reliable numbers for each category. At the moment, by the Government Equalities Office's own admission, 'No robust data on the UK trans population exists'. They 'tentatively estimate that there are approximately 200,000–500,000 trans people in the UK'.[32] As I write, the Office for National Statistics is currently preparing a voluntary 'gender identity' question for the 2021 Survey in England and Wales which asks 'Is your gender the same as the sex you were registered at birth?', and then invites people to put in what their gender identity is, if they wish. Yet, at the time of writing, the ONS apparently intends that the separate question 'What is your sex? Select either "Female" or "Male"' can be answered in terms of 'legal sex' not actual sex, allowing trans people with a Gender Recognition Certificate to describe themselves as of the opposite sex[33]. Meanwhile, Census authorities in Scotland and Northern Ireland apparently plan to advise respondents that they may answer in terms of gender identity, even without a GRC. In practice, this means there will be no fully robust way of cross-referencing sex information with other sources of information, including information about gender identity.
- The material and psychological effects on women of making women-only spaces accessible in terms of female gender identity, and especially on female victims

of sexual assault. Anecdotal reports include women using public toilets and changing rooms less, using some venues less and experiencing heightened anxiety. Since these are some of the very same conditions alleged on behalf of trans people in order to argue for 'gender neutral' spaces and/or increased access of trans women to women-only spaces, if borne out by data this information would surely be of relevance to the public conversation.

- How vulnerable trans people actually are to assault and violence in comparison to the general population. This data needs to be peer-reviewed according to standard academic norms, and not produced by trans activist organisations for the purposes of lobbying.

- What proportion of UK trans people medically transition, with separate information for types of surgery (facial, chest, genital) and for hormonal therapy.

- What the numbers of UK trans-identifying children are, who are *not* currently in the care of the NHS Gender Identity Development Service.

- What the outcomes are long term for children put on puberty blockers. It has recently become clear that, despite the NHS Tavistock GIDS using these drugs on adolescents since 2011, long-term outcomes are unknown.[34] As therapist Lisa Marchiano writes, generally speaking, 'there are few studies examining outcomes for children who are transgender'.[35]

- The true number of detransitioners, and their outcomes. There is reason to think existing studies don't show the whole picture: one focuses only on transsexuals, and one – quite bizarrely – focuses only on those who would still identify as transgender.[36]

Gender Identity Services do not keep track of those
who drop out of their programmes.

- What the experiences of 'trans widows' of late-
transitioning trans women are actually like, and what
their own political needs are.

- How a wide cross-section of trans people actually think
about their own needs and political interests, in relation
to those presented on their behalf by trans activist
organisations.

- What the material and psychological effects of the
political successes of gender identity theory have been
on older transsexuals, for whom the concept of gender
identity has played little part.

- What people in the UK generally understand by the
terms 'trans', 'trans woman', 'trans man', 'non-binary',
'gender' and 'gender identity'. It seems that there is still
a wide variety of interpretations of these terms in the
general population, potentially detrimentally affecting
public communication.

- What proportion of people in the UK believe that 'trans
women are women' and 'trans men are men', and what
exactly they mean by this. In Chapter 5 I cited one
survey, but it would be good to have others.

While activism and public discussion suffers from the lack
of availability of neutral, peer-reviewed data in these and other
areas, they also suffer from a surfeit of 'high' theory, infused
into activism via academics working in feminist theory, queer
theory and Trans Studies. High theory is abstract, totalising,
seductively dramatic in its conclusions, and relatively insulated
from any directly observable empirical consequences – which,
of course, makes it harder to dislodge. We have seen the
influence of some of this in Chapter 2 in discussion of Judith

Butler, who – with relatively few empirical observations in the entirety of her work on gender – has nonetheless managed to convince large numbers of people that biological sex doesn't exist. She argues from a lofty height, metaphorically speaking: from grand claims about concepts, language, reality and thought generally, and hardly ever via specific data about sex. Her claims and their consequences are supposed to be beyond mundane concepts like 'evidence' and 'empirical justification': precisely, she casts such notions, generally, into question. Just now, and also in Chapter 5, I discussed the influential idea that women, somehow uniquely of all the possible human groupings, aren't a fit or coherent subject for political activism. As with Butler, this conclusion is reached through a byzantine set of theoretical manoeuvres, few or none of which have anything to do with low-level empirical observation.

On the basis of these examples, I suggest a rule of thumb for activists: the less data provided, and the more complicated abstract theorising involved in the latest shiny position from academics, the more caution should be exercised before embracing it. This isn't the sweeping conclusion that theory is always bad. Indeed, we can't do without theory, since observation is nearly always inflected by presuppositions: what we see is partly influenced by what we think will be there. Mine is rather the point that the more dramatic and sexier the consequences of a new theory (e.g. 'there are no material biological sexes!', 'there are no women!') the more caution should be applied. Equally, the more heavily moralised the terms in which a theory is presented, the more suspicious readers should be about it in advance: for moralising language in a theory makes it psychologically harder for critics to reject it, even where it's false.

Finally, it should also be remembered that academia, like everywhere else, is subject to a constant demand for novel hot takes. There is strong pressure to publish and to have 'impact' – which in practice often means doing things that will grab headlines, irrespective of whether the work is valuable. Simply repeating true and interesting points made by others isn't enough to get a journal publication or make yourself a reputation: you have to (appear to) do something new and original, often irrespective of whether that thing is ultimately worth doing. It should be remembered, too, that many academics are themselves subject to wider social trends and a tendency towards broad ideological conformity, especially when their academic field is infused with a kind of inherent quasi-ethical purpose, as feminist theory, queer theory, and Trans Studies undoubtedly are. As trans scholar Emmett Harsin Drager says, strikingly candidly for someone working in Trans Studies: 'We are in the era of the trans child. It would be absolutely unfounded to imagine a Trans Studies scholar saying that perhaps, actually, trans children should not be given hormones. As a field we do not allow for those kinds of disagreements. Everything must be "gender affirming" (whatever that means).'[37]

In short: the societal problems to which political activism is (or should be) oriented – the problems that make material differences to people's lives – don't go away just because some academic wrote a hot new paper showing us there aren't women, gay or trans people as we used to understand them; or because what we used to think was the problem is really the solution, or what we used to think of as the solution is really the problem. Always beware the smart-looking reversal. Instead, social problems will get solved by time-honoured methods: finding out what exactly the problems are, with a focus on concrete evidence and listening to all affected parties; and finding out exactly what causes those problems, and what would practically help to make a difference. And then doing it.

Acknowledgements

Enormous thanks are due to my agent Caroline Hardman, for pushing me to write this book and fighting for it once born; and to my editor and publicist at Fleet, Ursula Doyle and Zoe Hood, for believing in it. My first and most brilliant reader was my darling wife, Laura Gibbon, and I thank her too for the thousands of conversations about sex and gender identity, as well as for picking me up off the floor at various points. My second brilliant reader was my father, Guy Stock. Many thanks to other generous readers of various bits: Heather Brunskell-Evans, Alex Byrne, Cathy Devine, Emma Hilton, Holly Lawford-Smith, Fiona Leach, Tony Lycholat, Lisa Marchiano, Susan Matthews, Jon Pike, Selina Todd and Nicola Williams; and to Ann Furedi and Brian Magowan for important conversations. All remaining mistakes are my own. Developing the arguments for this book has been psychologically punishing at times, and it's impossible to list all the wonderful people, known and unknown, who have encouraged me, supported me or inspired me with their own courage: there are just too many and I'm incredibly grateful to you all. But very special thanks go to Sophie Allen,

Elizabeth Finneron Burns, Holly Lawford-Smith, Mary Leng and Rebecca Reilly-Cooper, and to my feminist Queen, Julie Bindel.

Notes

Introduction

1. Julian Norman, '"Shifting sands": Six legal views on the transgender debate', *Guardian*, 19 October 2018, https://www.theguardian.com/society/2018/oct/19/gender-recognition-act-reforms-six-legal-views-transgender-debate
2. Equality Act Explanatory Notes, http://www.legislation.gov.uk/ukpga/2010/15/notes/division/3/2/1/4
3. Stonewall, 'The truth about trans', https://www.stonewall.org.uk/truth-about-trans#trans-people-britain
4. Government Equality Office, 'Trans people in the UK', https://assets.publishing.service.gov.uk/government/uploads/system/uploads/attachment_data/file/721642/GEO-LGBT-factsheet.pdf
5. Andrew Gilligan, 'Tavistock clinic reveals surge in girls switching gender', *Sunday Times*, 30 June 2019, https://www.thetimes.co.uk/article/surge-in-girls-switching-gender-pwqdtd5vk
6. Michael Biggs (2019), 'The Tavistock's Experiment With Puberty Blockers' http://users.ox.ac.uk/~sfos0060/Biggs_ExperimentPubertyBlockers.pdf
7. Health Research Authority, https://www.hra.nhs.uk/about-us/governance/feedback-raising-concerns/investigation-study-early-pubertal-suppression-carefully-selected-group-adolescents-gender-identity-disorders)
8. I. T. Nolan, C. J. Kuhner and G. W. Dy (2019), 'Demographic

and temporal trends in transgender identities and gender confirming surgery', *Translational Andrology and Urology*, 8 (3), 184–90

9. Stonewall, 'Glossary of terms', https://www.stonewall.org.uk/help-advice/faqs-and-glossary/glossary-terms

10. Woman's Place UK, 'Evidence of calls to remove single sex exemptions from Equality Act', https://womansplaceuk.org/references-to-removal-of-single-sex-exemptions/

11. MBM Policy Analysis, 'International evidence and the risks of reframing the sex question in the Census', https://murrayblackburnmackenzie.org/2020/11/30/international-evidence-and-the-risks-of-reframing-the-sex-question-in-the-census/. At the time of writing, as reported in the *Sunday Times*, 24 January 2021, the English Census authority (the Office for National Statistics) will drop its plan to officially interpret 'sex' as 'gender identity' in its Census, and will instead interpret it as 'legal sex'.

12. 'Police investigating bomb threat against Hastings meeting', *Hastings Observer*, 20 June 2018, https://www.hastingsobserver.co.uk/news/police-investigating-bomb-threat-against-hastings-meeting-1020623

13. 'J. K. Rowling Writes about Her Reasons for Speaking out on Sex and Gender Issues', https://www.jkrowling.com/opinions/j-k-rowling-writes-about-her-reasons-for-speaking-out-on-sex-and-gender-issues/

14. '"Trans women are women": Daniel Radcliffe speaks out after JK Rowling tweets', *Guardian*, 9 June 2020, https://www.theguardian.com/film/2020/jun/08/daniel-radcliffe-jk-rowling-transgender-tweets

15. 'JK Rowling and the publisher's staff revolt: Workers at publishing house Hachette threaten to down tools on her new children's book because of her "transphobic" views', *Daily Mail*, 16 June 2020, https://www.dailymail.co.uk/news/article-8424029/JK-Rowling-publishers-revolt-Workers-publishing-house-Hachette-threaten-tools.html

16. Andrea Long Chu and Emmett Harsin Drager (2019), 'After Trans Studies', *Transgender Studies*, 6 (1), 103–16

Chapter 1: A Brief History of Gender Identity

1. Céline Leboeuf (2016), 'One is not born, but rather becomes, a woman: the sex-gender distinction and Simone

de Beauvoir's account of woman', in K. Smits and S. Bruce (eds.), *Feminist Moments: Reading Feminist Texts*, Bloomsbury Academic. Leboeuf's image is borrowed from Nancy Bauer.

2. Simone de Beauvoir (2011 [1949]), *The Second Sex*, trans. C. Borde and S. Malovany-Chevallier, Vintage, p. 211

3. De Beauvoir, *The Second Sex*, p. 12

4. Ann Oakley (2016 [1972]), *Sex, Gender, and Society*, Routledge, pp. 21–2

5. Monique Wittig (1993), 'One Is Not Born A Woman', in H. Abelove, M. Barale and D. Halperin (eds.), *The Lesbian and Gay Studies Reader*, Routledge, p. 104

6. Judith Butler (1986), 'Sex and Gender in Simone de Beauvoir's Second Sex', *Yale French Studies*, No. 72, p. 35

7. John Money (1994), 'The concept of gender identity disorder in childhood and adolescence after 39 years', *Journal of Sex & Marital Therapy*, 20 (3), 164–5

8. Money, 'The concept of gender identity disorder', p. 169

9. Ibid.

10. Robert J. Stoller (1964), 'The hermaphroditic identity of hermaphrodites', *Journal of Nervous and Mental Disease*, 139, p. 456

11. M. Blackless et al. (2000), 'How sexually dimorphic are we? Review and synthesis', *American Journal of Human Biology: The official journal of the Human Biology Council*, 12 (2), 151–66

12. Anne Fausto-Sterling (1993), 'The Five Sexes: Why Male and Female are not Enough', *Science*, 33, 20–24

13. Anne Fausto-Sterling, 'Why Sex Is Not Binary', *New York Times*, 25 October 2018, https://www.nytimes.com/2018/10/25/opinion/sex-biology-binary.html

14. Fausto-Sterling, 'The Five Sexes'

15. Susan Stryker (2006), '(De)Subjugated Knowledges: An Introduction to Transgender Studies', in S. Stryker and S. Whittle (eds.), *The Transgender Studies Reader*, Routledge, p. 4; Stephen Whittle (2006), Foreword in S. Stryker and S. Whittle (eds.), *The Transgender Studies Reader*, Routledge, p. xi

16. Julia Serano (2007), *Whipping Girl: Transsexual Woman on Sexism and the Scapegoating of Femininity*, Seal Press

17. Serano talks mostly about 'cissexuals' and 'transsexuals' but makes clear she doesn't mean by this to identify any particular relation to medical transition, or the lack of it.

18. Max Valerio Wolf (2006), *The Testosterone Files: My*

Hormonal and Social Transformation from Female to Male,
Seal Press

19. GLAAD, 'Transgender FAQ', https://www.glaad.org/
transgender/transfaq

20. Stonewall, 'The Truth about Trans', https://www.stonewall.
org.uk/truth-about-trans#lesbian-trans-woman-gay-
trans-man

21. Stonewall, 'Glossary', https://www.stonewall.org.uk/
help-advice/glossary-terms#h

22. For instance, The Council of Europe's 2009 position paper
'Human Rights and Gender Identity', which cites the
Yogyakarta Principles, starts with the claim: 'Gender identity
is one of the most fundamental aspects of life', CommDH/
IssuePaper (2009) 2, https://rm.coe.int/16806da753, https://
yogyakartaprinciples.org/

23. Heather Brunskell-Evans (2019), 'The Medico-Legal
"Making" of "The Transgender Child"', *Medical Law
Review*, 27, 4

24. https://publications.parliament.uk/pa/cm201516/cmselect/
cmwomeq/390/39010.htm

25. 'Call to end "spousal veto" on trans people being recognised
as preferred gender', Metro, 15 September 2019, https://
metro.co.uk/2019/09/15/call-end-spousal-veto-trans-people-
recognised-preferred-gender-10745012/

26. 'Our successful Spousal Veto removal – amendments
68, 70 & 72', Scottish Trans Website, https://www.
scottishtrans.org/our-work/completed-work/equal-marriage/
spousal-veto-amendment/

27. Memorandum of Understanding on Conversion Therapy
in the UK, October 2017, https://www.psychotherapy.org.
uk/wp-content/uploads/2017/10/UKCP-Memorandum-of-
Understanding-on-Conversion-Therapy-in-the-UK.pdf

28. American Psychological Association, Guidelines for
Psychological Practice With Transgender and Gender
Nonconforming People, *American Psychological Association*,
Vol. 70, No. 9, 832–64, https://www.apa.org/practice/
guidelines/transgender.pdf

29. Verso Books Blog, 'Judith Butler on gender and the trans
experience: "One should be free to determine the course
of one's gendered life"', https://www.versobooks.com/
blogs/2009-judith-butler-on-gender-and-the-trans-experience-
one-should-be-free-to-determine-the-course-of-one-s-
gendered-life

30. Viv Smythe, 'I'm credited with having coined the word "Terf".

Here's how it happened', *Guardian*, 28 November 2018, https://www.theguardian.com/commentisfree/2018/nov/29/im-credited-with-having-coined-the-acronym-terf-heres-how-it-happened

31. Viv Smythe, 'An apology and a promise', *Finally, a Feminism 101 blog*, https://finallyfeminism101.wordpress.com/2008/08/19/an-apology-and-a-promise/

32. Myisha Cherry (2019), 'Rachel McKinnon on allies and ally culture', in M. Cherry, *Unmuted: Conversations on Prejudice, Oppression, and Social Justice*, Oxford University Press

33. Whittle, Foreword in Stryker and Whittle, p. xi

34. Sandy Stone (1992), 'The Empire Strikes Back: A Posttranssexual Manifesto', *Camera Obscura*, 10 (2 (29))

35. Stonewall, 'Glossary', https://www.stonewall.org.uk/help-advice/glossary-terms#h

36. 'Facebook's 71 gender options come to UK users', *Daily Telegraph*, 27 June 2014, https://www.telegraph.co.uk/technology/facebook/10930654/Facebooks-71-gender-options-come-to-UK-users.html

37. University of Kent, 'Trans Policy and Student Support Procedures', https://www.kent.ac.uk/studentservices/files/Trans%20Student%20Support%20Policy%2020%20Feb%202018.pdf

38. University of Essex, 'Working with Schools and Colleges: Trans Inclusion Guidance', https://www.essex.ac.uk/-/media/documents/study/outreach/transgender-guidance.pdf

39. University of Roehampton, 'Trans, Non-Binary and Intersex Equality: Policy and Guidance', https://www.roehampton.ac.uk/globalassets/documents/corporate-information/policies/transgender-non-binary-and-intersex-equality-policy-and-guidance.pdf

40. Stonewall, 'Creating an LGBT-inclusive primary curriculum', https://www.stonewall.org.uk/system/files/creating_an_lgbt-inclusive_primary_curriculum.pdf

41. Michael Paramo, 'Transphobia is a white supremacist legacy of colonialism', https://medium.com/@Michael_Paramo/transphobia-is-a-white-supremacist-legacy-of-colonialism-e50f57240650

42. In a 2019 tweet, Amnesty International's Rainbow Network described Hatshepsut as 'one of the most successful pharaohs in history: born a woman, used female pronouns but presented herself as a King', https://twitter.com/amnestyuk_lgbti/status/1098514489065066497?s=21

43. Hannah Barnes and Debora Cohen, 'Tavistock puberty blocker study published after nine years', BBC News website, https://www.bbc.co.uk/news/uk-55282113

44. Michael Biggs, 'The Tavistock's Experiment with Puberty Blockers', http://users.ox.ac.uk/~sfos0060/Biggs_ExperimentPubertyBlockers.pdf

45. Helen Joyce, 'The New Patriarchy: How trans radicalism hurts women, children and trans people themselves', *Quillette*, https://quillette.com/2018/12/04/the-new-patriarchy-how-trans-radicalism-hurts-women-children-and-trans-people-themselves/

46. 'Jazz Jennings Says She Is "Super Happy With The Results" Of Her 3rd Gender Confirmation Surgery', *Woman's Health Magazine*, 5 February 2020, https://www.womenshealthmag.com/health/a23828566/jazz-jennings-gender-confirmation-surgery-complication/

47. Emrys Travis, 'Choosing Top Surgery Was Choosing To Trust Myself To Know Who I Really Am', *Huffington Post*, 4 December 2018, https://www.huffingtonpost.co.uk/entry/non-binary-top-surgery_uk_5c06396ae4b0cd916faf5ade

48. Whittle, Forword in Stryker and Whittle, p. xi

49. Allison Gallagher, 'What does it mean to be a woman? It is not just about femininity', *Guardian*, 2 January 2019, https://www.theguardian.com/commentisfree/2019/jan/02/what-does-it-mean-to-be-a-woman-it-is-not-just-about-femininity

50. Bernice Hausman (1995), *Changing Sex: Transsexualism, Technology and the Idea of Gender*, Duke University Press, p. ix

51. Malhar Mali, 'Gender Trouble: Gender Feminism and the Blank Slate', *Areo* magazine, 16 March 2017, https://areomagazine.com/2017/03/16/gender-trouble-gender-feminism-and-the-blank-slate/

Chapter 2: What is Sex?

1. Woman's Place UK, 'Evidence of calls to remove single sex exemptions from equality act', https://womansplaceuk.org/references-to-removal-of-single-sex-exemptions/

2. Alex Byrne, 'Is Sex Binary?', *Arc Digital*, 2 November 2018, https://arcdigital.media/is-sex-binary-16bec97d161e

3. Richard Boyd (1991), 'Realism, Anti-Foundationalism and

the Enthusiasm for Natural Kinds', *Philosophical Studies*, 61, 127–48

4. Boyd talks about 'phenotypic' characteristics, but as 'phenotype' normally includes an organism's behaviour, I'm avoiding the term for purposes of clear explanation here.

5. Richard Boyd (1999), 'Homeostasis, Species, and Higher Taxa' in R. Wilson (ed.), *Species: New Interdisciplinary Essays*, pp. 141–86, MIT Press

6. Namely, the promotion in the early foetus of the Müllerian duct system, rather than the Wolffian one, due to the absence of the influence of androgens.

7. Julia Serano (2007), Whipping Girl: *Transsexual Woman on Sexism and the Scapegoating of Femininity*, Seal Press

8. Serano, *Whipping Girl*

9. Anne Fausto-Sterling (1993), 'The Five Sexes: Why Male and Female are not Enough', *Science*, 33, 20–4

10. M. Blackless et al. (2000), 'How sexually dimorphic are we? Review and synthesis', *American Journal of Human Biology: The official journal of the Human Biology Council*, 12 (2), 151–66

11. Leonard Sax (2002), 'How Common is Intersex? A Response to Anne Fausto-Sterling', *Journal of Sex Research*, 39 (3), 174–8

12. Sax, 'How Common is Intersex?'

13. Blackless et al., 'How sexually dimorphic are we?', p. 161

14. Fausto-Sterling, 'The Five Sexes'

15. Sax, 'How Common is Intersex?'

16. Peter Ludlow (2014), *Living Words*, Oxford University Press, pp. 41–6

17. Anne Fausto-Sterling, 'Why Sex Is Not Binary', *New York Times*, 25 October 2018, https://www.nytimes.com/2018/10/25/opinion/sex-biology-binary.html

18. The key texts here are *Gender Trouble* (1990) and *Bodies that Matter* (1993), both Routledge

19. In this she's inspired by French philosopher Michel Foucault, though she takes the idea in a much more radical direction than him.

20. Judith Butler (1990), *Gender Trouble*, Routledge, p. 44

21. Judith Butler (1993), *Bodies that Matter*, Routledge, p. 30

22. See, e.g., Martha Nussbaum, 'The Professor of Parody', *New Republic*, 22 February 1999, https://newrepublic.com/article/150687/professor-parody

23. Ian Hacking (1999), *The Social Construction of What?*, Harvard University Press, p. 67

24. Bruno Latour and Steve Woolgar (1986), *Laboratory Life: The Construction of Scientific Facts*, Princeton University Press, p. 180
25. f/Gender Critical, 'Before the Enlightenment the female skeleton didn't exist', https://www.reddit.com/r/GenderCritical/comments/b6qsmo/before_the_enlightenment_the_female_skeleton/
26. Thomas Laqueur (1990), *Making Sex: Body and Gender from the Greeks to Freud*, Harvard University Press, p. 23
27. *Laqueur, Making Sex*, p. 169
28. *Laqueur, Making Sex*, p. 21
29. *Laqueur, Making Sex*, p. 22
30. *Laqueur, Making Sex*, p. 153
31. *Laqueur, Making Sex*, p. 150
32. *Laqueur, Making Sex*, p. 11
33. *Laqueur, Making Sex*, p. 17
34. *Laqueur, Making Sex*, p. 22
35. *Laqueur, Making Sex*, p. 167
36. *Laqueur, Making Sex*, p. 96
37. Laqueur approvingly quotes philosopher W. V. O. Quine, also known for this view, on p. 68.
38. Laqueur, *Making Sex*, p. 96
39. For more on this see Alexander Bird (2000), *Thomas Kuhn*, Princeton University Press
40. Monique Wittig (1982), 'The Category of Sex', *Feminist Issues* 2, 63–8
41. Catharine MacKinnon (1983), 'Feminism, Marxism, Method, and the State: Toward Feminist Jurisprudence', *Signs*, 8 (4), 635–58
42. Wittig, 'The Category of Sex'
43. Donna Haraway (1991), *Simians, Cyborgs, and Women: The Reinvention of Women*, Free Association Books, p. 152
44. J. Christel et al. (2018), 'Breast Development in Transwomen After 1 Year of Cross-Sex Hormone Therapy: Results of a Prospective Multicenter Study', *The Journal of Clinical Endocrinology & Metabolism*, 103 (2), pp. 532–8
45. M. Klaver et al. (2018), 'Changes in regional body fat, lean body mass and body shape in trans persons using cross-sex hormonal therapy: results from a multicenter prospective study', *European Journal of Endocrinology*, 178 (2), 163, 17
46. See the Gender Recognition Act note 78; Equality Act point 7; Equality Act note 41

Chapter 3: Why Does Sex Matter?

1. C. L. Martin and D. N. Ruble (2010), 'Patterns of Gender Development', *Annual Review of Psychology*, 61, 353–81; Katie Alcock, 'But HOW CAN YOU TELL?', https://medium.com/@katieja/but-how-can-you-tell-7901324d0919

2. M. Strauss et al. (2012), 'The Development of Facial Gender Categorization in Individuals with and without Autism: The Impact of Typicality', *Journal of Autism and Developmental Disorders*, 42 (9), 1847–55

3. Office for National Statistics, 'Suicides in the UK: 2018 registrations', https://www.ons.gov.uk/peoplepopulationandcommunity/births deathsandmarriages/deaths/bulletins/suicidesintheunitedkingdom/2018registrations; 'One in five women have self-harmed, study reveals', *Guardian*, 4 June 2019, https://www.theguardian.com/society/2019/jun/04/one-in-five-young-women-have-self-harmed-study-reveals

4. A. F. Ceylan-Isik et al. (2010), 'Sex difference in Alcoholism: Who is at a greater risk for development of alcoholic complication?', *Life Sciences*, 87 (5–6), 133–8

5. https://www.womenshealth.gov/mental-health/mental-health-conditions/eating-disorders

6. 'The real reason girls are outperforming boys in school', *Daily Telegraph*, 5 November 2019, https://www.telegraph.co.uk/news/2019/11/05/real-reasons-girls-outperforming-boys-school/; 'UK's university gender gap is a national scandal, says thinktank', *Guardian*, 12 May 2016, https://www.theguardian.com/education/2016/may/12/university-gender-gap-scandal-thinktank-men; 'Women less inclined to self-promote than men, even for a job', *Harvard Gazette*, 7 February 2020, https://news.harvard.edu/gazette/story/2020/02/men-better-than-women-at-self-promotion-on-job-leading-to-inequities/

7. Sport England, 'Gender', https://www.sportengland.org/know-your-audience/demographic-knowledge/gender; '2016 Yoga in America Study', https://www.yogajournal.com/page/yogainamericastudy

8. 'Without women the novel would die: discuss', *Guardian*, 7 December 2019, https://www.theguardian.com/books/2019/dec/07/why-women-love-literature-read-fiction-helen-taylor

9. Chloë Taylor (2009), 'Foucault, Feminism, and Sex Crimes', *Hypatia*, 24 (4), 1–25

10. C. Ober et al. (2008), 'Sex-specific Genetic Architecture of Human Disease', *Nature reviews Genetics*, 9 (12), 911–22

11. L. C. Golden et al. (2017), 'The Importance of Studying Sex Differences in Disease: The example of multiple sclerosis', *Journal of Neuroscience Research*, 95 (1–2), 633–43

12. Choi et al. (2007), 'Why Men's Hearts Break: Cardiovascular effects of sex steroids', *Endocrinology & Metabolism Clinics of North America*, 36, 365–77

13. 'Why More Men Are Dying From COVID-19 Than Women – A Geneticist Explains', *Science Alert*, https://www. sciencealert.com/geneticist-explains-why-more-men-are-dying-from-covid-19-than-women

14. R. B. Fillingim et al. (2009), 'Sex, Gender, and Pain: A review of recent clinical and experimental findings', *The Journal of Pain: Official Journal of the American Pain Society*, 10 (5), 447–85

15. H. Whitley et al. (2009), Sex-based Differences in Drug Activity', *American Family Physician*, 80 (11), 1254–8

16. Institute of Medicine (US) Forum on Neuroscience and Nervous System Disorders, 'Sex Differences and Implications for Translational Neuroscience Research: Workshop Summary', National Academies Press (US); 2011. 2, 'Studying Sex Differences in Health and Disease' available from: https:// www.ncbi.nlm.nih.gov/books/NBK53393/

17. Caroline Criado Perez (2019), *Invisible Women: Exposing Data Bias in a World Designed for Men*, Chatto and Windus, Chapter 10

18. 'Anal Sex: What you need to know', *Teen Vogue*, https://www. teenvogue.com/story/anal-sex-what-you-need-to-know/amp

19. 'Smear test campaign drops the word "woman"' to avoid transgender offence', *The Times*, 5 June 2018, https://www. thetimes.co.uk/article/smear-test-campaign-drops-the-word-woman-to-avoid-transgender-offence-263mj7f6s

20. Planned Parenthood Action twitter feed, https://twitter.com/ ppact/status/771850195478908928?lang=en; 'The Guardian called women "menstruators" and these are the only responses you need', *The Poke*, https://www.thepoke.co.uk/2018/10/25/ guardian-called-women-menstruators-people-saw-red-favourite-responses

21. 'LGBTQIA Safe Sex Guide', *Healthline*, https://www. healthline.com/health/lgbtqia-safe-sex-guide

22. 'Accessibility and gendered language at Clue', Medium, https:// medium.com/clued-in/accessibility-and-gendered-language-at-clue-4b79a1dfc033#.2nublwhqx

23. Ann Furedi, correspondence with the author

24. 'Guidelines supporting single-sex sport policy development',

Fair Play For Women, https://fairplayforwomen.com/sport_policy/

25. A. Wiik et al. (2020), 'Muscle Strength, Size, and Composition Following 12 Months of Gender-affirming Treatment in Transgender Individuals', *Journal of Clinical Endocrinology and Metabolism*, 105 (3)

26. D. L. Coleman and W. Shreve, 'Comparing Athletic Performances: The Best Elite Women to Boys and Men', https://web.law.duke.edu/sports/sex-sport/comparative-athletic-performance/

27. Emma Hilton, 'Harder, better, faster, stronger: why we must protect female sports', https://fondofbeetles.wordpress.com/2018/10/01/harder-better-faster-stronger-why-we-must-protect-female-sports/

28. 'CIAC Transgender Policy', https://www.casciac.org/pdfs/Principal_Transgender_Discussion_Quick_Reference_Guide.pdf; 'The Challenges Ahead for Transgender Athletes and Title IX Under Trump', *Vice*, 28 July 2017, https://www.vice.com/en_us/article/59px8b/the-challenges-ahead-for-transgender-athletes-and-title-ix-under-trump

29. 'ACLU response to lawsuit attacking transgender student athletes', https://www.aclu.org/press-releases/aclu-responds-lawsuit-attacking-transgender-student-athletes

30. 'Durham University Trans and Intersex Inclusion Policy', https://www.dur.ac.uk/resources/equality.diversity/DurhamTransandIntersexInclusionPolicy.docx

31. D. J. Handelsman et al. (2018), 'Circulating Testosterone as the Hormonal Basis of Sex Differences in Athletic Performance', *Endocrine Reviews*, 39, (5), 803–29

32. Dr Antonia Lee, 'Myonuclei – the male to female sporting advantage', https://medium.com/@Antonia_Lee/myonuclei-the-male-to-female-sporting-advantage-ae205110d4b2

33. Rachel McKinnon, 'I won a world championship. Some people aren't happy', *New York Times*, 5 December 2019, https://www.nytimes.com/2019/12/05/opinion/i-won-a-world-championship-some-people-arent-happy.html

34. 'Transgender rugby player playing with "a smile on my face"', BBC Website, 22 August 2019, https://www.bbc.co.uk/sport/amp/rugby-union/49298550

35. Julian Savalescu, 'Ten ethical flaws in the Caster Semenya decision on intersex in sport', *The Conversation*, https://theconversation.com/ten-ethical-flaws-in-the-caster-semenya-decision-on-intersex-in-sport-116448

36. Hannah Mouncey, 'AFL's trans participation policy sets a

dangerous precedent for women', *Guardian*, 2 September 2018, https://www.theguardian.com/sport/2018/sep/03/afls-trans-participation-policy-sets-a-dangerous-precedent-for-women

37. Jonathan Liew, 'Why the arguments against trans, intersex and DSD athletes are based on prejudice and ignorance', *Independent*, 22 February 2019, https://www.independent.co.uk/sport/general/athletics/caster-semenya-news-gender-martina-navratilova-trans-cas-jonathan-liew-column-a8792861.html

38. 'Exclusive: Fallon Fox's latest opponent opens up to #WHOATV', *Violent Money*, 17 June 2014, https://whoatv.com/exclusive-fallon-foxs-latest-opponent-opens-up-to-whoatv/

39. Kathleen Stock (2019), 'Sexual Orientation: What Is It?', *Proceedings of the Aristotelian Society*, 119, 3, 295–319

40. Judith Halberstam (1998), *Female Masculinity*, Duke University Press, p. 52

41. Rictor Norton (1997), *The Myth of the Modern Homosexual: Queer History and The Search For Cultural Unity*, Cassell

42. A. J. Martos et al. (2015), 'Variations in Sexual Identity Milestones Among Lesbians, Gay Men, and Bisexuals', *Sexuality Research and Social Policy*, 12, 24–33

43. Edward Stein (1999), *The Mismeasure of Desire: The Science, Theory, and Ethics of Sexual Orientation*, Oxford University Press

44. K. W. Beard et al. (2015), Childhood and Adolescent Sexual Behaviors Predict Adult Sexual Orientations, *Cogent Psychology*, 2 (1), 1067568

45. K. L. Blair and R. A. Hoskin (2019), 'Transgender Exclusion from the World of Dating: Patterns of Acceptance and Rejection of Hypothetical Trans Dating Partners as a Function of Sexual and Gender Identity', *Journal of Social and Personal Relationships*, 36 (7), 2074–95

46. 'This Trans Woman Kept Her Beard And Couldn't Be Happier', *Buzzfeed*, 6 July 2015, https://www.buzzfeed.com/patrickstrudwick/this-transgender-woman-has-a-full-beard-and-she-couldnt-be-h

47. 'It feels like conversion therapy for gay children, say clinicians', *The Times*, 8 April 2019, https://www.thetimes.co.uk/article/it-feels-like-conversion-therapy-for-gay-children-say-clinicians-pvsckdvq2

48. 'Memorandum of understanding on conversion therapy in the UK', https://www.bacp.co.uk/events-and-resources/ethics-and-standards/mou/

49. 'NHS gender clinic "should have challenged me more" over transition', *BBC News*, 1 March 2020, https://www.bbc.co.uk/news/health-51676020

50. 'CTSG & CAPPE Conference | Gayness In Queer Times', http://arts.brighton.ac.uk/re/cappe/calendar/ctsg-and-cappe-conference-gayness-in-queer-times

51. Amia Srinivasan, 'Does anyone have the right to sex?', *London Review of Books*, 22 March 2018, https://www.lrb.co.uk/the-paper/v40/n06/amia-srinivasan/does-anyone-have-the-right-to-sex?referrer=https%3A%2F%2Fwww.google.com%2F

52. A. Sharpe (2016), 'Expanding Liability for Sexual Fraud Through the Concept of "Active Deception": A Flawed Approach', *The Journal of Criminal Law*, 80 (1), 28–44

53. Stonewall, 'A Vision for Change', https://www.stonewall.org.uk/system/files/a_vision_for_change.pdf

54. 'My Trans Youth Group Experience with Morgan Page', 4th Wave Now, https://4thwavenow.com/2019/01/26/my-trans-youth-group-experience-with-morgan-page/

55. Office for National Statistics, 'Families and households in the UK: 2019', https://www.ons.gov.uk/peoplepopulationandcommunity/birthsdeathsandmarriages/families/bulletins/familiesandhouseholds/2019

56. Fawcett Society, 'The Gender Pay Gap and Pay Discrimination – Explainer', https://www.fawcettsociety.org.uk/Handlers/Download.ashx?IDMF=7aed6cd4-5e2e-4542-ad7c-72dbbbe14ee3

57. 'Gender Equality' Athena SWAN, http://www.ecu.ac.uk/wp-content/uploads/2014/07/Gender-Equality-1.pdf

58. Labour Party NEC, 'NEC Statement on All Women Shortlists, women's officers and minimum quotas for women', https://labour.org.uk/about/how-we-work/nec-statement-women-shortlists-womens-officers-minimum-quotas-women/

59. '"Gender fluid" Credit Suisse director named on FT list of Top 100 Women in Business', *Evening Standard*, 22 September 2018, https://www.standard.co.uk/news/uk/gender-fluid-exec-named-on-list-of-top-100-women-in-business-a3942896.html

60. Office for National Statistics, 'Guidance for questions on sex, gender identity and sexual orientation for the 2019 Census Rehearsal for the 2021 Census', https://www.ons.gov.uk/census/censustransformationprogramme/questiondevelopment/genderidentity/guidanceforquestionsonsexgenderidentityandsexualorientationforthe2019censusrehearsalforthe2021census

61. Professor Alice Sullivan, Letter to three Census authorities,

https://www.parliament.scot/S5_European/General%20
Documents/CTEEA_2019.12.18_Sullivan.pdf

62. Office for National Statistics, 'Sexual offences in England
     and Wales: year ending March 2017', https://www.ons.gov.
     uk/peoplepopulationandcommunity/crimeandjustice/articles/
     sexualoffencesinenglandandwales/yearendingmarch2017

63. Rape Crisis, 'About sexual violence', https://rapecrisis.org.uk/
     get-informed/about-sexual-violence/statistics-sexual-violence/

64. Office for National Statistics, 'Domestic abuse in
     England and Wales: year ending March 2018', https://
     www.ons.gov.uk/peoplepopulationandcommunity/
     crimeandjustice/bulletins/domesticabuseinenglandandwales/
     yearendingmarch2018#prevalence-of-domestic-abuse

65. Steve Stewart-Williams, 'Nurture alone can't explain
     male aggression', *Nautilus*, http://nautil.us/blog/
     nurture-alone-cant-explain-male-aggression

66. Office for National Statistics, 'Sexual offences in
     England and Wales: year ending March 2017', https://
     www.ons.gov.uk/peoplepopulationandcommunity/
     crimeandjustice/articles/sexualoffencesinenglandandwales/
     yearendingmarch2017#which-groups-of-people-are-most-
     likely-to-be-victims-of-sexual-assault

67. Stonewall, 'Trans Inclusive Policies and Benefits:
     How to ensure your policies and benefits are trans
     inclusive', https://www.stonewall.org.uk/resources/
     trans-inclusive-policies-and-benefits

68. Prison Reform Trust, 'Information sheet for transgender
     people in prison', http://www.prisonreformtrust.org.uk/
     Portals/0/Documents/Prisoner%20Information%20Pages/
     Information%20sheet%20for%20transgender%20people%20
     in%20prison.pdf

69. 'Cardiff University Trans Policy', https://www.cardiff.
     ac.uk/__data/assets/pdf_file/0004/966532/Trans-Policy-v2.1-
     English-Dec-2019.pdf

70. 'University of Leeds Guidance to Support Trans Staff and
     Students', https://equality.leeds.ac.uk/support-and-resources/
     guidance-to-support-trans-staff-and-students/

71. 'UWE Bristol hits back at online trans toilet criticism', *BBC
     News*, 12 February 2019, https://www.bbc.co.uk/news/
     uk-england-bristol-47213433

72. 'Written evidence submitted by British Association of Gender
     Identity Specialists to the Transgender Equality Inquiry',
     http://data.parliament.uk/writtenevidence/committeeevidence.
     svc/evidencedocument/women-and-equalities-committee/

transgender-equality/written/
19532.pdf?fbclid=IwAR3leDByhYXoEKla1nr1k5jJWvkO4q
Za_eHIgMHXqSTCTtSp-iW8CDf-TOo

73. 'Shelter forced women to shower with person who identified
     as a transgender woman and sexually harassed them, lawsuit
     says', ABC30 Action News, 24 May 2018, https://abc30.com/
     homeless-women-harassed-in-shower-lawsuit-says/3514544/

74. 'Rights centre says trans activist Jessica Yaniv has filed new
     complaint against B.C. salon over waxing refusal', *National
     Post*, 7 January 2020, https://nationalpost.com/news/canada/
     rights-centre-says-trans-activist-jessica-yaniv-has-filed-new-
     suit-against-b-c-salon-over-waxing-refusal

75. 'Forced to share a room with transgender woman in Toronto
     shelter, sex abuse victim files human rights complaint',
     National Post, 2 August 2018, https://nationalpost.com/news/
     canada/kristi-hanna-human-rights-complaint-transgender-
     woman-toronto-shelter

76. 'Mum of supermarket toilet sex assault victim warns freed
     attacker could strike again', *Courier*, 1 February 2019,
     https://www.thecourier.co.uk/fp/news/local/fife/819644/
     mum-of-supermarket-toilet-sex-assault-victim-warns-freed-
     attacker-could-strike-again/

77. 'Transgender sex offender housed in female-only Fife hostel
     sparking furious response from sickened residents', *Scottish
     Sun*, 26 February 2019, https://www.thescottishsun.co.uk/
     news/3928585/transgender-sex-offender-female-only-fife-
     hostel-katie-dalatowski-furious-residents/

78. 'Karen White: how "manipulative" transgender
     inmate attacked again', *Guardian*, 11 February 2018,
     https://www.theguardian.com/society/2018/oct/11/
     karen-white-how-manipulative-and-controlling-offender-
     attacked-again-transgender-prison

79. Halberstam, *Female Masculinity*, p. 19

80. Halberstam, *Female Masculinity*, p. 21

Chapter 4: What is Gender Identity?

1.   California Legislative Information, SB-179 Gender identity:
     female, male, or nonbinary, https://leginfo.legislature.ca.gov/
     faces/billNavClient.xhtml?bill_id=201720180SB179

2.   Jan Morris (1974), *Conundrum*, Faber and Faber, p. 2

3.   '9 questions about gender identity and being transgender

you were too embarrassed to ask', *Vox*, 22 February 2017, https://www.vox.com/2015/4/24/8483561/ transgender-gender-identity-expression

4. Iris Marion Young (1980), 'Throwing Like a Girl: A Phenomenology of Feminine Body Comportment Motility and Spatiality', *Human Studies*, 3, 137–56

5. Simona Giordano (2013), *Children with Gender Identity Disorder: A Clinical, Ethical, and Legal Analysis*, Routledge, p. 48

6. D. Hoffman Fox (2017), 'You and Your Gender Identity: A Guide To Discovery', Seahorse

7. '9 questions about gender identity', *Vox*

8. http://www.getmariposa.com

9. Stonewall, 'Gender identity', 'Glossary of Terms', https://www.stonewall.org.uk/help-advice/faqs-and-glossary/glossary-terms#g

10. 'Growing up, girlhood and transitioning: an interview with Munroe Bergdorf', *gal-dem*, 22 October 2016, https://gal-dem.com/growing-up-girlhood-and-transitioning-an-interview-with-munroe-bergdorf/

11. Robert Winston (2017), *Help Your Kids With Growing Up: A No-Nonsense Guide to Puberty and Adolescence*, Dorling Kindersley, p. 24

12. Fox Fisher and Owl Fisher (2019), *Trans Teen Survival Guide*, Jessica Kingsley, p. 17

13. Stephanie Brill and Rachel Pepper (2008), *The Transgender Child: A Handbook for Families and Professionals*, Cleis Publishing, p. 16

14. Katie Kawa (2020), *What's Gender Identity?*, Kidhaven Publishing, p. 4

15. Brill and Pepper, *The Transgender Child*, p. 60

16. Baker Rogers (2020), *Trans Men in the South*, Rowman and Littlefield, p. 60

17. 'Transgender stories: "People think we wake up and decide to be trans"', *Guardian*, 10 July 2016, https://www.theguardian.com/society/2016/jul/10/transgender-stories-people-think-we-wake-up-and-decide-to-be-trans

18. Morris, *Conundrum*, p. 21

19. Bao et al. (2011), 'Sexual differentiation of the human brain: Relation to gender identity, sexual orientation and neuropsychiatric disorders', *Frontiers in Neuroendocrinology*, 32, 214–26

20. See for instance, Cordelia Fine and Daphna Joel, 'Can We Finally Stop Talking About "Male" and "Female" Brains?',

New York Times, 3 December 2018, https://www.nytimes.
com/2018/12/03/opinion/male-female-brains-mosaic.html;
Xin et al. (2019), 'Brain Differences Between Men and Women:
Evidence From Deep Learning', *Frontiers in Neuroscience*,
8 March 2019, https://www.frontiersin.org/articles/10.3389/
fnins.2019.00185/full

21. Jiska Ristori et al. (2020), 'Brain Sex Differences Related
    to Gender Identity Development: Genes or Hormones?',
    International Journal of Molecular Science, 21 (6), 2123

22. M. Lebow et al. (2016), 'Overshadowed by the amygdala:
    the bed nucleus of the stria terminalis emerges as key to
    psychiatric disorders', *Molecular Psychiatry*, 21, 450–63

23. Michelle Worth, 'Sex on the brain: The biology
    of sexual orientation', *Observer*, 8 April
    2010, https://ndsmcobserver.com/2010/04/
    sex-on-the-brain-the-biology-of-sexual-orientation/

24. 'The girls who are destined to grow up into tomboys', *The
    Times*, 6 June 2013, https://www.thetimes.co.uk/article/
    the-girls-who-are-destined-to-grow-up-into-tomboys-
    60pgv77cqxm

25. Bao et al., 'Sexual differentiation of the human brain'

26. C. Rodda et al. (1987), 'Muscle strength in girls with
    congenital adrenal hyperplasia', *Acta paediatrica
    Scandinavica*, 76 (3), 495–9; V. Pasterski et al. (2007),
    'Increased aggression and activity level in 3- to 11-year-old
    girls with congenital adrenal hyperplasia', *Hormones and
    Behaviour*, 52 (3), 368–74

27. Bao et al., 'Sexual differentiation of the human brain'

28. American Psychiatric Association (2013), *Diagnostic and
    Statistical Manual of Mental Disorders (DSM-5)*

29. Ayhan Alman, Gestalt Psychotherapy and Counselling, 'The
    Gender Identity/Gender Dysphoria Questionnaire', https://
    www.gestalt-psychotherapy.com/test/gidyq-aa-m/

30. Eva Kosofsky Sedgwick (1991), 'How to Bring Your Kids up
    Gay', *Social Text*, (29), 18–27. I'm grateful to Susan Matthews
    for the pointer.

31. 'Hundreds of transgender youths who had gender reassignment
    surgery wish they hadn't and want to transition back, says
    trans rights champion', *Daily Mail*, 5 October 2019, https://
    www.dailymail.co.uk/news/article-7541679/Hundreds-youths-
    gender-surgery-wish-hadnt-says-head-advocacy-network.html.
    In response to a similar criticism, a spokesperson for the NHS
    Tavistock and Portman Gender Identity Service said: 'The
    service is safe and all work we undertake is commissioned

and regulated by NHS England under strict guidance. The
service has a high level of reported satisfaction' ('David
Bell: Tavistock gender clinic whistleblower faces the sack',
The Times, 5 December 2020, https://www.thetimes.co.uk/
article/david-bell-tavistock-gender-clinic-whistleblower-faces-
the-sack-rtkl09907). Meanwhile, in response to criticism
of the continued use of puberty blockers for children at the
Scottish Young People's Gender Service, based in Glasgow,
First Minister Nicola Sturgeon said of the clinic: 'Young
people can be considered for puberty blockers only after
thorough psychological and endocrine assessment, as per
the clinical guidelines, and anyone who commences them
continues to receive regular psychological review and support
appointments.' ('Nicola Sturgeon refuses to stop Scots children
getting puberty blockers', *Glasgow Herald*, 10 December
2020, https://www.heraldscotland.com/news/18935834.nicola-
sturgeon-refuses-stop-scots-children-getting-puberty-blockers/)

32.   Judith Butler (2004), *Undoing Gender*, Routledge, p. 81
33.   Butler, *Undoing Gender*, p. 80
34.   Katie Herzog, 'They were transgender; until they
      weren't', *The Stranger*, 28 June 2017, https://www.
      thestranger.com/features/2017/06/28/25252342/
      the-detransitioners-they-were-transgender-until-they-werent
35.   University of Kent, 'Trans Policy and Student Support
      Procedures', https://www.kent.ac.uk/studentservices/files/
      Trans%20Student%20Support%20Policy%2020%20Feb%20
      2018.pdf; University of Essex, 'Working with Schools and
      Colleges: Trans Inclusion Guidance', https://www.essex.ac.uk/-
      /media/documents/study/outreach/transgender-guidance.pdf
36.   Joy Ladin (2010), *Through the Door of Life. A Jewish Journey
      Between Genders*, University of Wisconsin Press, p. 47
37.   Jay Prosser (1998), *Second Skins: Body Narratives of
      Transsexuality*, Columbia University Press, p. 32
38.   Alex Iantaffi and Meg-John Barker (2017), *How to
      Understand Your Gender: A Practical Guide for Exploring
      Who You Are*, Jessica Kingsley, p. 46
39.   Heinz Hartmann and Rudolph M. Loewenstein (1962), 'Notes
      on the Superego', *The Psychoanalytic Study of the Child*,
      17 (1), 42–81, p. 49
40.   D. D. Olds (2006), 'Identification: Psychoanalytic
      and Biological Perspectives', *Journal of the American
      Psychoanalytic Association*, 54 (1), 17–46
41.   Stuart Hall (1996), 'Who Needs "Identity"?', in S. Hall and
      P. DuGay (eds.), *Questions of Cultural Identity*, Sage, p. 3

42. As quoted in Susan Stryker (2008), *Transgender History: The Roots of Today's Revolution*, Seal Press, p.144

43. Morris, *Conundrum*, p. 39

44. Jack Halberstam (2018), *Trans*: A Quick and Quirky Account of Gender Variability*, University of California Press, p. 1

45. 'Growing up, girlhood and transitioning: an interview with Munroe Bergdorf'

46. Paris Lees, 'From bullied child to transgender woman: my coming of age', *Guardian*, 15 December 2013, https://www.theguardian.com/society/2013/dec/15/transgender-coming-of-age-paris-lees

47. 'Laverne Cox Opens Up About Childhood Bullying, Suicide Attempt', *Huffington Post*, 19 August 2014, https://www.huffingtonpost.co.uk/entry/laverne-cox-suicide_n_5691515?ri18n=true

48. Roi Jacobsen and Daphna Joel (2019), 'Self-Reported Gender Identity and Sexuality in an Online Sample of Cisgender, Transgender, and Gender-Diverse Individuals: An Exploratory Study', *The Journal of Sex Research*, 56 (2), 249–63

49. 'What It's Like to Be Trans and Live With Gender Dysphoria', *Teen Vogue*, 21 September 2018, https://www.teenvogue.com/story/what-its-like-to-be-trans-and-live-with-gender-dysphoria

50. Dr Az Hakeem (2018), *Trans: Exploring Gender Identity and Gender Dysphoria*, Trigger Press, p.52

51. Leslie Feinberg (2003), *Stone Butch Blues*, Allyson, p. 11

52. *Diagnostic and Statistical Manual of Mental Disorders (DSM-5)*, p. 284

53. Stonewall, 'An Introduction to Supporting LGBT Children and Young People', https://www.stonewall.org.uk/system/files/an_intro_to_supporting_lgbt_young_people_2020.pdf

54. Bernadette Wren (2019), 'Ethical issues arising in the provision of medical interventions for gender diverse children and adolescents', *Clinical Child Psychology and Psychiatry*, 24 (2), 203–22; H. Z. Gastgeb and M. Strauss (2012), 'Categorization in ASD: The Role of Typicality and Development', *Perspectives on Language Learning and Education*, 19 (2), 66–74

55. Hakeem, *Trans*, p. 55

56. Domenico Di Ceglie (1998), 'Management and therapeutic aims with children and adolescents with gender identity disorders and their families', in D. Di Ceglie and D. Freedman (eds.), *A Stranger in My Own Body: Atypical gender identity development and mental health*, Karnac, p. 14

57. Hakeem, *Trans*, p. 54

58. 'Butterfly: Teen transgender drama "inflates suicide risk"',

Sunday Times, 4 October 2018, https://www.thetimes.co.uk/article/teen-transgender-drama-butterfly-inflates-suicide-risk-9ng3z22mv

59. Helen Joyce, 'Speaking up for female eunuchs', *Standpoint*, February 2020, https://standpointmag.co.uk/issues/february-2020/speaking-up-for-female-eunuchs/

60. Helen Joyce, 'Speaking up for female eunuchs', *Standpoint*, 30 January 2020, https://standpointmag.co.uk/speaking-up-for-female-eunuchs/

61. Bernice Hausman (1995), *Changing Sex: Transsexualism, Technology and the Idea of Gender*, Duke University Press, p. 3

62. See Finn Mackay (2019), 'No woman's land? Revisiting border zone denizens', *Journal of Lesbian Studies*, 23 (3), 397–409

63. Judith Halberstam (1998), *Female Masculinity*, Duke University Press, p. 71

64. Halberstam, *Female Masculinity*, p. 68

65. Equality Act 2010, Section 7, http://www.legislation.gov.uk/ukpga/2010/15/section/7

66. Gender reassignment discrimination, EHRC website, https://www.equalityhumanrights.com/en/advice-and-guidance/gender-reassignment-discrimination

67. Stonewall Youth, 'Gender Identity', https://www.youngstonewall.org.uk/lgbtq-info/gender-identity

Chapter 5: What Makes a Woman?

1. Jack Halberstam (2018), *Trans*: A Quick and Quirky Account of Gender Variability*, University of California Press, p. 5

2. John Dupré (1993), *The Disorder of Things: Metaphysical Foundations of the Disunity of Science*, Harvard University Press, p. 19

3. This shouldn't be confused with the different claim that some things are dependent on human beings for their existence. That's certainly true of funny jokes and arguably also true of poison, depending on further assumptions too distracting to go into here.

4. There's a philosopher's side issue here, about whether in this sort of case an old concept is being replaced by a different concept altogether, or whether a version of the same concept is being replaced by another version. I will take the latter route.

5. Angela Onwuachi-Willig, 'Race and Racial

Identity Are Social Constructs', *New York Times*,
6 September 2016, https://www.nytimes.com/
roomfordebate/2015/06/16/how-fluid-is-racial-identity/
race-and-racial-identity-are-social-constructs

6. 'Race is a social construct, scientists argue', *Scientific American*, 5 February 2016, https://www.scientificamerican.com/article/race-is-a-social-construct-scientists-argue/

7. Alex Byrne makes this point in his (2020) 'Are women adult human females?', *Philosophical Studies*

8. Marilyn Frye (1983), *The Politics of Reality: Essays in feminist theory*, Crossing Press, p. 16

9. J. A. Collins and I. R. Olson (2014), 'Knowledge is Power: How conceptual knowledge transforms visual cognition', *Psychonomic Bulletin & Review*, 21, 843–60

10. Philip J. Kelmann and Christine M. Massey (2013), 'Perceptual Learning, Cognition, and Expertise', *Psychology of Learning and Motivation*, Brian H. Ross (ed.), 58, 117–65

11. Stonewall, 'Statement on the ruling against Freddy McConnell', 29 April 2020, https://www.stonewall.org.uk/about-us/news/statement-ruling-against-freddy-mcconnell

12. Office for National Statistics, 'The nature of violent crime in England and Wales: year ending March 2017', https://www.ons.gov.uk/peoplepopulationandcommunity/crimeandjustice/articles/thenatureofviolentcrimeinenglandandwales/yearendingmarch2017

13. IPSO, 'Guidance on researching and reporting stories involving transgender individuals', September 2016, https://www.ipso.co.uk/media/1275/guidance_transgender-reporting.pdf

14. In later editions, this was changed to 'Transgender woman, 41 ...'

15. 'Police forces let rapists record their gender as female', *The Times*, 20 October 2019, https://www.thetimes.co.uk/article/police-forces-let-rapists-record-their-gender-as-female-d7qtb7953

16. Simone de Beauvoir (2011 [1949]), *The Second Sex*, trans. C. Borde and S. Malovany-Chevallier, Vintage, p. 211, p. 3

17. J. L. Austin (1962), *Sense and Sensibilia*, Oxford University Press, p. 70

18. C. Brezina (2005), *Sojourner Truth's 'Ain't I a Woman?' Speech: A Primary Source Investigation*, The Rosen Publishing Group

19. Elizabeth V. Spelman (1998), *Inessential Woman: Problems of Exclusion in Feminist Thought*, Beacon Press

20. Diana Fuss (1989), *Essentially Speaking*, Routledge, p. 36

21. 'The controversy over Chimamanda Ngozi Adichie and trans
     women, explained', *Vox*, 5 March 2017, https://www.vox.com/
     identities/2017/3/15/14910900/chimamanda-ngozi-adichie-
     transgender-women-comments-apology
22. Elinor Burkett, 'What makes a woman?', *New York Times*,
     6 June 2015, https://www.nytimes.com/2015/06/07/opinion/
     sunday/what-makes-a-woman.html
23. Catharine MacKinnon (1989), *Towards a Feminist Theory of
     the State*, Harvard University Press, p. 178
24. Sally Haslanger (2000), 'Gender and Race: (What) are they?
     (What) do we want them to be?', *Noûs*, 34, 31–55. Later on, in
     a startling volte-face, Haslanger confessed in relation to earlier
     writing: 'by appropriating the terms "woman" and "man,"
     I problematically excluded some women from being counted
     as women.' ('Going on, not in the same way', in A. Plunkett,
     H. Cappelen, and D. Burgess (eds.) (2020), *Conceptual Ethics
     and Conceptual Engineering*, Oxford University Press
25. Kate Bornstein (2012), *A Queer and Pleasant Danger*, Beacon
     Press, p. 198
26. Joy Ladin (2010), *Through the Door of Life. A Jewish Journey
     Between Genders*, University of Wisconsin Press, p. 38
27. Andrea Long Chu (2019), *Females*, Verso, p. 11
28. 'Sex, Gender, and Sexuality: The Trans Advocate
     interviews Catharine A. MacKinnon', *Trans Advocate*,
     7 April 2015, https://www.transadvocate.com/
     sex-gender-and-sexuality-the-transadvocate-interviews-
     catharine-a-mackinnon_n_15037.htm

Chapter 6: Immersed in a Fiction

1. 'Gender Recognition Bill', Hansard, https://api.parliament.uk/
    historic-hansard/bills/gender-recognition-bill
2. Ibid.
3. '11 Feb 2004: Column 1093', Hansard, https://publications.
    parliament.uk/pa/ld200304/ldhansrd/vo040211/
    text/40211-01.htm
4. 'Gender Recognition Bill', Hansard, 3 February 2004, https://
    api.parliament.uk/historic-hansard/lords/2004/feb/03/
    gender-recognition-bill-hl#S5LV0656P0_20040203_HOL_411
5. 'Gender Recognition Bill', Hansard, 29 January 2004, https://
    api.parliament.uk/historic-hansard/lords/2004/jan/29/
    gender-recognition-bill-hl#S5LV0656P0_20040129_HOL_228

6. 'Gender Recognition Bill', Hansard, 19 January 2004, https://api.parliament.uk/historic-hansard/written-answers/2004/jan/19/gender-recognition#S5LV0657P0_20040119_LWA_42

7. Equality Act Explanatory Notes, http://www.legislation.gov.uk/ukpga/2010/15/notes/division/3/2/1/4

8. https://onlinelaw.wustl.edu/blog/legal-english-legal-fiction/

9. Sidney T. Miller (1910), 'The Reasons for Some Legal Fictions', *Michigan Law Review*, 8 (8), (Jun., 1910), 623–36

10. 'Gender Recognition Bill', Hansard, 18 December 2003, https://api.parliament.uk/historic-hansard/lords/2003/dec/18/gender-recognition-bill-hl#S5LV0655P0_20031218_HOL_58

11. 'The General Guide for all Users, Gender Recognition Act 2004', https://assets.publishing.service.gov.uk/government/uploads/system/uploads/attachment_data/file/786910/t455-eng.pdf

12. 'Gender Recognition Act 2004', http://www.legislation.gov.uk/ukpga/2004/7/pdfs/ukpga_20040007_en.pdf

13. Debbie Hayton, 'Defend Me or Expel Me', https://debbiehayton.wordpress.com/2020/04/14/defend-me-or-expel-me/

14. Miranda Yardley, 'Why I Disavow "Woman" And Am No Longer "Gender Critical"', https://medium.com/@mirandayardley/why-i-disavow-woman-and-am-no-longer-gender-critical-8352586e7aab

15. Fionne Orlander, 14 November 2018, https://twitter.com/FionneOrlander/status/1062728906304827392

16. I'm not saying that all acting is like this. Denis Diderot denied it was, as did Bertolt Brecht. My claim is only that it sometimes is.

17. Samuel Kampa (2018), 'Imaginative Transportation', *Australasian Journal of Philosophy*, 96 (4), 10

18. 2018 Populus poll, commissioned by 'Women Ask Questions', accessible at https://fairplayforwomen.com/wp-content/uploads/2018/11/gender_recognition_act-1.pdf. These numbers add up to 101 per cent because they are rounded up.

19. 'Woman billboard removed after transphobia row', *BBC News*, 26 September 2018, https://www.bbc.co.uk/news/uk-45650462

20. Talia Mae Bettcher (2007), 'Evil Deceivers and Make-Believers: On Transphobic Violence and the Politics of Illusion', *Hypatia*, 22 (3), 43–65

21. Susanna Schellenberg (2013), 'Belief and Desire in Imagination and Immersion', *Journal of Philosophy*, 110, 508

22. Mark J. Miller (1980), 'Role-Playing as a Therapeutic Strategy: A Research Review', *The School Counselor*, 27 (3), 217–26

23. 'Cultural sexism in the world is very real when you've lived on both sides of the coin', *Time*, https://time.com/transgender-men-sexism/

24. A. K. Przybylski et al. (2012), 'The Ideal Self at Play: The Appeal of Video Games That Let You Be All You Can Be', *Psychological Science*, 23 (1), 69–76

25. Abigail Shrier (2020), *Irreversible Damage*, Regnery, p. 7

26. Judith Halberstam (1998), *Female Masculinity*, Duke University Press

27. Shrier, *Irreversible Damage*, p. 7.

28. Stéphanie Laconi et al. (2017), 'Internet Gaming Disorder, Motives, Game Genres and Psychopathology', *Computers in Human Behavior*, 75, 652–9

29. Katie Herzog, 'The Detransitioners: They Were Transgender, Until They Weren't', *The Stranger*, 28 June 2017, https://www.thestranger.com/features/2017/06/28/25252342/the-detransitioners-they-were-transgender-until-they-werent

30. Sasha Sioni et al. (2017), 'Internet gaming Disorder: Social phobia and identifying with your virtual self', *Computers in Human Behavior*, 71, 11–15

31. See below, in the section on the Stroop Effect, for some relevant context.

32. See, e.g., Alex Sharpe (2016), 'Expanding Liability for Sexual Fraud Through the Concept of "Active Deception": A Flawed Approach', *The Journal of Criminal Law*, 80 (1), 28–44

33. Bernadette Wren (2019), 'Ethical issues arising in the provision of medical interventions for gender diverse children and adolescents', *Clinical Child Psychology and Psychiatry*, 24 (2), 203–22

34. San Francisco Aids Foundation, 'Q&A: Gynecologic and vaginal care for trans men', https://www.sfaf.org/collections/beta/qa-gynecologic-and-vaginal-care-for-trans-men/

35. Stonewall, 'Trans Inclusive Policies and Benefits: How to ensure your policies and benefits are trans inclusive', https://www.stonewall.org.uk/resources/trans-inclusive-policies-and-benefits

36. Stonewall, 'Glossary', https://www.stonewall.org.uk/help-advice/glossary-terms#t

37. Stonewall, 'LGBT in Britain: Hate Crime and Discrimination', https://www.stonewall.org.uk/system/files/lgbt_in_britain_hate_crime.pdf

38. Stonewall, 'Trans Inclusive Policies and Benefits: How to ensure your policies and benefits are trans inclusive'

39. Stonewall blog, 'It's International Pronouns Day, and it's

time for all of us to step up as trans allies', 16 October 2019, https://www.stonewall.org.uk/about-us/blog/it%E2%80%99s-international-pronouns-day-and-it%E2%80%99s-time-all-us-step-trans-allies

40. Stonewall, 'Delivering LGBT-inclusive Higher Education: Academic provision, accommodation, catering, facilities, induction, recruitment, registry, societies, sports and student services', https://www.stonewall.org.uk/resources/delivering-lgbt-inclusive-higher-education

41. 'Radical feminist warned to refer to transgender defendant as a "she" during assault case', *Daily Telegraph*, 12 April 2018, https://www.telegraph.co.uk/news/2018/04/12/radical-feminist-warned-refer-transgender-defendant-assault/

42. 'Judge rules against researcher who lost job over transgender tweets', *Guardian*, 18 December 2019, https://www.theguardian.com/society/2019/dec/18/judge-rules-against-charity-worker-who-lost-job-over-transgender-tweets

43. Crown Prosecution Service, 'Trans Equality Statement', https://www.cps.gov.uk/sites/default/files/documents/publications/Trans-equality-statement-July-2019.pdf

44. *Equal Treatment Bench Book*, Judicial College, https://www.judiciary.uk/wp-content/uploads/2018/02/equal-treatment-bench-book-february-v6-2018.pdf

45. Helga Varden (2020), *Sex, Love and Gender: A Kantian Theory*, Oxford University Press, p. xvi

46. Mary Leng, 'Harry Potter and the Reverse Voltaire', https://medium.com/@mary.leng/harry-potter-and-the-reverse-voltaire-4c7f3a07241

47. 'Are academics freely able to criticise the idea of "gender identity" in UK Universities?', Kathleen Stock, 3 July 2019, https://medium.com/@kathleenstock/are-academics-freely-able-to-criticise-the-idea-of-gender-identity-in-uk-universities-67b97c6e04be

48. 'Gender Dysphoria Isn't A "Social Contagion," According To A New Study', *Buzzfeed*, 22 April 2019, https://www.buzzfeednews.com/article/shannonkeating/rapid-onset-gender-dysphoria-flawed-methods-transgender; 'New paper ignites storm over whether teens experience "rapid onset" of transgender identity', *Science*, 30 August 2018, https://www.sciencemag.org/news/2018/08/new-paper-ignites-storm-over-whether-teens-experience-rapid-onset-transgender-identity

49. 'Doctor fired from gender identity clinic says he feels "vindicated" after CAMH apology, settlement', *The Globe and Mail*, 7 October 2018, https://www.theglobeandmail.

com/canada/toronto/article-doctor-fired-from-gender-identity-clinic-says-he-feels-vindicated/

50. 'Staff at trans clinic fear damage to children as activists pile on pressure', *Sunday Times*, 16 February 2019, https://www.thetimes.co.uk/article/staff-at-trans-clinic-fear-damage-to-children-as-activists-pile-on-pressure-c5k655nq9

51. Michael Biggs, 'The Tavistock's Experiment with Puberty Blockers', http://users.ox.ac.uk/~sfos0060/Biggs_ExperimentPubertyBlockers.pdf

52. https://andersen.sdu.dk/vaerk/hersholt/TheEmperorsNewClothes_e.html

53. L. van Maanen et al. (2009), 'Stroop and picture-word interference are two sides of the same coin', *Psychonomic Bulletin & Review*, 16, 987–99

54. Barra Kerr, 'Pronouns are Rohypnol', *Fairplay for Women*, https://fairplayforwomen.com/pronouns/

55. James Kirkup, 'Why was a transgender rapist put in a women's prison?', *Spectator*, 7 September 2018, https://www.spectator.co.uk/article/why-was-a-transgender-rapist-put-in-a-women-s-prison-

Chapter 7: How Did We Get Here?

1. Stonewall, 'A Vision for Change', https://www.stonewall.org.uk/system/files/a_vision_for_change.pdf

2. 'Government Response to the Women and Equalities Committee Report on Transgender Equality', https://assets.publishing.service.gov.uk/government/uploads/system/uploads/attachment_data/file/535764/Government_Response_to_the_Women_and_Equalities_Committee_Report_on_Transgender_Equality.pdf

3. 'Trans people to be able to register new identities more easily', *Guardian*, 3 July 2018, https://www.theguardian.com/society/2018/jul/03/trans-people-to-be-able-to-register-new-identities-more-easily

4. 'A timeline of LGBTQ communities in the UK', The British Library, https://www.bl.uk/lgbtq-histories/lgbtq-timeline

5. 'Against The Law Review: A fitting tribute to gay men whose persecution in 1950s paved way for new rights', *The Conversation*, 26 July 2017, https://theconversation.com/against-the-law-review-a-fitting-tribute-to-gay-men-whose-persecution-in-1950s-paved-way-for-new-rights-74785

6. 'Homosexuality', British Social Attitudes survey, https://www.
    bsa.natcen.ac.uk/latest-report/british-social-attitudes-30/
    personal-relationships/homosexuality.aspx
7. Stonewall tweet, 'It's been 32 years since the introduction
    of Section 28, the devastating legislation banning
    discussion of LGBT identities in schools. We've come a
    long way since then but there is still more to do to ensure
    acceptance without exception for everyone in the LGBT
    community', 24 May 2020, https://twitter.com/stonewalluk/
    status/1264571946236366854
8. 'British Social Attitudes 36', Natcen Social Research, https://
    www.bsa.natcen.ac.uk/media/39363/bsa_36.pdf
9. 'David Cameron apologises to gay people for section 28',
    Guardian, 2 July 2009, https://www.theguardian.com/
    politics/2009/jul/02/david-cameron-gay-pride-apology
10. Hubert C. Kennedy (1981), 'The "Third Sex" Theory of Karl
    Heinrich Ulrichs', *Journal of Homosexuality,* 6 (1–2), 103–11
11. Richard von Krafft-Ebing (1927), *Psychopathia Sexualis: A
    medico-forensic study*, Heinemann, p. 399
12. Judith Green, 'Health care is a human right', Woman's
    Place UK, https://womansplaceuk.org/2020/06/14/
    health-care-human-right/
13. 'Directive-type Memorandum-19-004', https://drive.google.
    com/file/d/1tQugAtmmg-cDrhwQVRPtCGNBA6c7b3x2/view
14. Stonewall, 'Transgender Day of Remembrance', https://www.
    stonewall.org.uk/node/21888
15. Transgender Day of Remembrance, https://tdor.info/
16. Stonewall, 'Step 4: Communicating an Inclusive Service',
    https://www2.le.ac.uk/offices/equalities-unit/documents/
    step4Communication.pdf
17. 'Jeremy Corbyn's Statement on Transgender Day of
    Remembrance', https://jeremycorbyn.org.uk/articles/jeremy-
    corbyns-statement-on-transgender-day-of-remembrance/
    index.html; 'Labour's Dawn Butler vows to build a world
    where transphobia is a thing of the past', *Pink News*, 20
    November 2019, https://www.pinknews.co.uk/2019/11/20/
    dawn-butler-labour-transgender-gra-reform-women-equalities-
    minister-exclusive/
18. Woman's Place UK, 'Evidence of calls to remove single sex
    exemptions from Equality Act', https://womansplaceuk.org/
    references-to-removal-of-single-sex-exemptions/; Stonewall,
    'Inaccurate reporting', https://www.stonewall.org.uk/
    node/79306
19. https://transrespect.org/wp-content/uploads/2019/11/

TvT_TMM_TDoR2019_SimpleTable.pdf

20. 'TvT TMM UPDATE TRANS DAY OF REMEMBRANCE 2019', https://transrespect.org/wp-content/uploads/2018/11/TvT_TMM_TDoR2018_SimpleTable_EN.pdf

21. '"A devastating scenario": Brazil sets new record for homicides at 63,880 deaths', *Guardian*, 9 August 2018, https://www.theguardian.com/world/2018/aug/09/brazil-sets-new-record-for-homicides-63880-deaths

22. 'Brazil's Murder Rate Finally Fell—and by a Lot', *FP*, 22 April 2019, https://foreignpolicy.com/2019/04/22/brazils-murder-rate-finally-fell-and-by-a-lot/

23. 'Murder Rate by Country 2020', World Population Review, https://worldpopulationreview.com/countries/murder-rate-by-country/

24. 'The vicious circle of violence: Trans and gender-diverse people, migration, and sex work', TGEU, https://transrespect.org/wp-content/uploads/2018/01/TvT-PS-Vol16-2017.pdf

25. Talia Mae Bettcher (2014), 'Transphobia', *Transgender Studies Quarterly*, 1 (1–2), 249–51

26. E. Evens et al. (2019), 'Experiences of gender-based violence among female sex workers, men who have sex with men, and transgender women in Latin America and the Caribbean: a qualitative study to inform HIV programming', *BMC International Health and Human Rights*, 19 (1), 9

27. R. L. Stotzer (2017), 'Data Sources Hinder Our Understanding of Transgender Murders', *American Journal of Public Health*, 107 (9), 1362–3; A. Dinno (2017), 'Homicide Rates of Transgender Individuals in the United States: 2010–2014', *American Journal of Public Health*, 107 (9), 1441–7

28. Macrotrends, 'U.K. Murder/Homicide Rate 1990-2020', https://www.macrotrends.net/countries/GBR/united-kingdom/murder-homicide-rate

29. Stonewall, 'The truth about trans', https://www.stonewall.org.uk/truth-about-trans#trans-people-britain

30. Stonewall, 'Stonewall to work with trans charities to reduce discrimination in key public services', 4 July 2019, https://www.stonewall.org.uk/about-us/news/stonewall-work-trans-charities-reduce-discrimination-key-public-services

31. Samaritans, 'Media Guidelines for Reporting Suicide', https://media.samaritans.org/documents/Samaritans_Media_Guidelines_UK_Apr17_Final_web.pdf

32. Mermaids, 'An open letter from Mermaids on World Suicide Prevention Day', 10 September 2019, https://mermaidsuk.org.uk/news/world-suicide-prevention-day

33. Office for National Statistics, 'Suicides in the UK: 2017 registrations', https://www.ons.gov.uk/peoplepopulationandcommunity/birthsdeathsandmarriages/deaths/bulletins/suicidesintheunitedkingdom/2017registrations#suicide-patterns-by-age

34. Stonewall, 'School Report: The experiences of lesbian, gay, bi and trans young people in Britain's schools in 2017', https://www.stonewall.org.uk/system/files/the_school_report_2017.pdf

35. Transgender Trend, 'Stonewall School Report: What Does The 45% Attempted Suicide Rate Really Mean?', https://www.transgendertrend.com/stonewall-school-report-what-does-suicide-rate-mean/

36. GIDS, 'Evidence base', https://gids.nhs.uk/evidence-base

37. Michael Biggs, 'Suicide by trans-identified children in England and Wales', Transgender Trend, https://www.transgendertrend.com/suicide-by-trans-identified-children-in-england-and-wales/

38. Helen Joyce, 'Speaking up for female eunuchs', *Standpoint*, February 2020, https://standpointmag.co.uk/issues/february-2020/speaking-up-for-female-eunuchs/

39. In the National Lottery Community Fund's 2019 review into their previous £500,000 grant to Mermaids, the allegation that 'Mermaids promotes questionable statistics in relation to suicidality in children and young people with gender identity issues' was raised. In response, Mermaids were quoted as saying: 'This allegation is denied. Mermaids stand by their use of statistics and have cited a number of other studies including the Williams Institute Study (2014), the Life in Scotland for LGBT Young People (2017) and the Canadian Trans Youth Health Study Alberta which support their expressed view that transgender young people experience a higher risk of suicide.' ('Review into the award of a Reaching Communities Grant to Mermaids', https://www.tnlcommunityfund.org.uk/media/documents/Mermaids-UK-Review-Report_February-2019.pdf?mtime=20190219142027&focal=none)

40. Transgender Trend, 'A Scientist Reviews Transgender Suicide Stats', https://www.transgendertrend.com/a-scientist-reviews-transgender-suicide-stats/

41. Linda Stupart, 'I Want To Show You A Body: Thinking Through Gender, Bodies, and Building Different Worlds', Tate London, https://www.tate.org.uk/file/i-want-show-you-body

42. 'Hate crimes double in six years with transphobic abuse recording biggest rise, police figures show', *Daily Telegraph*, 15 October 2019, https://www.telegraph.co.uk/

news/2019/10/15/hate-crimes-double-six-years-transphobic-abuse-recording-biggest/

43. 'Hate crimes double in five years in England and Wales', *Guardian*, 15 October 2019, https://www.theguardian.com/society/2019/oct/15/hate-crimes-double-england-wales

44. College of Police, 'Responding to Hate', https://www.app.college.police.uk/app-content/major-investigation-and-public-protection/hate-crime/responding-to-hate/#perception-based-recording

45. Crown Prosecution Service, 'Homophobic, Biphobic and Transphobic Hate Crime – Prosecution Guidance', https://www.cps.gov.uk/legal-guidance/homophobic-biphobic-and-transphobic-hate-crime-prosecution-guidance

46. 'Less than one in 10 hate crimes prosecuted despite record attacks', *Independent*, 27 December 2019, https://www.independent.co.uk/news/uk/crime/hate-crime-attacks-jews-muslims-gay-prosecutions-police-falling-a9257256.html

47. Crown Prosecution Service, 'Hate Crime Data', https://www.cps.gov.uk/cps/hate-crime-data

48. Kathleen Stock, 'Presence of Mind', Forum for Philosophy blog, https://blogs.lse.ac.uk/theforum/presenceofmind/

49. Lynda Nead (1990), 'The Female Nude: Pornography, Art, and Sexuality', *Signs*, 15 (2), 323–35

50. Guerrilla Girls, 'Do women have to be naked to get into the Met. Museum?', National Gallery of Art, https://www.nga.gov/collection/art-object-page.139856.html

51. https://artuk.org/discover/stories/the-eight-women-artists-of-the-national-gallery

52. Jade King, 'The eight women artists of The National Gallery', Art UK, 11 February 2019, https://news.artnet.com/womens-place-in-the-art-world/female-artists-represent-just-2-percent-market-heres-can-change-1654954

53. 'Fashion Photography Has A Real Gender Equality Problem', *Fashionista*, 5 October 2018, https://fashionista.com/2018/04/female-fashion-photographers-2018

54. 'Sexism in advertising: "They talk about diversity, but they don't want to change"', *Guardian*, 14 April 2019, https://www.theguardian.com/media/2019/apr/14/sexism-in-advertising-industry-gender-pay-gap-diversity

55. D. M. Quinn et al. (2006), 'The Disruptive Effect of Self-Objectification on Performance', *Psychology of Women Quarterly*, 30 (1), 59–64

56. John Berger (1972), *Ways of Seeing*, Penguin, p. 47

57. 'Selfie City London', http://www.selfiecity.net/london/

58. C. P. Butkowski et al. (2020), 'Quantifying the feminine self(ie): Gender display and social media feedback in young women's Instagram selfies', *New Media & Society*, 22 (5), 817–37

59. Joshua B. Grubbs et al. (2019), 'Internet pornography use and sexual motivation: a systematic review and integration', *Annals of the International Communication Association*, 43 (2), 117–55

60. Anne A. Lawrence (2017), 'Autogynephilia and the Typology of Male-to-Female Transsexualism', *European Psychologist*, 22 (1), 39–54

61. Alice Dreger (2015), *Galileo's Middle Finger: Heretics, Activists, and One Scholar's Search for Justice*, Penguin

62. J. Michael Bailey (2003), *The Man Who Would Be Queen: The Science of Gender Bending and Transsexualism*, Joseph Henry Press, p. 174

63. Lawrence, 'Autogynephilia'

64. Ibid.

65. Andrea Long Chu (2019), *Females*, Verso, p. 74

66. Charles Moser (2009), 'Autogynephilia in Women', *Journal of Homosexuality*, 56, 539–47

67. Anne A. Lawrence (2009), 'Something Resembling Autogynephilia in Women: Comment on Moser (2009)', *Journal of Homosexuality*, 57 (1), 1–4

68. '"I Cross-Dress. Do You Still Love Me?": The Secret Lives of Sissies', *Vice*, 28 July 2016, https://www.vice.com/en_us/article/9aeevy/i-cross-dress-do-you-still-love-me-the-secret-lives-of-sissies

69. Chu, *Females*, pp. 78–9

70. Sheila Jeffreys (2014), *Gender Hurts: A Feminist Analysis of the Politics of Transgenderism*, Routledge, p. 95

Chapter 8: A Better Activism in Future

1. 'English Freemasons Open the Doors to Transgender Members', *New York Times*, 1 August 2018, https://www.nytimes.com/2018/08/01/world/europe/uk-freemasons-transgender.html

2. R. Claire Snyder (2008), 'What Is Third-Wave Feminism? A New Directions Essay', *Signs*, 34 (1), 175–96

3. Snyder, 'What is Third-Wave Feminism?'

4. Julia Long, 'A Meaningful Transition?', *Uncommon*

Ground, 12 May 2020, https://uncommongroundmedia.
com/a-meaningful-transition-julia-long/

5.   Ibid.

6.   'Why Everyday Feminism Is For Everyone', *Everyday
Feminism*, 5 July 2012, https://everydayfeminism.
com/2012/07/feminism-is-for-everyone/

7.   Meghan Murphy, 'Vancouver Women's March becomes
opportunity for misogynist threats against women', *Feminist
Current*, 22 January 2018, https://www.feministcurrent.
com/2018/01/22/vancouver-womens-march-becomes-
opportunity-misogynist-threats-women/

8.   Kitty-It blog https://web.archive.org/save/
https://kittyit.tumblr.com/post/177744771682/
kittyit-there-is-currently-a-video-going-around

9.   'Ideals of Equality: feminisms in the twenty-first century',
LSE, 27 February 2016, https://blogs.lse.ac.uk/theforum/
from-the-vaults-feminisms-in-the-twenty-first-century/

10. 'BFI criticised for naming trans activist Munroe Bergdorf
as speaker at women's summit', *Guardian*, 15 June
2018, https://www.theguardian.com/film/2018/jun/15/
bfi-munroe-bergdorf-women

11. Stonewall, 'A Vision for Change', https://www.stonewall.org.
uk/system/files/a_vision_for_change.pdf

12. Alex Sharpe (2017), 'Blind desire: the troubling
case of Gayle Newland', *Inherently Human*, https://
inherentlyhuman.wordpress.com/2017/06/29/
blind-desire-the-troubling-case-of-gayle-newland/

13. K. W. Crenshaw (2010), 'Close Encounters of Three Kinds:
On teaching dominance feminism and intersectionality', *Tulsa
Law Review*, 46 (1), 162

14. Douglas Murray (2019), *The Madness of Crowds: Gender,
Race, and Identity*, Bloomsbury

15. Combahee River Collective Statement, 1977, https://
americanstudies.yale.edu/sites/default/files/files/Keyword%20
Coalition_Readings.pdf

16. K. W. Crenshaw (1989), 'Demarginalizing the Intersection of
Race and Sex: A Black Feminist Critique of Antidiscrimination
Doctrine, Feminist Theory, and Antiracist Politics', reprinted
in K. Bartlett and R. Kennedy (eds.) (1992), *Feminist Legal
Theory: Readings in law and gender*, Routledge

17. Kimberlé Crenshaw (1991), 'Mapping the Margins:
Intersectionality, Identity Politics, and Violence against
Women of Color', *Stanford Law Review*, 43 (6), 1241–99

18. Crenshaw, 'Demarginalizing'

19. bell hooks (1984), *Feminist Theory: From Margin to Center*, pp. 133–4

20. All statistics are from 'Women in Prison: Key Facts', https://www.womeninprison.org.uk/research/key-facts.php

21. W. Bailey (1999), 'The Socioeconomic Patterns of Forcible Rape for Major U.S. Cities', *Sociological Focus*, 32 (1), 57–8

22. 'Unisex changing rooms put women in danger', *The Times*, 2 September 2018

23. Woman's Place UK, 'Spousal Consent and the Liberal Democrats', https://womansplaceuk.org/2019/09/21/spousal-consent-and-the-liberal-democrats/

24. Rachel Anne Williams, 'What is girldick?', https://medium.com/@transphilosophr/what-is-girldick-9363515e0bfd

25. I. T. Nolan et al. (2019), 'Demographic and temporal trends in transgender identities and gender confirming surgery', *Translational Andrology and Urology*, 8 (3), 184–90

26. Michael Biggs, 'LGBT facts and figures', http://users.ox.ac.uk/~sfos0060/LGBT_figures.shtml

27. Stonewall, 'Transphobia at Pride in London', https://www.stonewall.org.uk/node/82236

28. Ibid.

29. 'Lottery thousands pay for former trans stripper to sway public opinion', *Sunday Times*, 23 December 2018, https://www.thetimes.co.uk/article/lottery-thousands-pay-for-former-trans-stripper-to-sway-public-opinion-6lw9xbwgr

30. Morgan Page (2012), publicity material for the workshop 'Overcoming the Cotton Ceiling: Breaking Down Sexual Barriers for Queer Trans Women', Planned Parenthood Toronto

31. Buck Angel, Twitter, 23 December 2019, https://twitter.com/BuckAngel/status/1209236297140834304

32. Government Equalities Office, 'Trans People In the UK', https://assets.publishing.service.gov.uk/government/uploads/system/uploads/attachment_data/file/721642/GEO-LGBT-factsheet.pdf

33. 'Sex question back on census in blow to trans lobby', *Sunday Times*, 24 January 2021

34. Michael Biggs, 'The Tavistock's Experiment with Puberty Blockers', http://users.ox.ac.uk/~sfos0060/Biggs_ExperimentPubertyBlockers.pdf

35. Lisa Marchiano, 'The Ranks of Gender Detransitioners Are Growing. We Need to Understand Why', *Quillette*, 2 January 2020, https://quillette.com/2020/01/02/the-ranks-of-gender-detransitioners-are-growing-we-need-to-understand-why/

36. Ibid.
37. Andrea Long Chu and Emmett Harsin Drager (2019), 'After Trans Studies', *Transgender Studies Quarterly*, 6 (1), 103–16